Zen Cart

E-commerce Application Development

A step-by-step developer's guide

Suhreed Sarkar

PUBLISHING

BIRMINGHAM - MUMBAI

Zen Cart
E-commerce Application Development

First published: July 2008

Production Reference: 1150708

Published by Packt Publishing Ltd.
32 Lincoln Road
Olton
Birmingham, B27 6PA, UK.

ISBN 978-1-847191-17-5

www.packtpub.com

Cover Image by Parth Thakkar (p.bestpics@gmail.com)

Credits

Author

Suhreed Sarkar

Reviewer

Kanudan Rohadiya

Acquisition Editor

Bansari Barot

Technical Editors

Bhupali Khule

Sashank Iyer

Copy Editor

Sumathi Shridhar

Editorial Team Leader

Akshara Aware

Project Manager

Abhijeet Deobhakta

Project Coordinator

Rajashree Hamine

Indexer

Monica Ajmera

Proofreader

Dirk Manuel

Claire Lane

Production Coordinator

Shantanu Zagade

Cover Work

Shantanu Zagade

About the Author

Suhreed Sarkar is an IT consultant, trainer, and technical writer. He studied Marine engineering, served on board for two years, and then started with his journey in to IT world with MCSE in Windows NT 4.0 track. Recently he has earned an MBA from the University of Dhaka. He has several BrainBench certifications on various topics including PHP4, Project Management, RDBMS Concepts, E-commerce, Web Server Administration, Internet Security, Training Development, Delivery and Evaluation, and Technical Writing.

As a trainer, Suhreed taught courses on system administration, web development, e-commerce, and MIS. He has consulted several national and international organizations including the United Nations, and has helped clients build and adopt their enterprise portals, large scale databases, and management information systems. He is a renowned technical author in Bengali, having a dozen books published on subjects covering web development, LAMP, networking, and system administration. As an open source enthusiast, he is active in several forums and takes every opportunity to promote open source CMSs and shopping carts.

While not busy with hacking some apps, blogging on his blog (www.suhreedsarkar. com), reading philosophy of Bertrand Russel, or the management thought of Peter F Drucker, he likes to spend some special moments with his family. Suhreed lives in Dhaka, Bangladesh and can be reached at suhreedsarkar@gmail.com.

I would like to thank Packt team for their excellent professional support, and special thanks to Bansari Barot, without whose support it would not have been possible for me to write this book. I would also like to thank all three Project Coordinators I have worked with—Aboli Mendhe, Abhijeet Deobhakta, and Rajashree Hamine— who have helped me a lot throughout the process. I would also like to express my gratitude to Kanudan Rohadiya for being the technical reviewer and providing insightful comments on first drafts of this book. I thank my kids—Sabyasachi and Sanchita—for giving me time, which should be theirs. I dedicate this book to my loving wife Sharmin, who kept me away from so many things to keep me busy with what I like.

About the Reviewer

Kanudan Rohadiya's academic background includes a Bachelor of Engineering in Computer Science. He is an IBM certified VAJ 4.1 web developer, is currently pursuing his MBA Degree from ICFAI University, and has more than three years of experience in web application development. His expertise is in PHP, MySQL technology with Open source customization such as ZenCart, OsCommerce, Joomla, Drupal, Wordpress, Typo3, and so on. He is capable of providing cost effective and appropriate open-source solutions to small businesses. He has good command over the logical and physical design of an application. He also has a strong understanding of the business logic required for projects. He is very enthusiastic about handling challenges encountered by him while at work. He has good troubleshooting skills which he uses for the benefit of his team and his tasks whenever required. He always takes initiative to implement upcoming technologies.

Currently he is working with Rightway Solution (I) Pvt. Ltd. as Team Leader in PHP and Open Source technologies.

Rightway Solution is one of the leading offshore outsourcing companies in India. The company is trusted by software and technology enabled enterprises to deliver cutting edge technology solutions.

Rightway offers web design and development, portal development, open source customization, RIA application development, customized software development, e-commerce site development, enterprise application development, and the supply of dedicated services to enterprises world-wide.

Table of Contents

Preface

Zen Cart is a popular open-source PHP/MySQL-based e-commerce solution available under GPL that is designed to put the merchants' and shoppers' requirements first. Not only does Zen Cart offer a very long list of features, but the system is designed with both store owners and web developers in mind. There's no sacrifice of usability or power.

Zen cart is a branch of osCommerce—another popular open-source e-commerce application. Although it was derived from the code base of osCommerce, it surpassed osCommerce in respect of usability, design flexibility, and power. More and more people are now using Zen Cart for running their online shops. This is because Zen Cart gives much flexibility in customizing its look and feel and running the shop.

With the increasing popularity of Zen Cart, a lot of people are migrating from other shopping carts, especially osCommerce, to Zen Cart. Also, the need increasingly arises to integrate Zen Cart with other content management system.

What This Book Covers

Chapter 1 introduces you to the world of Zen Cart. It explains what Zen Cart is, what features it includes, and how it compares to other shopping cart solutions. It also shows the differences between osCommerce and Zen Cart. You will get a complete overview of Zen Cart before starting work with it.

Chapter 2 discusses installation and basic configuration for Zen Cart. It shows you preprequisites for installation, the step-by-step installation process—both from Fantastico and by file uploading, upgradation from an earlier version of Zen Cart, and finally the basic configuration of Zen Cart shop. It shows you how to edit the configuration file for Zen Cart shop, and how to start using the administration panel after completing the installation.

Chapter 3 shows you how to configure a Zen Cart store. It discusses all configuration options for the store, customers, zones, taxes and currencies, and the product catalog. This will show you how to manage the product catalog and how to install and configure payment and shipping modules.

Chapter 4 discusses customization of the look and feel of a Zen Cart shop. The step-by-step guide in this chapter enables you to configure the look and feel from the administration panel, apply different templates, change the text and graphics displayed in the front-end, customize the look and feel by editing files, understand and apply the template override system, modify and create new templates, and finally modify email templates. The skills gained through this chapter will enable you to attract more customers by designing attractive look and feel for your Zen Cart shop.

Chapter 5 explains the localization of Zen Cart. It shows you how to localize regions and taxes, use multiple currencies, add new languages to the shop, translate Zen Cart languages, and modify the status of order status. This chapter enables you to suite your Zen Cart shop to local context and help attract customer niche.

Chapter 6 discusses the promotion and public relations features of Zen Cart. It shows you how to use Zen Cart's promotion and public relation features, such as cross-sell, up-sell, gift certificates and coupons to attract more customers, and maintain the existing customer base through constant communication using newsletters and product notifications. It also shows you how to implement search engine friendly URLs for your Zen Cart shop.

Chapter 7 shows how to migrate from osCommerce to Zen Cart. This chapter covers points to be considered before migration, a brief discussion of the differences between osCommerce and Zen Cart database structure, and finally actual data migration from osCommerce to Zen Cart, converting osCommerce modules for Zen Cart, and common problems during migration. This chapter enables you to migrate your old osCommerce shop to Zen Cart without losing vital data.

Chapter 8 shows you how to integrate Zen Cart with several popular content management systems. It enables you to integrate Zen Cart with Drupal, WordPress, e107, Gallery2, phpBB, and XOOPS.

Chapter 9 discusses maintenance and troubleshooting tasks for your Zen Cart shop. First, it shows you the maintenance tasks such as backing up the database and files, restoring database and files when needed, taking the shop offline for maintenance, auditing, and hardening security. Then it discusses some common problems you may face and enables you to solve those problems.

The *Appendix* shows you how to set up a development environment for Zen Cart and where to find useful resources for Zen Cart. It lists all of the modules and contributions discussed in the book and links to other contributions and resources.

What You Need for This Book

First of all you need an Apache-MySQL-PHP environment to run a Zen Cart shop. We have used Zen Cart v. 1.3.8 for this book. All descriptions and screenshots are based on this version. For some activities in this book, for example installing Zen Cart through *Fantastico*, you need a hosting account on a Linux server with *cPanel* access. If you do not have access to a webhosting service, you can still use Zen Cart, and learn using your own computer. In that case, you need to setup development environment by installing WAMP (`www.wampserver.com`) on windows machine. For more information on setting up a development environment on your Windows computer, please see the *Appendix*. To get the exact results described in this book, all examples should be followed sequentially.

In addition to an Apache-MySQL-PHP environment and Zen Cart, you need to be familiar with HTML, CSS, and PHP. A basic skill in creating MySQL databases through phpMyAdmin will also be necessary.

Who is This Book For

This book is primarily written for developers interested in building, enhancing, or extending Zen Cart sites for customers.

This book can also act as a useful reference for those who have implemented Zen Cart for their own store, and want to improve it.

It can also help those developers who want to migrate from osCommerce or other engines to Zen Cart.

Conventions

In this book, you will find a number of styles of text that distinguish between different kinds of information. Some examples of these styles, and an explanation of their meaning, are given below.

Code words in text are shown as follows: "In most of the cases, you may need to change the `DIR_WS_CATALOG` and `DIR_WS_HTTPS_CATALOG` variables to reflect your installation directory".

Blocks of code are set as follows:

```
define('DIR_FS_DOWNLOAD', DIR_FS_CATALOG . 'download/');
define('DIR_FS_DOWNLOAD_PUBLIC', DIR_FS_CATALOG . 'pub/');
define('DIR_WS_UPLOADS', DIR_WS_IMAGES . 'uploads/');
define('DIR_FS_UPLOADS', DIR_FS_CATALOG . DIR_WS_UPLOADS);
define('DIR_FS_EMAIL_TEMPLATES', DIR_FS_CATALOG . 'email/');
```

When we wish to draw your attention to a particular part of a code block, the relevant lines or items will be shown in bold:

```
define('HEADING_TITLE', 'Congratulations! You have successfully
installed  your Zen Cart&trade; E-Commerce Solution.');
} elseif ($category_depth == 'nested') {
  // This section deals with displaying a subcategory
 /*  Replace this line with the headline you would like for your shop.
For example: 'Welcome to My SHOP!' */
```

All command-line input and output is written as follows:

```
chmod -R 777 ./includes/languages/english/html_includes
```

New terms and **important words** are introduced in bold-type font. Words that you see on the screen, in menus or dialog boxes for example, appear in our text like this: " Click **activate** next to the Zen Cart listing on the module page".

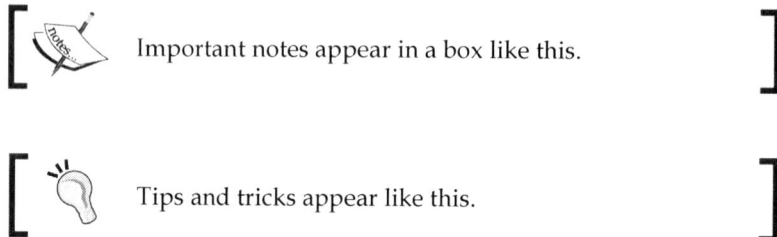

Important notes appear in a box like this.

Tips and tricks appear like this.

Reader Feedback

Feedback from our readers is always welcome. Let us know what you think about this book, what you liked or may have disliked. Reader feedback is important for us to develop titles that you really get the most out of.

To send us general feedback, simply drop an email to feedback@packtpub.com, making sure to mention the book title in the subject of your message.

If there is a book that you need and would like to see us publish, please send us a note via the **SUGGEST A TITLE** form on www.packtpub.com or email suggest@packtpub.com.

If there is a topic that you have expertise in and you are interested in either writing or contributing to a book, see our author guide on www.packtpub.com/authors.

Customer Support

Now that you are the proud owner of a Packt book, we have a number of things to help you to get the most from your purchase.

Downloading the Example Code for the Book

Visit http://www.packtpub.com/files/code/1175_Code.zip to directly download the example code.

The downloadable files contain instructions on how to use them.

Errata

Although we have taken every care to ensure the accuracy of our contents, mistakes do happen. If you find a mistake in one of our books—maybe a mistake in text or code—we would be grateful if you would report this to us. By doing this you can save other readers from frustration, and help to improve subsequent versions of this book. If you find any errata, report them by visiting http://www.packtpub.com/support, selecting your book, clicking on the **let us know** link, and entering the details of your errata. Once your errata are verified, your submission will be accepted and the errata added to the list of existing errata. The existing errata can be viewed by selecting your title from http://www.packtpub.com/support.

Questions

You can contact us at questions@packtpub.com if you are having a problem with some aspect of the book, and we will do our best to address it.

1
Introduction to Zen Cart

Zen Cart is an open-source e-commerce shopping cart based on PHP and MySQL. It is one of the major derivatives of osCommerce shopping cart. This chapter introduces you to Zen Cart and answers the following questions:

- What is Zen Cart
- What are the main features of Zen Cart
- What are the similarities in and differences between Zen Cart and osCommerce
- What are the advantages of using Zen Cart over osCommerce
- Where does Zen Cart stand when compared to other shopping carts

What is Zen Cart?

First, you have to be clear what Zen Cart is. Let's hear from the creators of Zen Cart who said the following, on Zen Cart's website www.zen-cart.com :

> *Zen Cart™ truly is the art of e-commerce; free, user-friendly, open-source shopping cart software. The e-commerce website design program is being developed by a group of like-minded shop owners, programmers, designers, and consultants who think e-commerce web design could be and should be done differently.*

From the above lines, it is clear that:

- Zen Cart is a shopping cart software application
- Zen Cart is open-source
- Zen cart was developed by a group of programmers, designers, and consultants

Let's see what all of these mean. First, you come to the point of it being a shopping cart. In your daily life, you know what a shopping cart is. Whenever you are in a store, you browse the goods and put the ones you want to buy in the shopping cart. Once you are done with the shopping, you take that shopping cart to the checkout counter and pay for the goods. Once the payment is made in full, the goods you have put in the shopping cart are yours. Similarly, in online shopping carts, when you are visiting an online store you browse the products in the catalogue, put the products you want to buy in the cart, and at the end you checkout from the shop, making the payment. Once the payment is made, you can instantly get the products (for downloadable products) or the store may arrange shipment of the goods to your address. Shopping cart software manages the whole process—from maintaining a catalogue to ensuring delivery of the purchased products to customers. Zen Cart is a software application that can be used to build and run our online shop.

Zen Cart is open-source software. Open-source means that its code is open to programmers. Programmers have freedom to modify the code for their own purposes. Zen Cart is itself an open-source software and is also built using some other open-source software. Zen Cart uses PHP as the programming language and runs on most Web servers that support PHP. At the backend, it uses MySQL—another robust, open-source database server—to store products and other information in the database.

Like other open-source software, development of Zen Cart is a collaborative effort. Although there is a core team of Zen Cart developers, others also contribute and develop modules to enhance its functionality. You can interact with the Zen Cart community at Zen Cart's forum `http://www.zen-cart.com/forum`.

Zen Cart is a branch of another open-source e-commerce application, osCommerce. osCommerce also uses PHP and MySQL. However, there is lot of debate as to which one is better—osCommerce or Zen Cart. You will also learn about the merits and demerits of both these shopping carts in this chapter.

The Main Features of Zen Cart

Zen Cart is built for entrepreneurs, by entrepreneurs. Zen cart developers claim that the program is built by programmers and designers who understand the online selling process from start to finish. Existing users of Zen Cart know that it contains all of the necessary tools required to build a successful online store. Zen Cart is also being constantly improved and upgraded based on users' requirements.

The major features included in Zen Cart are outlined in the following sections:

Easy Installation and Upgradation

Zen Cart has a very easy installation and upgradation system. Its native web-based installer checks the database and server requirements before proceeding to install Zen Cart. It guides you systematically through installation of the store. Each step is well-documented, guiding you through online help tips with a ready to help community of Zen Cart users. The installation tool prepopulates the basic store information, which helps you to quickly set up the shop. From the installation tool, you can also populate optional demo products to explore Zen Cart's features.

Easy Localization

Zen Cart has some useful features for localization. It supports multiple languages, multiple currencies, multiple payment methods, shipping methods, and multiple tax rates for different tax regions. Some of the language packs, including Arabic, Spanish, Dutch, French, German, and Polish are readily available from Zen Cart website's download section. You can also add new languages and translate the interface into your desired language.

Similarly, you can show your product prices in any currency. You can add currencies of your choices, set conversion rates against base currency, and product prices will be shown in any currency the customer wants. You also have an auto-update facility for updating the currency conversion rates based on available market data.

Tax rates can vary depending on the shipping address or billing address. You can apply different tax rates to different types of products, based on the regions you are shipping or billing to. You can also create custom tax and shipping regions as per your needs.

You have an array of options for payment methods. Most of the major online payment gateways are supported for online payment processing. Besides online payment, you also have options for offline payments such as money order, bank transfer, cash on delivery, and so on. You have the full freedom to apply appropriate payment methods for specific regions.

Customer Management

Zen Cart has excellent features both for customers and shop administrators, especially in managing customers and products.

In a normal Zen Cart shop, customers can browse the products, view the details, and register themselves to order a product. Once registered with Zen Cart shop, customer information is stored in the database. Then, they can log in to Zen Cart shop each time they visit your store. Customers can maintain up to five shipping and billing addresses, which can be used when they shop. They can also subscribe to newsletters and product notifications of their choice and manage these subscriptions from the account details page.

The administrator of the shop can allow customer unrestricted shopping. You can also make registration mandatory for customers to see the prices of the products. Administrators have the right to enable or disable any customer at any time. There is an excellent way to communicate with a single customer or a group of customers from the Zen Cart administration panel. You do not need external email program to communicate with customers — Zen Cart handles it for you.

The administrator of the shop can set the shop to be only a showroom. This means that products will be displayed in the shop, customers will be able to browse the items but they cannot make a purchase. While using it as a showroom, you have the option to either hide, or show the prices of the products. At any time, the showroom can be brought online and customers allowed to purchase products.

In normal shopping mode, often you may need to make the shop offline for some maintenance work. In that case, you can simply switch on the shop in maintenance mode, which will show a notice to the customers that you are in maintenance mode and will be back soon.

Categories and Products

In Zen Cart, there is no limit to how big the catalog can be. You can build your catalog with thousands of products and keep the products in categories. Zen Cart allows you to create unlimited nested categories. You also have the ability to copy, move, or link a product to another category.

Your catalog may contain both — physical merchandise and downloadable virtual products. You can assign attributes to products, and price the products according to these attributes. Product options can be shown as drop-downs, option buttons, checkboxes, and text inputs. Products can also be marked as "Free" or "Call for Price". A product marked "Free" does not require the buyers to pay for it. However, shipping charges may apply to it.

Customer Retention Tools

Zen Cart has many customer retention tools that allows the store owner to communicate with the customers. Zen Cart maintains a customer-base from where the administrator can contact any customer through email. The store owner can notify customers about new products, promotions, discounts, and many other things. The store owner can send order status emails whenever the status of an order is changed. This allows the customers to be informed about their orders.

The administrators can send periodic newsletters to customers in plain text or HTML format. Customers can subscribe and unsubscribe to newsletters when creating their account, or from the account details page. Zen Cart also has referral tools that can track customer referrals. Customers can also send the product details to others by using the "**Tell a Friend**" feature. It has a system for gift certificate and discount coupon generation and distribution. Customers can use these gift certificates and discount coupons for purchasing products from the store.

Promotions, Sales, and Discounts

Promotions, sales, and discounts are common to all shops. Zen Cart also has features for adding promotions, sales, and discounts. The administrator can specify special prices and sale reductions for individual products, or can apply category-wide sales prices. Moreover, the administrator has the opportunity to generate discount coupons and send them to customers, who can then use the coupon codes to get discounts while shopping. The discount coupons may be configured for specific customer groups or for specific quantities of products purchased. This discount may be in the form of a one-time value deduction, or percentage deduction. Minimum and maximum purchases per product can also be configured.

Another great feature of Zen Cart is pricing by attributes. Some products may have various attributes and choosing those will add or deduct from product-base price.

Powerful Administration Tool

Zen Cart has a powerful administration tool. Zen Cart's administration panel is password-protected and only users with administrative privilege can log in to this area. From this administrative panel, the administrator can configure minimum and maximum values, image sizes, and customer details. Further more, the administrator can also:

- Choose layout settings for spotlight listings
- Pick details to be displayed on the product details page
- Edit policy pages with HTML
- Add, delete, move, link, or copy products
- Create and manage product attributes
- Manage product reviews, featured products, specials, and storewide sales.
- Install and manage the shipping and payment module
- Control banner advertising, price, and taxation
- Create and send newsletters

Besides, Zen Cart also has several tools for content management and adding new content pages to the shop.

Fully Customizable Catalog Templates

Zen Cart has an easy-to-use template system, which is XHTML 1.0 compliant and utilizes a nearly table-less layout. The administrator can:

- Change the colors, fonts, and many graphics using **Cascading Stylesheets** (CSS)
- Add, move, and remove sideboxes using the administration tool

Zen Cart template system uses overriding functionality, which means that configuration changes do not get overwritten during upgrades. Override functionality can be used even without knowing PHP. Using this, the administrator can create as many different looks as needed. These templates are easily administered and applied to the site from the administration panel.

Third-Party Modules

Zen Cart supports a large number of third-party modules that can build on or enhance the functionality of Zen Cart. Zen Cart website's download section lists almost every conceivable type of third-party module. The administrators can download the third-party modules and install them as per the easy-to-follow instructions that come with the module. Most of the modules are designed in such a way that they do not need to modify or overwrite Zen Cart core files.

For a working Zen Cart shop, the administrator may need to install such third-party modules. For example, to facilitate administration of Zen Cart shop, the administrator may install, 'Backup MySQL Plugin', 'Barcode product field', 'Credit Card Fraud Detection', 'Easy Populate', 'Email Archive Manager', 'PayPal Session Viewer', 'Sales Report', and so on. From the buttons and graphics category, you may also download appropriate buttons in the language that you need, and use appropriate graphic icons for your shop.

Third-party modules categorized as marketing tools may be used for product marketing and promotion. For example, the 'cross-sell', 'advanced cross-sell', and 'better-together' modules can be used for adding cross-sell and up-sell features in your shopping carts. These modules are discussed in detail in Chapter 6, *Promotion and Public Relations*.

There are more than 100 third-party modules for payment processing. These modules can be used for accepting different types of payments and using payment processors ranging from PayPal, 2CheckOut, eWay, Google Checkout, LinkPoint, MoneyBooker, WorldPay, and so on.

Third-party shipping modules can be used for using different shipping methods ranging from Free Shipping, AusPost, UPS, RoyalMail, FedEx, and so on. There are some other third party modules that can be used for search engine friendly URL generation, adding lightbox effects, changing look and feel, adding header graphics and logos, and so on.

Zen Cart versus osCommerce

osCommerce is an open-source application licensed under the GPL and is available for free without warranty. For production, the latest milestone release osCommerce 2.2 milestone 2, released in 2003, is recommended. Although the last release was a long time ago, this is a testimony to the stability of osCommerce. Like Zen Cart, osCommerce will work on any machine that can run PHP (4.x+) and has access to a MySQL database. It is also possible to run osCommerce on a WAMP (Windows/Apache/MySQL/PHP) or even a WIMP (Windows/IIS/MySQL/PHP).

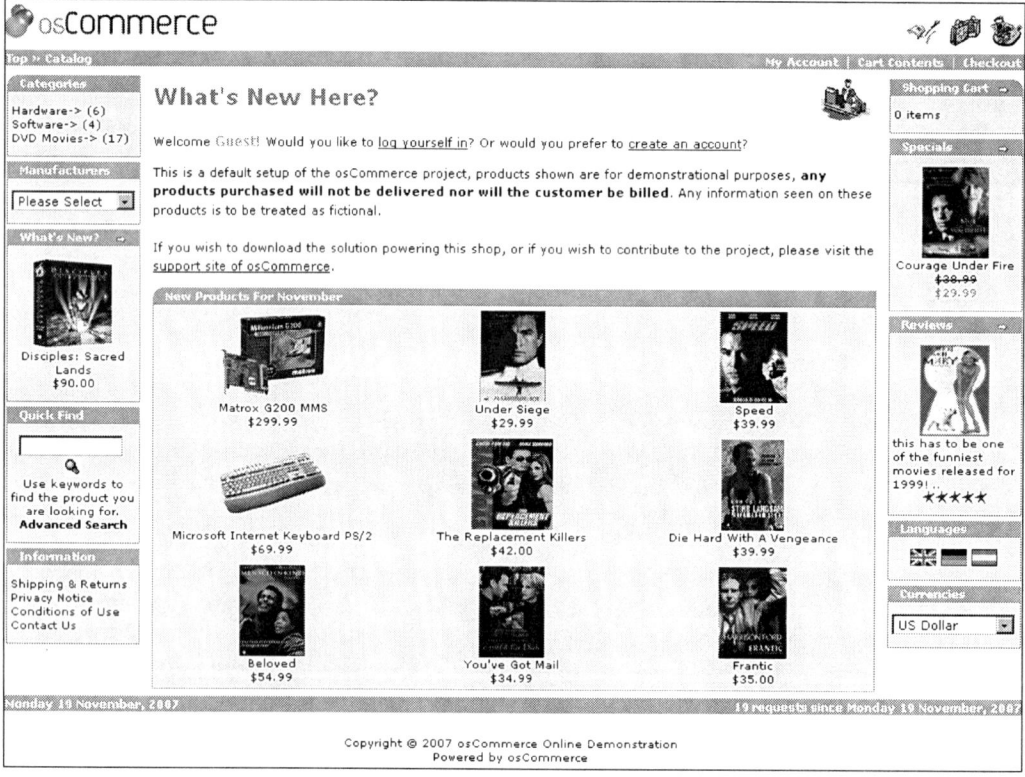

The idea that drove Zen Cart developers was to make the osCommerce easier for users as well as for developers. With this in mind, Zen Cart was built on osCommerce. Now, they are two separate products. The programming structure has also been changed in Zen Cart, and extra functionalities added.

According to its users, Zen Cart is a better cart than osCommerce, as it is being actively developed by a good group who release new versions regularly. osCommerce has not had a release for more than two years now. Zen Cart is more dynamic, yet is also stable.

The only drawback to Zen Cart is that it does not have many modules as compared to osCommerce. But if you consider its age, it has progressed a lot in developing third-party contributions, and more developers are interested in developing such modules for Zen Cart.

Users have the choice of using either osCommerce or Zen Cart. But having some experience of both carts, one would easily be convinced that Zen Cart is a more secure and easy-to-use shopping cart than osCommerce.

Feature Comparison

After discussing the general differences between osCommerce and Zen cart, let's point out the specific differences between their features. The following sections will show how features differ in these two carts.

Default and Contributed Modules

By default, Zen Cart has most of the required modules. You can start using Zen Cart for a live shop without installing additional modules. Its administration area is, by default, protected and you do not need to install an additional module to protect it. Common payment and shipping modules are also installed.

osCommerce has fewer default modules installed as compared to Zen Cart. However, there are hundreds of user-contributed modules to help add desired features. The only caveat is that there is no official rating system on the osCommerce site for the quality of any of the modules contributed by the third-party developers. As per the site's disclaimer, shop owners have to use the modules at their own risk. Zen Cart is behind in terms of the number of modules available at its site. However, the modules available are clearly-described, and users will not be confused about which one to download for what purpose.

Security

By default, Zen Cart has better security than osCommerce. From a security point of view, the default installation of osCommerce should not be used in a production environment. It must first be customized to harden security.

In osCommerce's default installation, there is no specific admin-login authentication protection built into it. If you keep everything unchanged from the default installation, anyone can simply visit `http://[our site]/catalog/admin` and have access to the store's administration interface. However, there are user-contributed modules for securing the administration area in osCommerce.

You can use passwords to protect the administration area through the `.htaccess` file. If there is no time-based cookie authentication system, even with `.htaccess` (and you do access the admin screen), any user that has access to the URL from your Web browser can also access the administration system by following that URL.

On the other hand, Zen Cart has a built-in administrative login system. The administrative username and password are configured during installation. Whenever you want to access the admin area, you must type that administrative username and password. You can create additional administrative accounts from the admin area via **Tools | Admin Settings**.

Categories and Products Management

Both osCommerce and Zen Cart support multiple nested categories for products. However, osCommerce allows the addition of products and categories at the same level, while Zen Cart does not. In Zen Cart, a category may contain only other categories or products, but not both.

There are differences on the page for adding new products. In osCommerce, it has fewer fields as compared to Zen cart. It simply gives the stock status, availability date, tax class, price, product description, quantity, model, image, URL, and weight. On the other hand, in Zen Cart, you can also add whether a product is virtual, call for price, priced by attributes, if the product is virtual whether shipping address will be displayed or not, whether free shipping will be used or not, and so on.

For adding product images in Zen Cart, you have two options: upload an image to a specified directory, or use an existing image from the Web server. In both the cases, you have the option to either specify the directory from which the image will be used, or to where the image will be uploaded. In osCommerce, you cannot specify the image directory, or specify the URL of an image located on the Web server. The only option is to upload an image for the product.

Product type is an excellent feature of Zen Cart. It helps us show different products with different information and layout. The product type feature allows you to configure the display of products based on the product's attributes. By default, Zen Cart will have **Product – General** and **Product – Music** types of products. You can add additional product types, for example, for selling books, you can add 'Product - Books'.

Template Customization

The osCommerce default template is unusable for serious e-commerce storefronts. Therefore, users want to customize its look and feel at the very beginning. But osCommerce has no easy-to-customize templates. The default template and text are not easily editable and users must go through each line of the code on the appropriate pages to make the changes. The template structure is also table-based, and complex to understand, especially because logic and layout are not adequately separated.

Zen Cart has an easily-customizable template system where overrides can be used to apply customization to the base template. Using this override, you can apply multiple templates to a site and get the desired look and feel. Zen Cart templates are almost table-less, and fully XHTML 1.0 compliant. It has a developer tool to locate strings for translation and modification, which makes it easy to customize the templates.

Promotion and Public Relations

Several promotion and public relation tools are built into Zen Cart. It has a built-in gift certificate and discount coupon feature which can better promote your products. In osCommerce, you need to install a third party module separately to add this feature. Similarly, Zen Cart has a SaleMaker, through which you can manage all sales. osCommerce has no such built-in feature. In osCommerce, the only way to configure a special price is through menu **Catalog | Specials**.

User and Developer Community

It's hard to say which one has the largest user community. According to osCommerce's claim, it has over 13,000 live shops. For Zen Cart, although the number of shops has not been estimated, it may not be an insignificant number. Most modern stores run on Zen Cart, as it is easy to use and does not compromise on security and flexibility in customization.

osCommerce's biggest strength is its large developer community and a wide variety of contributed modules. While a large number of contributed modules may be considered as strength, at the same time, this also creates a lot of confusion for newbies to osCommerce.

Programmatic Differences

Although Zen Cart has been developed from they osCommerce code base, there are programmatic differences between the two. Understanding the programming differences can help solve migration-related problems when migrating from one cart to another. It will be especially helpful when you convert some osCommerce modules for use in Zen Cart.

The most significant programmatic difference between osCommerce and Zen Cart is that you need `register_globals` **on** for osCommerce, whereas Zen Cart recommends this setting be kept **off**. For security reasons, most of the hosting servers keep this setting **off**. Running osCommerce on these servers will be difficult unless you work out some way to enable `register_globals`.

Another major difference between osCommerce and Zen Cart are their use of functions and classes. The naming convention for functions is different in both carts. Zen Cart functions start with `zen_` prefix, whereas osCommerce functions start with `osc_` or `tep_` prefix.

In osCommerce, `tep_db_query()` function is used to run a query against the database, then a `while()` loop is used. In Zen Cart, `$db->Execute()` function is used to run the query, and the `while()` loop is used differently.

There are also some differences in the database structure. osCommerce has 54 database tables, whereas Zen Cart has 93. In osCommerce, the `products` table contains 12 fields, whereas in Zen Cart, it contains around 35 fields. The `Product_attributes` table in Zen Cart also contains a much higher number of fields as compared to osCommerce.

Zen Cart has a splendid and easy-to-navigate template system while osCommerce doesn't have one at all. In Zen Cart, all template files are located in `includes/templates` folder. There is a template override system that can be used to apply multiple templates to a site and to customize the template easily. In osCommerce, template files are located in the osCommerce installation directory and are difficult to customize. The administrators need to override the original files during the installation of a new template in osCommerce.

Zen Cart and Other CMS/Shopping Carts

There are other shopping carts and CMSs that can be compared with Zen Cart. The following sections describe the main features of these carts/CMSs and compare them with Zen Cart.

Joomla-VirtueMart

VirtueMart is a component for the award winning content management system Joomla!. It is quite powerful and easy to use. Most of the features of Zen Cart are available in VirtueMart component. However, VirtueMart lacks Zen Cart's coupon administration system. VirtueMart is a good choice if you are building a content-based website using Joomla! and want to sell some products from that site. However, you cannot use it independently. It must be used together with Joomla! or Mambo.

Joomla provides the core system and the framework on which VirtueMart can run. Using these two will provide a complete Shopping Cart Solution within a content-based website, together with many other plug-ins such as Forums, FAQ, Guestbooks, Galleries, and so on. Changing the look and feel of VirtueMart shop is also easy as it uses Joomla's easy to customize CSS and XML/HTML based templates.

CubeCart

CubeCart is a powerful eCommerce script written with PHP & MySQL. CubeCart is not open-source software and is not redistributable. With CubeCart, you can set up a powerful online store as long as you have hosting that supports PHP and a MySQL database.

CubeCart v4 requires, at the least, PHP 4.3.0, MySQL 4.1, and GD (Image Library). It can run on both a Linux/Unix or a Windows webserver, but a Linux/Unix server is recommended.

CURL with SSL support is required for some shipping/payment modules. ZendOptimizer or Ioncube will need to be installed on Windows servers in order to run CubeCart v4. On Linux/Unix servers, ZendOptimizer is not required but the hosting account must be able to load IonCube loader files.

Considering the features and licensing requirements of CubeCart, Zen Cart is a better choice than CubeCart if you are building an online shop from the scratch.

AgoraCart

AgoraCart is a free open-source ecommerce shopping cart software application that offers a wide range of features. It has limitless flexibility in many areas including full design control through Cascading Style Sheets (CSS), template systems, customizable layouts, custom individual product category layouts and templates, modular 'drop-in and go' code as well as AgoraScript, AgoraCart's own scripting language inside parsed HTML pages, which experienced programmers will appreciate.

Although AgoraCart has most of the features of Zen Cart, it is not based on PHP. AgoraCart is programmed in Perl 5. Therefore, you need to install a Unix/Linux based hosting server, supporting Perl 5.6 and runing cgi scripts to host AgoraCart. As PHP has better performance and easier templating as compared to Perl, Zen Cart will be easier and more attractive than AgoraCart for new online shop owners.`

x-Cart

x-Cart is a commercial shopping cart. Its web-based administrator area and installation wizard make setup and maintenance of the shopping cart easy. 24x7 technical support is also available from its vendor.

x-Cart has no logical limitations on the number of products. Its code is optimized for smooth performance for up to 20,000 products. Depending on server configuration, x-Cart can run with up to 500,000 products.

x-Cart is neither free, nor open-source. The user interface and the operation of x-cart remains similar to Zen Cart. X-cart uses the smarty template language, which is not any easier than Zen Cart's templating. Moreover, third party modules for Zen Cart are mostly free, whereas those for X-cart are sold separately involving a significant investment by the shop owner.

Summary

This chapter has introduced Zen Cart and its functionalities. Zen Cart has some great features for online shop owners and shoppers. Shoppers can register and keep themselves updated on new products at the shop.

Although Zen Cart is a branch of osCommerce, it has advanced a lot in terms of added security, ease of templating and an array of features. Unlike osCommerce, some essential features are readily-available in Zen Cart. As Zen Cart has developed, it has adopted a simpler and powerful templating system that enables programmers to easily customize the look and feel. There are differences in function names and database structure in Zen Cart and osCommerce. One should be aware of these differences while converting some modules from osCommerce to Zen Cart.

Finally, you have seen how different shopping carts compare to Zen Cart. With this little introduction to Zen Cart, you can proceed to its installation and basic configuration in the next chapter.

2

Installation and Basic Configuration

If you are not using Zen Cart or have not installed it yet, then you need to learn about installing Zen Cart, before proceeding to the next chapter. In fact, installation of Zen Cart takes very little effort. If you are familiar with other shopping carts/ CMS installations, it will not be very difficult for you. In this chapter, you are going to learn about installing Zen Cart on your server and making the required configuration.

On completion of this chapter, you will be able to:

- Describe the prerequisites for installing Zen Cart
- Install Zen Cart using Fantastico
- Install Zen Cart by uploading files
- Upgrade from previous versions
- Configure shop for your use

 If you have already installed Zen Cart, or you have been using it for a long time, then you may skip this chapter.

Prerequisites

Before installing Zen Cart on your server, ensure that you have the required server environment. As prerequisites, you need a web server that can support PHP and run MySQL database server. The following sections describe the prerequisites for installing Zen Cart in more detail.

The minimum recommended server requirements for Zen cart installation is:

- PHP 4.3.2 or higher (PHP 4.4.x for optimal performance),
- Apache 1.3.x and higher; and
- MySQL 3.2.x or higher.

Although Register Globals may be on or off, it is recommended to keep safe_mode off. For many shipping and payment modules, CURL has to be installed/compiled with PHP.

Support for HTTPS may be required depending on the payment methods being accepted. The use of SSL during account creation and check out is also recommended.

At present, Zen Cart does not officially support PHP5. However, many shops are successfully running on servers, using PHP5. In August 2007, it was announced on Zen Cart's website that Zen Cart version 1.4 and higher will require PHP 5.2 as the minimum.

Web Server

You can use Zen Cart on Apache, Microsoft IIS and other web servers that can support PHP. If you are using Zen Cart for development or testing purposes, you may have local web servers—such as Apache or IIS—installed. For live shops, you must have a web server running for live websites. You may have a dedicated web host server or a shared web server for hosting. There are a lot of web hosting companies offering budget web hosting on Linux-Apache-MySQL-PHP hosting. On windows server, PHP or MySQL may not be available in a standard hosting package.

For your local computer, you may install web server, PHP and MySQL server separately, or install one of the following bundled packages :

- WAMP: WAMP is a package of Apache-MySQL-PHP for Windows computers. You can download it from www.wampserver.com and install it as a windows application. You can get Apache, MySQL and PHP running within a few minutes. You will also have phpMyAdmin pre-installed to administer MySQL databases.
- EasyPHP: EasyPHP, a package of Apache-MySQL-PHP, is simple to install and use. You can download it free of charge at www.easyphp.org.
- XAMPP: XAMPP is an easy-to-install Apache distribution containing MySQL, PHP and Perl. XAMPP is very easy to install and use—just download, extract and start. You can download a version for Linux, Windows, Mac, or Solaris. It is available at www.apachefriends.org/en/xampp.html.

Installing any of these packages will ease your administration task for web server and MySQL database. However, you are free to install and configure Apache, MySQL, and PHP separately.

 If you are playing around with Zen Cart, I recommend using a development server. You will also need a development environment for customizing themes and testing third party contributions. In Linux, you can set it up by installing Apache, MySQL, and PHP packages. For Windows machines, you need to use one of the above-mentioned Apache-MySQL-PHP packages. In *Appendix A*, we will show how to set up a development environment by installing and configuring WAMP on a Windows machine.

PHP

If you plan to use Zen Cart, I am sure that you know about PHP. PHP is the hot scripting language for the web. You can get the latest version of PHP from www.php.net. You can download and install PHP package with your web server. For IIS, PHP can be configured as CGI or ISAPI; you can use either modes. For Linux, Apache-PHP-MySQL is installed by default. If you use WAMP, EasyPHP, or XAMPP web server package, you don't have to install and configure PHP separately.

Database

At present, Zen Cart supports only MySQL. MySQL version 4.1.x is recommended. However, Zen Cart can run on MySQL 5 server, but advanced features of MySQL 5 cannot be used in Zen Cart tables.

The data structure of Zen Cart is given in the mysql_zencart.sql file located in the zc_install/sql directory. Database tables will automatically be built during installation. However, you have to create the database and the user for login to that database before hand.

If you have installed WAMP or XAMPP, you will get MySQL server installed automatically. You can also use phpMyAdmin for managing databases in MySQL server. If you are using Linux hosting and cPanel, you can also use cPanel's database management tool and phpMyAdmin to create, delete, and manage databases and users.

Step-by-Step Installation

Once all prerequisites have been met, you can proceed to the installation of Zen Cart. The following sections describe the installation process for Zen Cart systematically, by using Fantastico and by uploading files to the server.

Through Fantastico

Fantastico is an excellent tool for installing a number of PHP applications on a server. Most of the Linux hosting services will give you access to your account through cPanel. Along with cPanel, you may also get Fantastico support. One of the benefits of installing a PHP application using Fantastico is that you don't need to bother about creating databases and uploading Zen Cart files separately.

A detailed discussion of use of cPanel is beyond the scope of this book. It is assumed that you know how to login and use cPanel. To learn more about cPanel administration, please refer to *cPanel User Guide and Tutorial*, published by Packt.

Step-by-step guidelines for installing Zen Cart using Fantastico are given below:

1. Login to cPanel and click on the Fantastico icon.

2. A list of available PHP applications will be displayed. Go to the E-commerce section and click on **Zen Cart** link.

3. A short description of Zen Cart, current installations, and a link for new installation will be displayed. You will be informed about the space required for the new installation too. Click on the **New Installation** link to install Zen Cart.

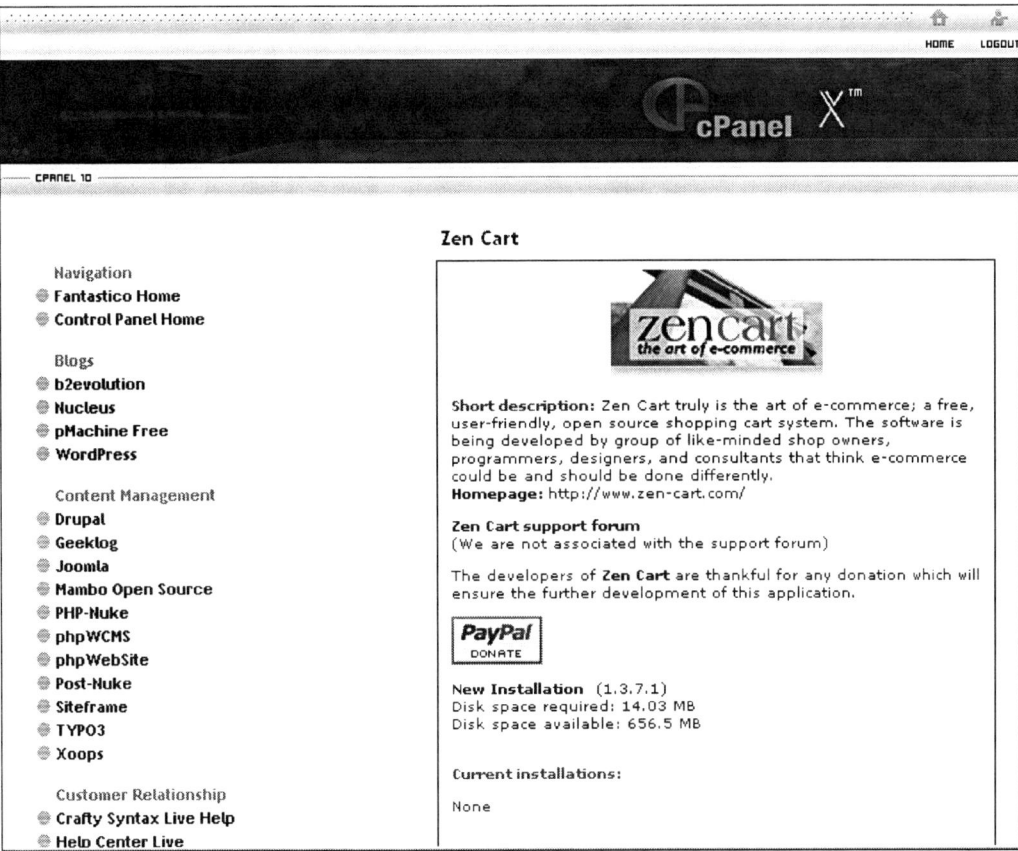

4. Steps 1 to 3 for Zen Cart installation will be shown. Then , you have to provide the following information:

- **Install on domain**: Select the domain on which Zen Cart will be installed. If you have a sub-domain of, say, shop.yourdomain.com, you can select it, or you can install on yourdomain.com domain.

- **Install on directory**: Enter the name of the directory on which Zen Cart will be installed. The directory should not already-exist; Fantastico will create a new one. If you want to install Zen Cart in the shop directory under your domain's root directory, just type shop in this field. Keep it blank to install it in that domain's root directory.

- **Administrator-username**: Enter the name of administrative account. This will be used to login to Zen cart administration panel.

- **Password**: Enter a password in this field. This will be needed to access the administrative panel.

- **Site name**: Give your shop an attractive name, which will be displayed in the browser title bar.

- **Admin email**: Enter the email address of the administrative user. All emails regarding administration will be sent to this address. If you forget the administrator account's password, a new password will be sent to this email address.

Once these fields are filled in, click on the **Install Zen Cart** button.

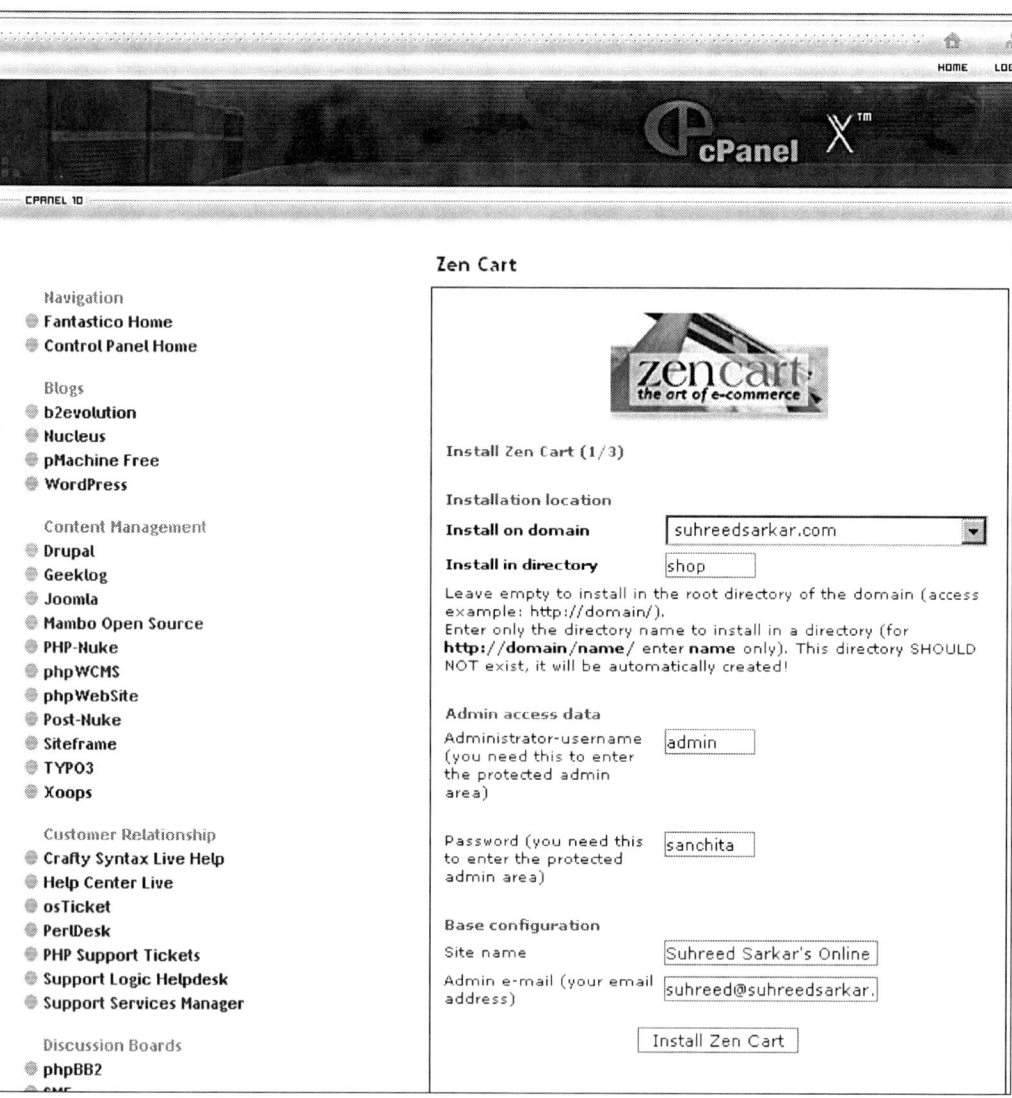

5. In the next step, a summary of your chosen configuration will be displayed. Click on the **Finish Installation** button.

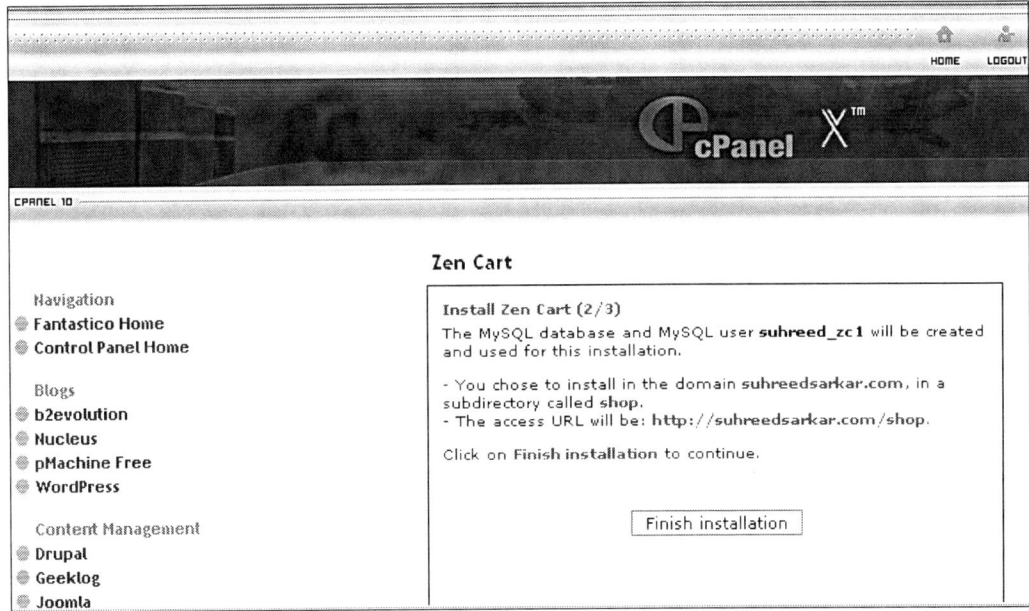

6. On clicking **Finish Installation**, the required files are copied to the target directory and a database is created with a user and password. The configuration file for Zen cart will also be created automatically. Then, a screen will indicate that you have installed Zen Cart successfully. You can notify others about this installation by entering their email address and pressing **Send E-mail** Button. You will also see links to your shop catalog and the administrative area in this screen.

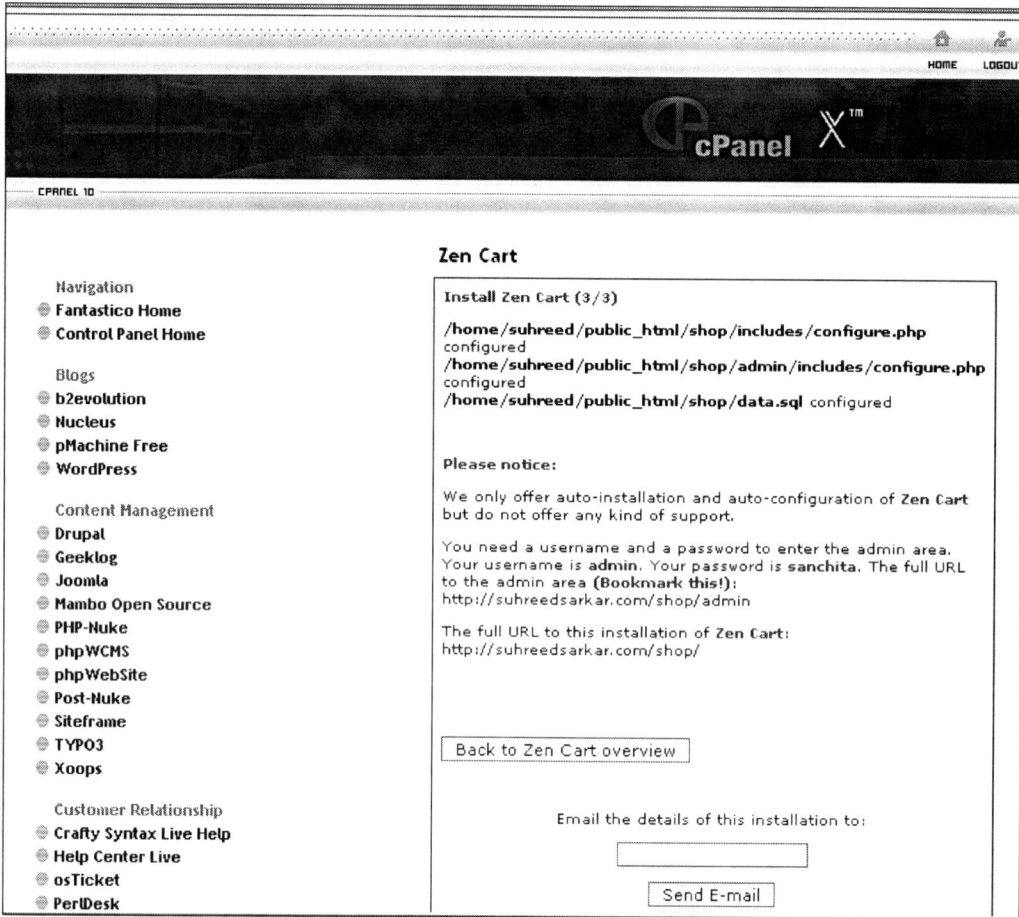

By Uploading Files

If you do not have Fantastico, do not worry. You can easily install Zen Cart by uploading the required files to the web server. Before doing this, you must download the latest version of Zen Cart from www.zen-cart.com. Unzip the zipped or gzipped package on your computer. Then, create the directory on your web server's webroot, and a database for Zen Cart on the MySQL server. Also, configure a database user to have the appropriate permissions (SELECT, INSERT, UPDATE, DELETE, CREATE, ALTER, INDEX, DROP) on this database. If you are using cPanel, you can use its tools such as phpMyAdmin for this.

You need an FTP program for uploading files to the server. FileZilla is a nice choice for this.

Web hosts have their preferences in naming folders for running a website. You can have many files that don't even get shown to the public. The ones that are available for access via a browser are usually in a specific folder, for example, `/home/yourname/public_html` or `/var/www/yourname/httpdocs` or `/usr/accounts/a/b/yourname/httpd` and so on.

You need to upload your files to one of these folders. If you want the shop to be in a directory different to that of the webroot, you must create a directory, say `shop`, in the webroot.

Before running the installer, you need to know the following facts:

- The physical path to your new Zen Cart directory, for example, `/home/suhreed/public_html/shop`
- The Virtual HTTP path (the URL of your domain and the directory for your shop), for example, `http://www.suhreedsarkar.com/shop`
- The Virtual HTTPS server or the secure URL to your domain, for example, `https://www.suhreedsarkar.com`. You can have a shared certificate on a virtual server, for example, `https://suhreedsarkar.secureservername.net/` or `https://secure.sharedservername.net/~suhreed`.
- The Virtual HTTPS path or the secure URL to your domain and directory for your shop, for example, `https://www.suhreedsarkar.com/shop` or `https://secure.sharedservername.net/~suhreed/shop`.

You must take note of these paths before starting the installation. You should also know your database name, username, and the password to access it. You have now uploaded the files to the `shop` directory, and you will use it for the following examples.

Once you have all of the information at hand, and have completed uploading all the files to the web server, you must start the installation with the following steps:

1. Open the browser and point to `http://www.yourdomain.com/shop/` `zc_install/`. You will find the following Zen Cart Setup, **Welcome** screen :

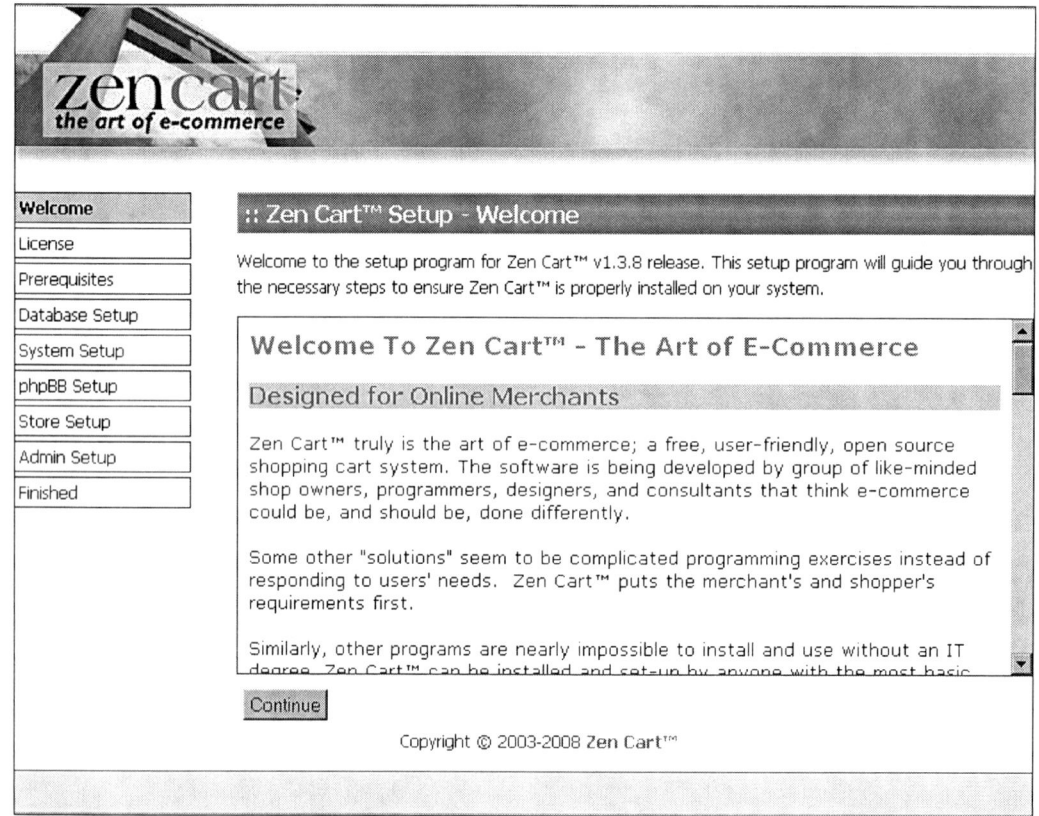

2. You can see a brief description in the **Welcome** page. To see the full description, you must scroll down and click on the **Continue** button to start the installation. On clicking the **Continue** button, the following **License Confirmation** page is shown:

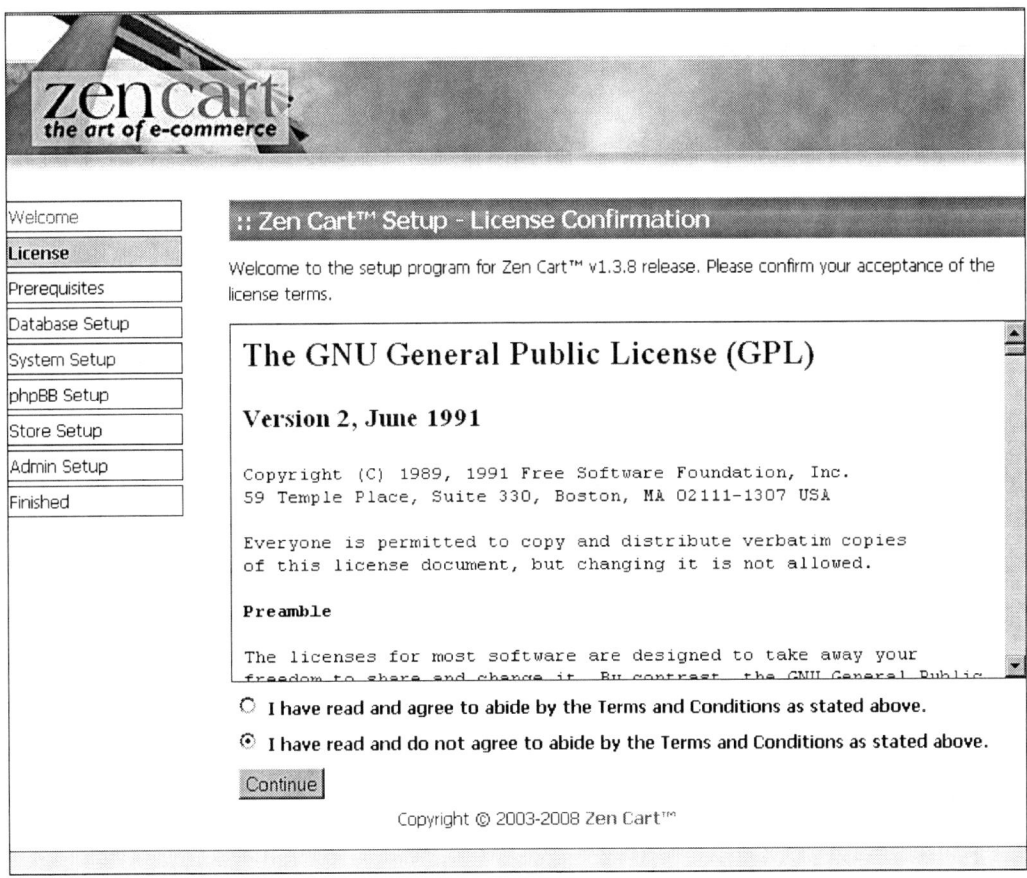

3. Zen Cart uses **GNU General Public License (GPL)**. To accept the licensing conditions, you must read and select **I have read and agreed to abide by the Terms and Conditions as stated above**. On clicking the **Continue** button, the **System inspection** screen will be shown.

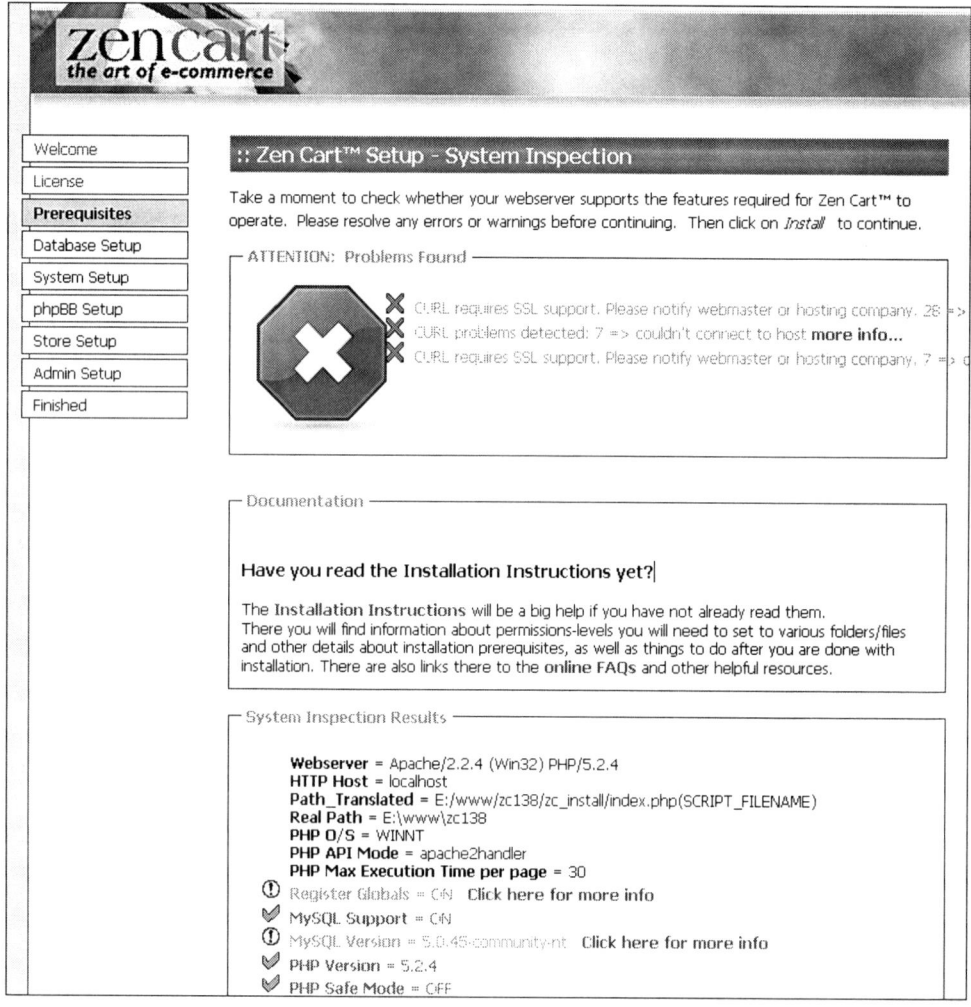

4. The **System Inspection** screen will show your server environment variables. Variables suitable for Zen Cart installation are shown in green. Any variable configuration not suitable for Zen Cart installation will be shown in red. To know about that variable's desired configuration click on **Click here for more info** link. If you find any variable in red, you must reconfigure it on your server and click on the **Recheck** button at the bottom. If everything is alright, then click on the **Install** button. The following **Database Setup** screen is then shown:

:: Zen Cart™ Setup - Database Setup

Next we need to know some information on your database settings. Please carefully enter each setting in the appropriate box and press *Save Database Settings* to continue.'

Database Information

Database Type
Choose the database type to be used. more info...   MySQL

Database Host
What is the database host? The database host can be in the form of a   localhost
host name, such as 'db1.myserver.com', or as an IP-address, such as '192.168.0.1'. more info...

Database Username
What is the username used to connect to the database? An example   root
username is 'root'. more info...

Database Password
What is the password used to connect to the database? The password
is used together with the username, which forms your database user account. more info...

Database Name
What is the name of the database used to hold the data? An example   zc138
database name is 'zencart' or 'myaccount_zencart'. more info...

Database - OPTIONAL Settings

It is recommended to leave these settings as-is unless you have a specific reason for altering them.

Store Identifier (Table-Prefix)
What is the prefix you would like used for database tables? Example: zen_
Leave empty if no prefix is needed.
You can use prefixes to allow more than one store to share the same database. more info...

Database Sessions
Do you want store your sessions in your database? Click 'yes' if you are unsure.   ⦿ YES ⦾ NO
more info...

SQL Cache Method
Select the method to use for SQL caching. more info...   None

Session/SQL Cache Directory
Enter the directory to use for   E:/www/zc138/cache
file-based caching. more info...

Save Database Settings

Copyright © 2003-2008 Zen Cart™

5. In the **Database Setup** screen, you have to configure the following options for the database:

    • **Database Type**: Select the type of database to be used for the Zen Cart shop. At present, you can only select **MySQL** as the **Database Type**.

- **Store Identifier (Table-Prefix)**: If you are using the same database for another application, it is better to separate Zen Cart tables with a prefix. Type a prefix for the tables, for example, **zen**, in this field.

- **Database Host**: Enter the database server's name in this field. Usually, it is localhost. If not, you can enter the hostname as dbserver. yourdomain.com in the **Database Host** field.

- **Database Username**: For connecting to the database, you need a database username. Remember that for shared hosting on the linux server, the username used to log into cPanel is prefixed to the database username, for example suhreed_zen, where suhreed is the account on that server, and zen is the database username.

- **Database Password**: Enter password for that database user in this field. This password must match with the existing database user's password.

- **Database Name**: You have to specify the name of the database that will be used for the Zen Cart Shop, for example, zencart or yourname_zencart. You must provide the name of an existing database. Therefore, you need to create this database beforehand. However, **Zen Cart Setup** can create the tables in the database.

- **Database Sessions**: You can store your session information in the database or separate file system. For storing sessions in the database, select **Yes** in this field.

- **SQL Cache method**: Caching SQL queries improves the performance of the Zen Cart shop. You can store SQL queries in the database or in file systems. Select the method that you want to use.

- **Session/SQL Cache Directory**: If you select a file system as SQL Cache method, specify the directory to be used for caching. By default, this is the cache directory under the Zen Cart installation.

6. Click on the **Save Database Settings** button to proceed to the next step. The installation process will create the database structures for Zen Cart. You will see an **Installation in progress ...** message while the database creation is ongoing. Once the database creation is complete, the following **System Setup** screen is shown:

Welcome
License
Prerequisites
Database Setup
System Setup
phpBB Setup
Store Setup
Admin Setup
Finished

:: Zen Cart™ Setup - System Setup

We will now setup the Zen Cart™ System environment. Please carefully review each setting, and change if necessary to suit your directory layout. Then click on *Save System Settings* to continue.

Server/Site Settings

Physical Path To Zen Cart™
Physical Path to your
Zen Cart™ directory.
Leave no trailing slash. more info...

E:/www/zc138

URL to your Zen Cart™ store
Virtual Path/URL to your
Zen Cart™ directory.
Leave no trailing slash. more info...

http://localhost/zc138

SSL Details

Do you already have an SSL Certificate? If so, enter the details below. If this is your first install, the supplied values are *only best-guesses*. Please verify the information with your hosting company if you are unsure of the correct details.

HTTPS Domain
Virtual server for your
secure Zen Cart™ directory.
Leave no trailing slash. more info...

https://localhost

HTTPS Server URL
Full Virtual Path to your
secure Zen Cart™ directory.
Leave no trailing slash. more info...

https://localhost/zc138

If your SSL certificate is already working, choose your SSL settings below.
DO NOT enable SSL here if you do not already have SSL enabled on your hosting account.
If you enable SSL but the SSL address you provide does not work, you will not be able to access your admin site nor log in to your store. You can activate SSL later by editing settings in your configure.php file.

Enable SSL
Would you like to enable Secure Sockets Layer in Customer area?
Leave this set to NO unless you're SURE you have SSL working. more info...

○ YES ◉ NO

Enable SSL in Admin Area
Would you like to enable Secure Sockets Layer for Admin areas?
Leave this set to NO unless you're SURE you have SSL working. more info...

○ YES ◉ NO

Save System Settings | Redetect defaults for this host

7. You have to provide some more information on the **System Setup** screen. First, enter the physical path to your Zen Cart directory in the **Physical Path** field. This will look like /home/Suhreed/public_html/shop or, for windows host, e:/www/shop. Then, enter the virtual path/URL of your Zen Cart shop in **URL to your Zen Cart™ store** field, For all paths, do not include a trailing slash, '/ ' at the end of the path. For an explanation of a fields, click on the **more info...** link beside the field. In the SSL Details section enter the URL of virtual directory for secure Zen Cart shop in **HTTPS Domain** field. The full virtual path of this secure directory should be mentioned in **HTTPS Server URL** field. If you want to use SSL to provide enhanced security for your shop, select **Yes** in the **Enable SSL** field. Select **Yes** in the **Enable SSL in Admin Area** field if you want to use SSL for access to the admin section. Usually, this screen will show the detected values for your server as defaults. Click on the **Redetect defaults for this host** button to get new values for these fields. Once you have entered all required paths and configurations, click on the **Save System Settings** button. The following **phpBB Setup** screen is shown:

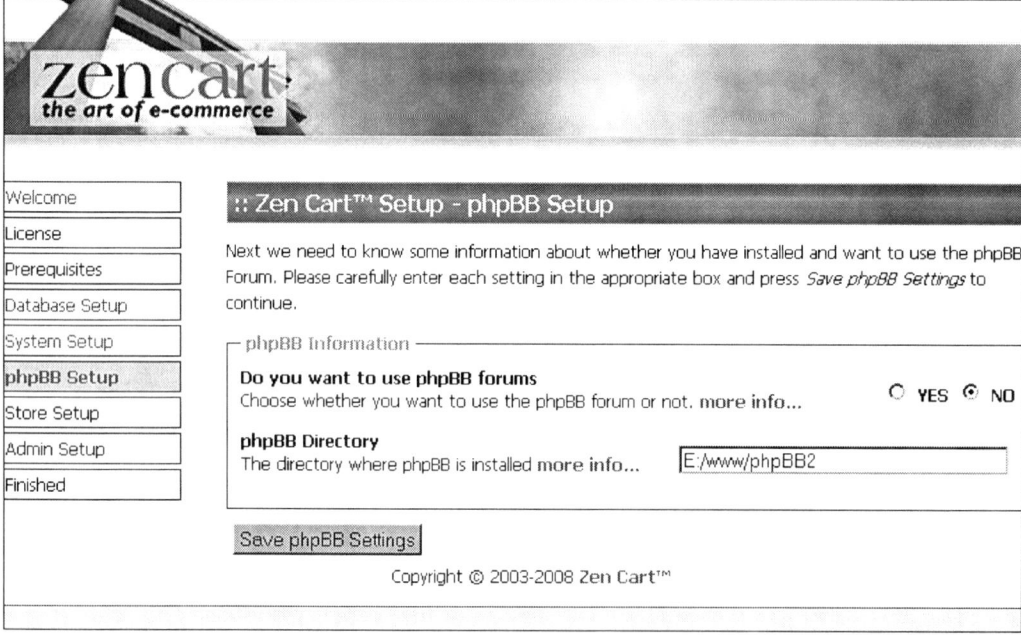

8. The phpBB screen gives you an option to integrate the phpBB forum with your shop. If you want to use phpBB with Zen Cart shop, select **YES** and then type the path of the phpBB installation in **phpBB Directory** field. You can get an explanation of these setting by clicking on the **more info…** link. Now, click on the **Save phpBB settings** button. The **Store Setup** screen is shown.

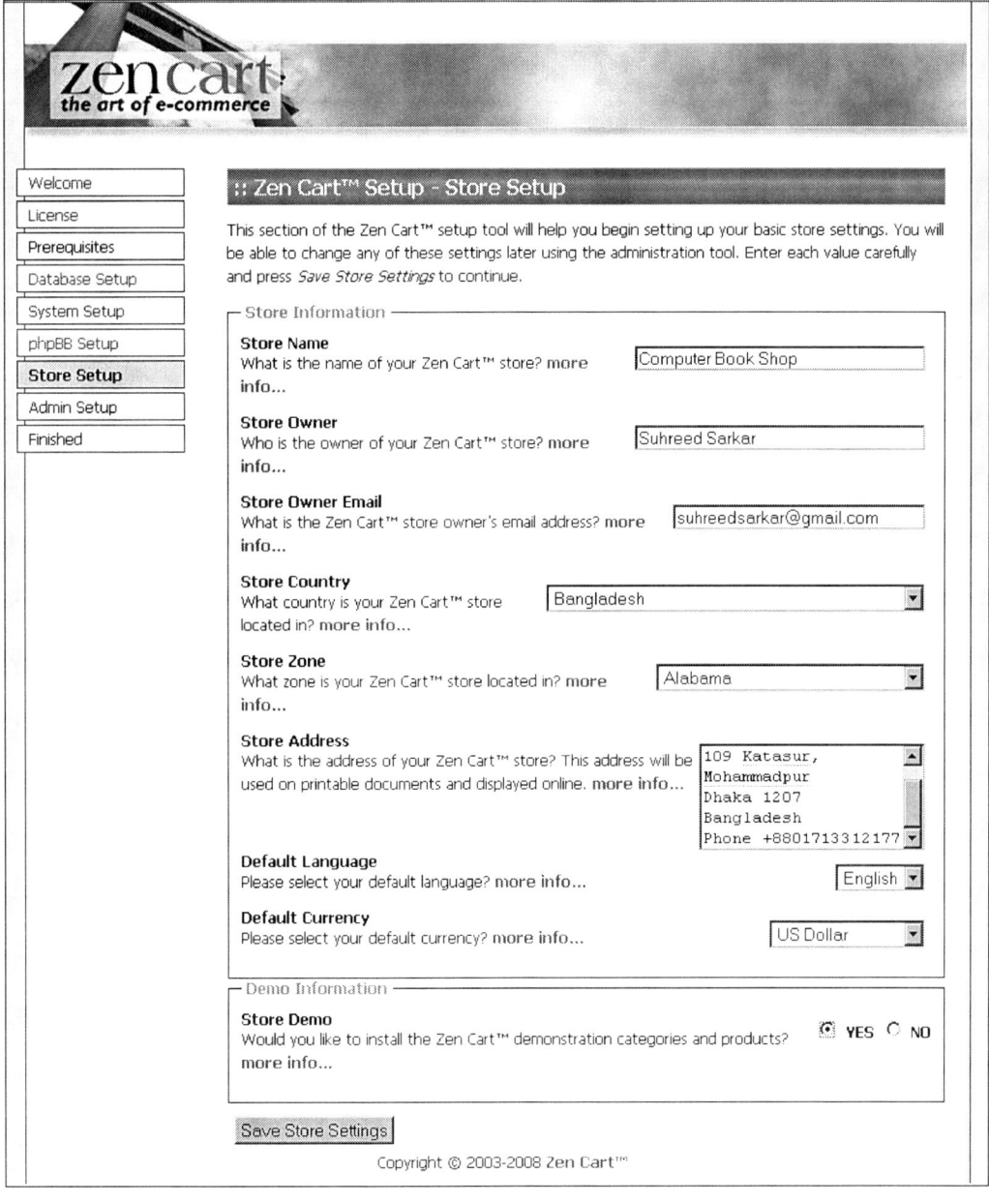

9. In the **Store Setup** screen, you must provide the **Store Name**, **Store Owner**, **Store Owner Email**, **Store Country**, **Store Zone**, **Store Address**, **Default Language** and **Default Currency**. Zen Cart comes with some example products and categories. To load these demo categories and products, select **Yes** in the **Store Demo** field. If you want to build a completely new product catalog, select **No**. Once these options are configured, click on the **Save Store Settings** button to proceed to the next step. The **Administrator Account Setup** screen appears, as shown below:

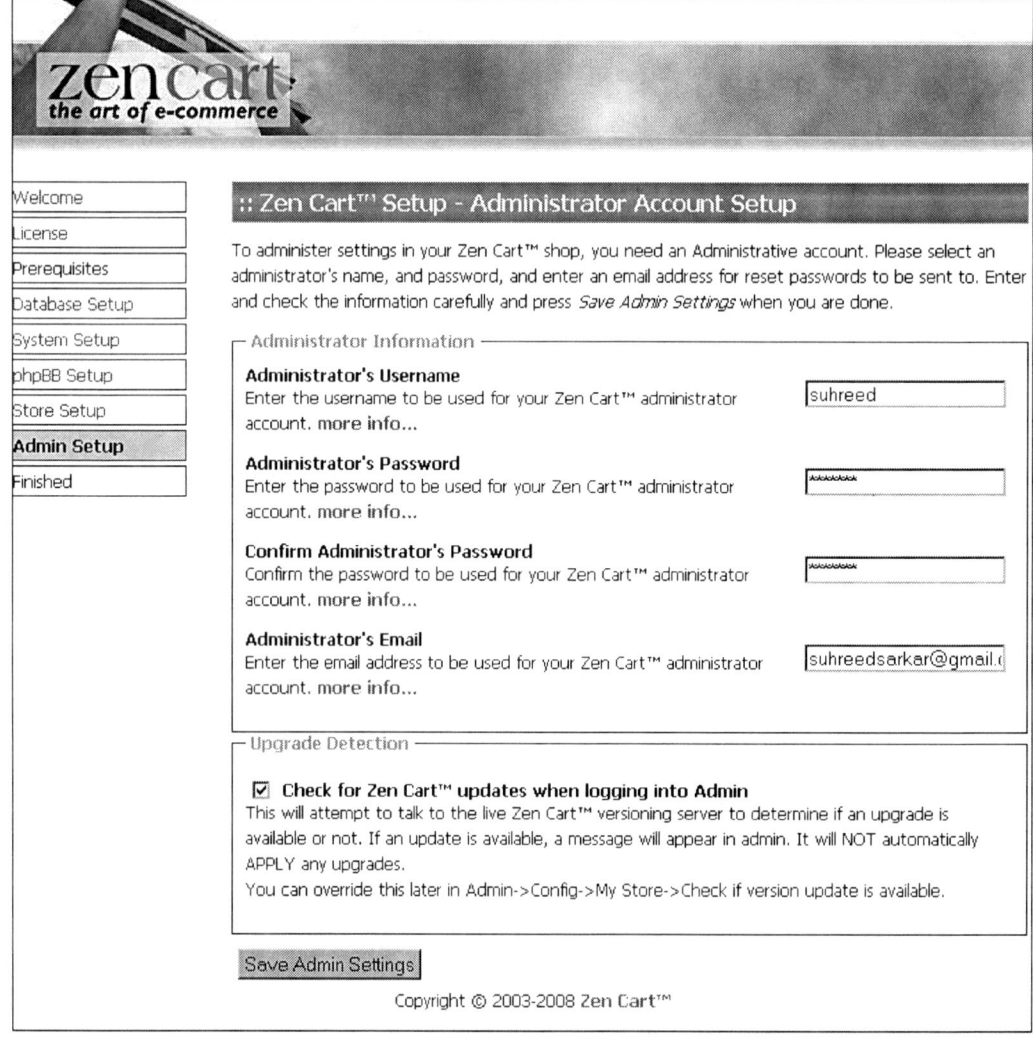

10. In the **Administrator Account Setup** screen, enter an **Administrator's Username**, **Administrator's Password** and **Administrator's email**. These will be used to login into the Administration panel for your shop. You have to confirm the administrator's password by retyping it in the **Confirm Administrator's Password** field. If you select **Check for Zen Cart updates when logging into Admin**, you will be notified about new versions of the Zen Cart release when you (as the administrator) log on. Click on the **Save Admin Settings** button.

11. Now, the **Zen Cart Setup Finished** screen is displayed. This screen will congratulate you on the successful installation of Zen Cart. It will also tell you about the next steps—setting permissions to the `configure.php` file, `zc_install` and `admin/includes/` folders. It will also show you some links for getting help. At the bottom of this page, you will see two buttons: **Click here to go to the Store** and **Click here to open the Admin area**. First check the store, and then try the admin area. You are going to explore these in a few minutes.

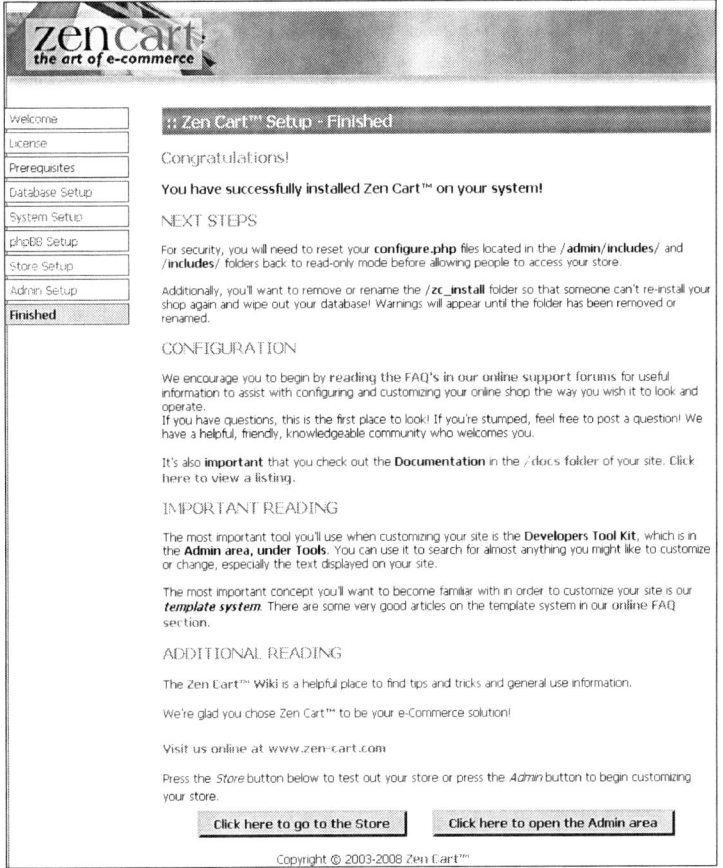

Upgrading from Previous Versions

Although installation of Zen Cart is very straightforward, you have to think twice before upgrading to a newer version of Zen Cart. The main concern during upgrading is to keep the existing product catalog and customer base intact. As you are running a live shop, you must always try to minimize offline time for maintenance. You will also need to ensure that your custom look and feel for the shop works flawlessly with the newer version of Zen Cart.

Before starting the upgrade, you need to experiment with it to ensure that it does not disrupt your shop's operations. For each new release, there are important documents in the /docs folder of the Zen Cart ZIP file. Please check the 2.readme_how_to_upgrade.html file for any special notes about the version you are upgrading from and upgrading to. Always keep a backup of your database and your files before starting the upgrade.

> During the upgrade, a file-comparison tool such as WinMerge, Beyond Compare or ExamDiff (Linux) may be very helpful to you. These tools will help you compare file changes, and understand implication of these changes. Once you understand the changes, you may have a clearer picture of what to expect after upgrading.

It is better if you can install the new version as a separate shop, with demo data, and browse through it to understand the new features. Doing so will help you understand whether that version will be compatible with your previous version of Zen Cart.

Preparation for Upgrading

First, unzip a copy of the new version of Zen Cart, upload it on to your web server, into a demo folder, install the new version into a separate database, and also include the demo products (these can be deleted after the conversion is complete).

Then, study the new features, and the changes to the template structures, as well as the change log. Use the demo products in the demo shop as examples. Also read the supporting documentation provided with the new release.

Take a full backup of your database by exporting it to an SQL file. Then, make a full backup of all of your site files and keep the backup on your computer. You may want to call this backup zen_backup.

Now, unzip a copy of the original Zen Cart files for your installed version. This should be placed in a separate working folder on your PC, perhaps \zen_orig. Then, make a list of any add-ons that you may have installed, for later reference.

Run a tool such as WinMerge to compare the original Zen Cart files in `\zen_orig` against your working backup files in `\zen_backup`. Note all of the files that are different - these are the files that you have changed or configured. In WinMerge, double-click on each file and note what the differences are. If the differences are just language definitions for display text, they will be simple to carry forward.

If the differences are actual programming/code differences, you will need to make detailed notes in order to replicate those changes in the new version. Any mods/add-ons you've installed are likely to contain many programming changes, and may not be fully compatible with the newer Zen Cart release.

Replicating File Changes

After identifying the changed files, go through each changed file, and copy your changes from the old version into the new version. Simple language edits will be just a matter of copy and paste. Programming changes to core components will be more difficult and may require significant testing.

Note that there will be several changes you will have to make to files that you have overridden using the template overrides system. Thus, you'll want to compare files from `/includes/templates/MYTEMPLATE/*` to `/includes/template/template_default/*`. Similarly, you will have to compare and change language files and sidebox overrides.

Testing and Upgrading

As indicated earlier, it is better to have a new database for the upgraded version, as the database structure may be different to the previous version. Therefore, you have to create a new database in which to install the new version of Zen Cart. Make a fresh database backup for your existing shop to include the last order that might have been processed, or the last customer registration. Now, restore your database to the new database you just created.

Now, you have to edit the `includes/configure.php` file to reflect the new database. If your `/zen_new` folder doesn't have `/includes/configure.php` and `/admin/includes/configure.php` files, copy them from the old store folder. Then, edit the `/zen_new/includes/configure.php` file to ensure that your **DATABASE_NAME** matches the new database that you have created. Make sure that the database username and password have also been changed. Now, save these changes so that you can upload the files to the web server.

Upload the modified files from the /zen_new folder to your web server into an alternate folder, for example, /zen_138. Once you have uploaded the files, run the /zc_install/index.php file, and choose **Upgrade** when prompted. Don't select **Install** at this stage as it will overwrite your database. If you do not find the **upgrade** option, then it may be the case that the installer was unable to connect to your database and confirm the database's version. In this case you should check your configure.php settings and correct accordingly.

Before going live, place the shop in **Down for Maintenance** mode from the admin area. Then, you need to add your IP address to the list of allowed addresses to get into the site for previewing. You must test the site to ensure that things are operating as planned. If you have any small problems to repair, turn **Down for Maintenance** on and off again as required.

Basic Configuration of the Store

On finishing the installation or upgrade, you may be tempted to check the new face of your shop. You may go straight to the store on completion of the installation process by clicking a button. Alternatively, you could open your browser and point it to http://www.yourdomain.com/shop/. Here, **shop** is the folder where you have installed Zen Cart. This will show the store with the demo categories and products and using the default design of of the store.

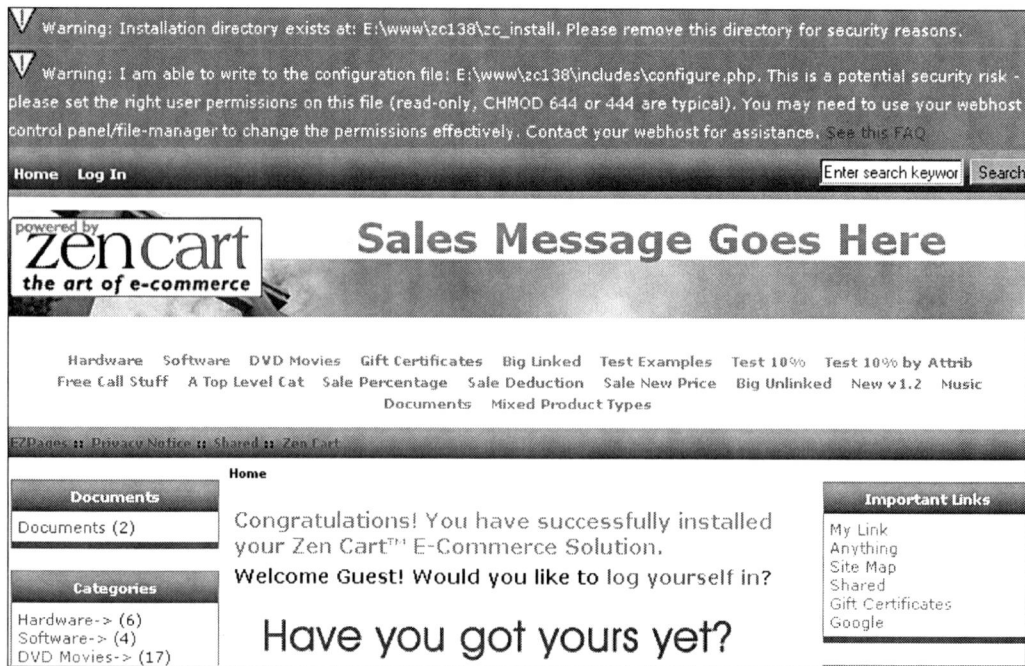

Note that, at the top, there are two warnings in red. These warnings ask you to remove the `zc_install` directory and make the `includes/configure.php` file read-only. You must resolve these problems before proceeding to change anything else.

Removing the Installation Directory

The first step after installation is to remove the installation directory, `zc_install`. Keeping this directory threatens the security of your site, as other people may point their browser to `www.yourdomain.com/shop/zc_install/` and override the installation settings. Therefore, you should either delete the whole directory, or rename it (in which case the name should be complex and hard to guess).

Setting Appropriate Directory and File Permissions

Some of the files and folders need special permissions to be set. For security reasons, you need to ensure that appropriate permissions are set to these files and folders. If appropriate permissions are not set, the browser will issue some warning messages. This section describes how to set up appropriate permissions on the Zen Cart folders and files.

Using FTP Programs

Most of the FTP programs allow you to change file permissions. Connect to your site using the FTP program, navigate to your `public_html` directory, and perhaps into your `zencart` folder underneath `public_html`. Then, look for a **Properties** command that can be applied to that directory. If you right-click on the folder, you will find **Properties** as one of the options.

If you are using FileZilla, you have to right-click on the folder and select **File Attributes**. Then, you change the permissions to the required settings for the following folders, as indicated below:

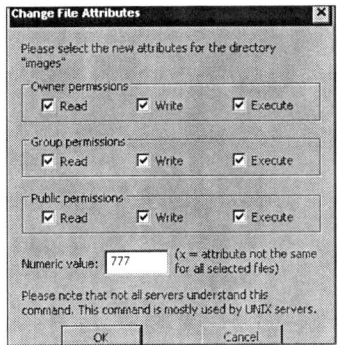

Set 777 (read, write, execute for all) to all of these folders:

- /cache
- /pub
- /images
- /includes/languages/english/html_includes
- /admin/backups
- /admin/images/graphs

Set 444 (read only) or 644 (read-write for owner, for others read-only) to these files:

- /includes/configure.php
- /admin/includes/configure.php

Using cPanel

If you are using cPanel, you can use its file manager to set permissions on the files and folders. Open **File Manager**, and browse to the folder where you have put your Zen Cart files. Click on the link of the file or folder (not on the icon), and then click on the **Change Permission** link on the right. You will see a permission setting box on the right, as shown below.

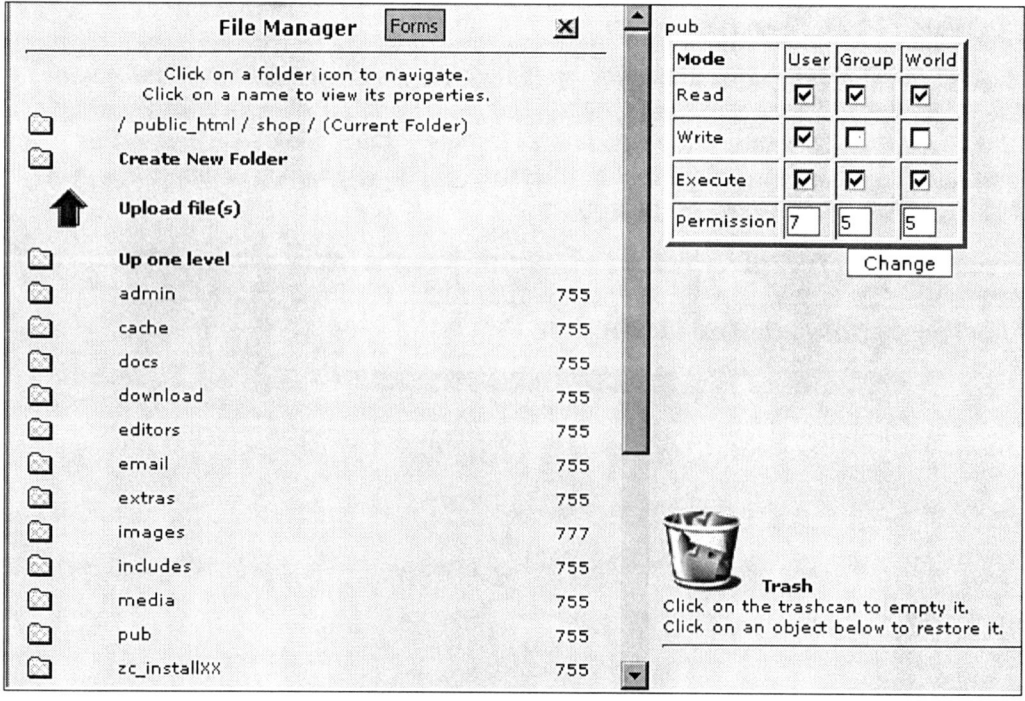

Set permissions to read, write and execute for the User, Group, and World groups by checking the appropriate nine checkboxes. You will see the permissions as numerical values (such as 644) in the Permission field. If there is an option to process all files under this subdirectory, check that box. Then, click **Change** or **OK** (or whatever) button to process the changes.

Using SSH

If you have SSH access instead of cPanel, you could type the following commands:

```
chdir /home/suhreed/public_html/shop (substitute your actual
working directory).
chmod -R 777 ./cache
chmod -R 777 ./pub
chmod -R 777 ./images
chmod -R 777 ./includes/languages/english/html_includes
chmod -R 777 ./admin/backups
chmod -R 777 ./admin/images/graphs
chmod 444 ./includes/configure.php
chmod 444 ./admin/includes/configure.php
```

Note that, uppercase R is important in these commands.

If you are using shared hosting, access to your server through SSH may not be available. In that case, using cPanel file manager is the best choice.

On a Windows Server

If you are using Windows server for your Zen Cart shop, you can set permissions to the folders and files as follows:

1. Navigate to the wwwroot folder or to the path where your Zen Cart files are in.
2. From the list of folders and files, right-click on a particular file or folder.
3. Choose **Properties** from the pop-up menu.
4. Click on the **Security** tab.
5. Now, add the **IUSR_xxxx** user account where xxxx is the computer name and give it read write permissions. **IUSR_xxxx** account is the local account for accessing your folders.
6. Click on **OK** to close the Properties box.
7. If you do not see a Security tab in step 4 above, you have to simply select the Read and Write boxes. Deselect the read-only checkbox if it is already select.
8. Repeat these steps for all required files/folders, as indicated earlier in this section.

On a Windows PC

You can also try your Zen Cart on Windows PC (Windows 2000 Professional, Windows XP, and so on). In such cases, you have to set the following folder and files permissions:

1. Navigate to the `wwwroot` folder or the path your Zen Cart files are in.
2. Right-click on the required files or folders as listed earlier.
3. Choose **Properties**.
4. Set the read-only flag on or off depending on your requirements
5. Click **Apply** or **OK**.
6. Repeat for all the required files/folders.

> You may be interested to know more about CHMOD and the permission system. For getting a good lesson on CHMOD and linux permission system, you can—visit the following sites: `http://en.wikipedia.org/wiki/Chmod` and `http://en.wikipedia.org/wiki/File_system_permissions`. You can also use this online CHMOD calculator to calculate CHMOD values: `http://www.classical-youbdesigns.co.uk/resources/whatchmod.html`.

Changing Configuration File

Zen Cart's configuration options are set in the database. However, for connecting to the database and locating the required files and directories, a configuration file is used. Zen Cart's main configuration file is `includes/configure.php`. This file contains the directory and database connectivity variables. Usually, you don't have to edit this file manually - it is configured during installation. However, you may need to edit it manually if you want to change the database name, user, or password. If you relocate a directory, you will also need to reflect this in the file.

Now, let's have a look at the main variables in this file and understand what each variable means:

```
// Define the webserver and path parameters
// HTTP_SERVER is your Main webserver: eg, http://www.yourdomain.com
// HTTPS_SERVER is your Secure webserver:
                                    eg, https://www.yourdomain.com
  define('HTTP_SERVER', 'http://www.suhreedsarkar.com');
  define('HTTPS_SERVER', 'https://www.suhreedsarkar.com');
// Use secure webserver for checkout procedure?
  define('ENABLE_SSL', 'false');
```

```
// NOTE: be sure to leave the trailing '/' at the end of these lines
// if you make changes!
// * DIR_WS_* = webserver directories (virtual/URL)
// these paths are relative to top of your webspace ... (ie: under the
// public_html or httpdocs folder)
  define('DIR_WS_CATALOG', '/shop/');
  define('DIR_WS_HTTPS_CATALOG', '/shop/');

  define('DIR_WS_IMAGES', 'images/');
  define('DIR_WS_INCLUDES', 'includes/');
  define('DIR_WS_FUNCTIONS', DIR_WS_INCLUDES . 'functions/');
  define('DIR_WS_CLASSES', DIR_WS_INCLUDES . 'classes/');
  define('DIR_WS_MODULES', DIR_WS_INCLUDES . 'modules/');
  define('DIR_WS_LANGUAGES', DIR_WS_INCLUDES . 'languages/');
  define('DIR_WS_DOWNLOAD_PUBLIC', DIR_WS_CATALOG . 'pub/');
  define('DIR_WS_TEMPLATES', DIR_WS_INCLUDES . 'templates/');

  define('DIR_WS_PHPBB', '/');

// * DIR_FS_* = Filesystem directories (local/physical)
// the following path is a COMPLETE path to your Zen Cart files.
// eg: /var/www/vhost/accountname/public_html/store/
  define('DIR_FS_CATALOG', '/home/suhreed/public_html/shop/');

  define('DIR_FS_DOWNLOAD', DIR_FS_CATALOG . 'download/');
  define('DIR_FS_DOWNLOAD_PUBLIC', DIR_FS_CATALOG . 'pub/');
  define('DIR_WS_UPLOADS', DIR_WS_IMAGES . 'uploads/');
  define('DIR_FS_UPLOADS', DIR_FS_CATALOG . DIR_WS_UPLOADS);
  define('DIR_FS_EMAIL_TEMPLATES', DIR_FS_CATALOG . 'email/');

// define your database connection
define('DB_TYPE', 'mysql');
define('DB_PREFIX', '');
define('DB_SERVER', 'localhost');
define('DB_SERVER_USERNAME', 'suhreed_shop');
define('DB_SERVER_PASSWORD', '******');
define('DB_DATABASE', 'suhreed_zencart');
define('USE_PCONNECT', 'false'); // use persistent connections?
define('STORE_SESSIONS', 'db'); // use 'db' for best support, or ''
for file-based storage

// The next 2 "defines" are for SQL cache support.
// For SQL_CACHE_METHOD, you can select from:  none, database, or file
// If you choose "file", then you need to set the DIR_FS_SQL_CACHE to
// a directory where your apache or webserver user has write privileges
// (chmod 666 or 777). We recommend using the "cache" folder inside
// the Zen Cart folder ie: /path/to/your/webspace/public_html/zen/
// cache -- leave no trailing slash
 define('SQL_CACHE_METHOD', 'none');
 define('DIR_FS_SQL_CACHE', '/home/suhreed/public_html/shop/cache');
```

This file is self-explanatory. For most of the variables, instructions are given inside comments (lines starting with //). In most cases, you may need to change the DIR_WS_CATALOG and DIR_WS_HTTPS_CATALOG variables to reflect your installation directory. Also, you may need to change the DB_SERVER_USERNAME, DB_SERVER_PASSWORD, and DB_DATABASE variables. Note the differences between DIR_WS_* and DIR_FS_* variables. DIR_WS_* variables are for the webserver. This means that DIR_WS_CATALOG represents the webserver path to the catalog directory, for example, http://www.suhreedsarkar.com/shop. On the other hand, DIR_FS_* is for the file system path. This means that DIR_FS_CATALOG represents the path in the files system, for example, /home/suhreed/public_html/shop/.

There is another file for the admin section—admin/includes/configure.php. This file is completely different from the includes/configure.php file and must not be accidentally overwritten. The admin/includes/configure.php file contains settings for the secured admin area. Some of the variables in this file are:

```
//following settings are webserver paths
define('DIR_WS_ADMIN', '/shop/admin/');
define('DIR_WS_CATALOG', '/shop/');
define('DIR_WS_HTTPS_ADMIN', '/shop/admin/');
define('DIR_WS_HTTPS_CATALOG', '/shop/');
define('DIR_WS_IMAGES', 'images/');
define('DIR_WS_ICONS', DIR_WS_IMAGES . 'icons/');
define('DIR_WS_CATALOG_IMAGES', HTTP_CATALOG_SERVER . DIR_WS_CATALOG .
'images/');
define('DIR_WS_CATALOG_TEMPLATE', HTTP_CATALOG_SERVER . DIR_WS_CATALOG
. 'includes/templates/');
define('DIR_WS_INCLUDES', 'includes/');
define('DIR_WS_BOXES', DIR_WS_INCLUDES . 'boxes/');
define('DIR_WS_FUNCTIONS', DIR_WS_INCLUDES . 'functions/');
define('DIR_WS_CLASSES', DIR_WS_INCLUDES . 'classes/');
define('DIR_WS_MODULES', DIR_WS_INCLUDES . 'modules/');
define('DIR_WS_LANGUAGES', DIR_WS_INCLUDES . 'languages/');
define('DIR_WS_CATALOG_LANGUAGES', HTTP_CATALOG_SERVER . DIR_WS_
CATALOG . 'includes/languages/');

//following settings are file system settings
define('DIR_FS_ADMIN', '/home/suhreed/public_html/shop/admin/');
define('DIR_FS_CATALOG', '/home/suhreed/public_html/shop/');
define('DIR_FS_CATALOG_LANGUAGES', DIR_FS_CATALOG . 'includes/
languages/');
define('DIR_FS_CATALOG_IMAGES', DIR_FS_CATALOG . 'images/');
define('DIR_FS_CATALOG_MODULES', DIR_FS_CATALOG . 'includes/
odules/');
define('DIR_FS_CATALOG_TEMPLATES', DIR_FS_CATALOG . 'includes/
```

```
templates/');
define('DIR_FS_BACKUP', DIR_FS_ADMIN . 'backups/');
define('DIR_FS_EMAIL_TEMPLATES', DIR_FS_CATALOG . 'email/');
define('DIR_FS_DOWNLOAD', DIR_FS_CATALOG . 'download/');
```

There are also settings for the database and cache folders. Database settings are the same as the `includes/configure.php` file.

Using the Administration Panel

Once you have installed Zen Cart, you can try to log in to the admin area. Point your browser to `http://www.youdomain.com/shop/admin/`. Then, type the administrative username and password, which you had defined during installation. You can click on the **Login** button to proceed.

The administration panel is the area from where you will configure your store for public use, and add products to your catalog. This panel will also be used for managing customers, products, and orders.

When you first enter the administration panel, you will see a dashboard with a summary of products available, orders received, orders unfulfilled, new customers, new orders, and other statistics for your shop. This information is very useful for a shop owner for monitoring day to day operations.

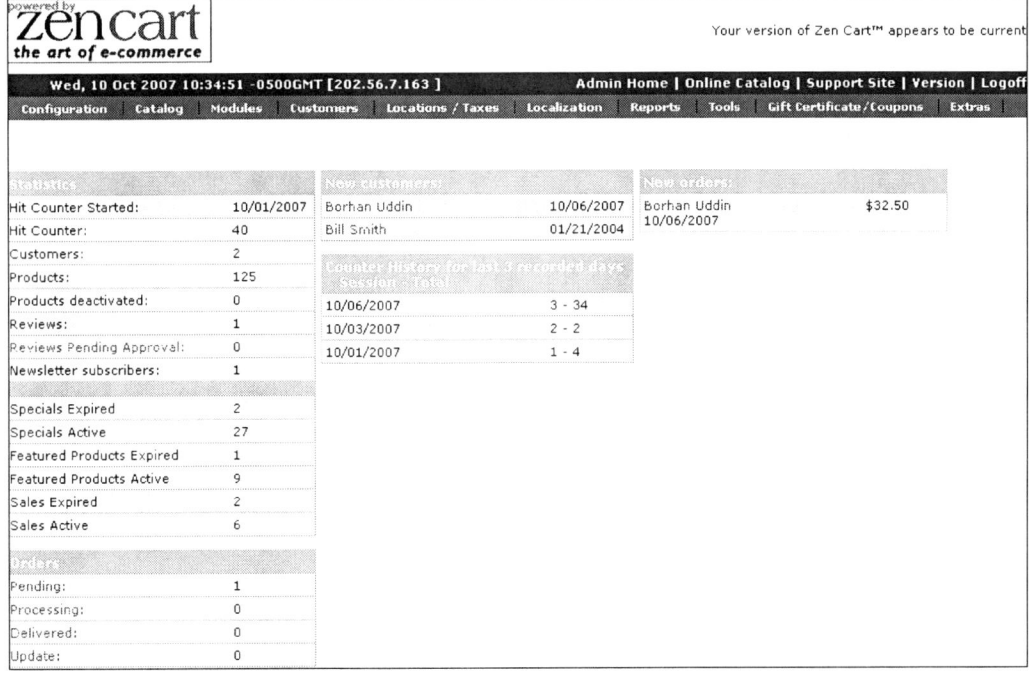

To make your store usable for others, you have to configure your store first, that is configure its name, address, shop owner's email, email transportation method, and so on. You can configure your shop from **Configuration | My Store**. We will learn about these configuration options in the next chapter.

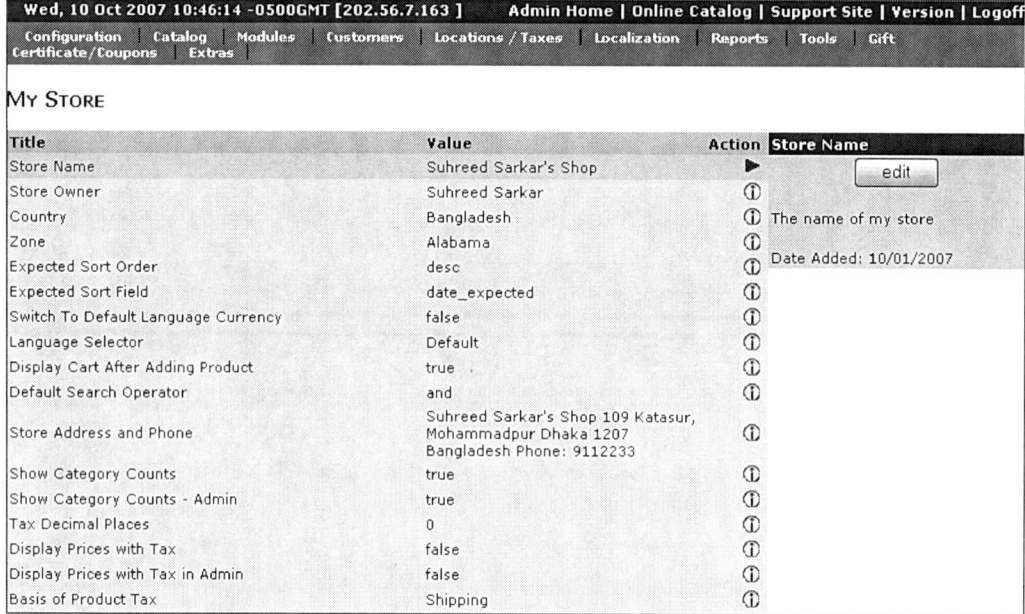

Summary

In this chapter, you have learned about prerequisites to installing Zen Cart. You have also learned the step-by-step procedures for installing Zen Cart using Fantastico, and by file uploading. Then you learned about upgrading from an older version to a newer version of Zen Cart.

You have also learned about the file and folder permissions that need to be set for effective operation of the Zen Cart shop. You have seen that certain files and folders need special permission for read and write. Finally you have learned how to login to the admin areas and configure the shop's name, address, and so on.

Once the installation is complete, the shop has to be configured for the customers' use. Zen Cart includes a lot of configuration options. In the next chapter, you will learn about configuring the shop. Until then, you can reward yourself with a mug of coffee for having installed Zen Cart successfully!

3
Configuring the Store

By now, you have learned how to install Zen Cart and log into the administration area. In this chapter, you are going to learn about different configuration options for the store.

On completion of this chapter, you will know:

- How to set global configuration options for a Zen Cart store
- How to manage the product catalogue
- How to install and configure payment, shipping, and order total modules for Zen Cart store
- How to manage customers and orders

The configuration options introduced in this chapter are essential.

Shop Configuration

Before launching your shop online, you have to configure several aspects of your shop. First, you configure the store's name, address, store owner's name, login options, product listing, payment, and shipping options, and so on. Then, you add categories and products to your product catalog. Once the shop is live, customers will place orders and you will have to manage those orders.

Store Name and Address

Before launching your online shop, you need to specify your store's name and address. You can define these via **Configuration | My Store**. You should at least change the **Store Name, Store Owner, Country, Zone, Store Address**, and **Phone**. These are the essentials for starting your online shop.

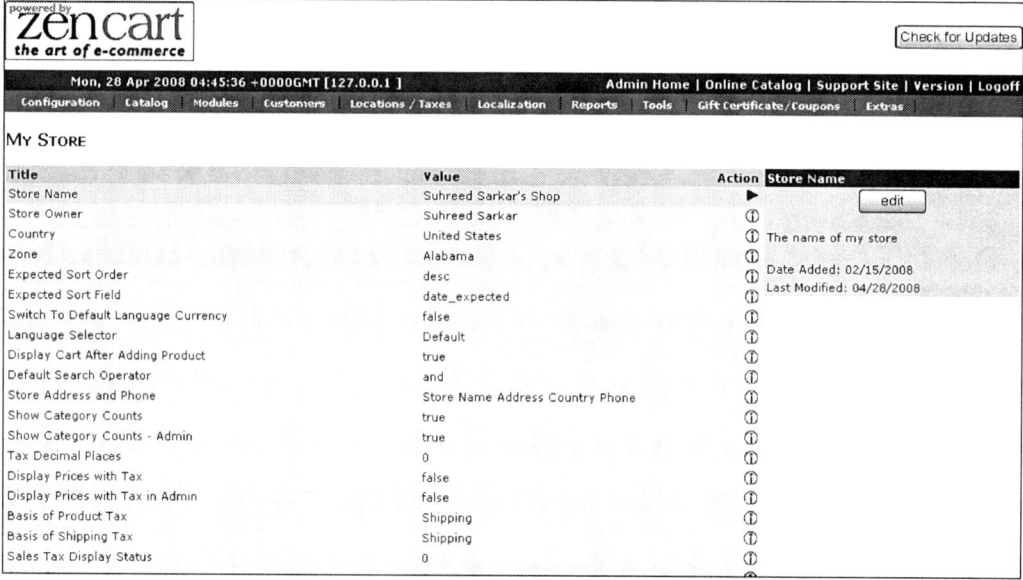

There are some interesting settings on this screen. If your store is multilingual, then you can specify in what language the store will be shown—based on the store's default language or on the browser's language settings. Select **Default** or **Browser** in the **Language Selector** field, as required.

When showing the category lists, you may want to know how many products are there in each category. Select **true** in the **Show Category Counts** field to show the product counts. Similarly, you can show the products count in the admin area by selecting **true** in the **Show Category Counts – Admin** field.

Product prices can be shown with tax. Set **Display Prices with Tax** to display the prices inclusive of tax. You can also specify the basis on which the product and shipping taxes are computed. This may be based on the tax rules in the originating country (where store is located), billing address (from where the bill will be paid), or destination country (where the product is shipped to). You have to select the appropriate settings in these fields.

You can use a Zen Cart store as a showcase or as a normal store by setting the following values in the **Store Status** field:

- **0 (=Normal Store)**: Setting **0** in **Store Status** field will display the store in normal mode where customers can buy products from the store.

- **1 (=showcase no prices)**: Setting this value will display the shop as a showcase, where customers will not be able to place orders. This option will only show the product listing and descriptions, but not the prices.

- **2 (=Showcase with prices)**: setting this value in **Store Status** field will display the shop in showcase mode and also display the product prices.

Another important setting on the **My Store** screen is the **Currency Conversion Ratio**. You can automatically update currency exchange rates in Zen Cart. In this case, you may want to uplift the conversion by a certain ratio. This will be added to the conversion rate. As the bank rate is obtained from the currency-exchange servers, this conversion ratio will enable you to charge extra in order to make up the difference between the bank rate and the consumer rate.

Customer Information

You can define the extent to which you are going to collect information on customers. From the **Configuration | Customer Details** screen, you can define the fields that are going to be presented during account creation, and identify the absolute essentials for purchasing a product from your store.

You may want to know the customer's age to be sure that the person who is buying a product is an adult and legally authorized to transact online. For this, you require the birth date of each customer during account creation. Set the **Date of Birth** option to **true**. This will show the **Date of Birth** field during account creation. However, the customers could leave it blank. To make it a required field, set the value **>0** in the **Date of Birth** field in the **Configuration | Minimum Values** screen.

You can show or hide the Company, Address Line 2, State, and Fax Number fields. If you want to show the states as a drop-down list, set the **State - Always display as pulldown?** field to **true**. Further, if you can set a default country from the **Create Account Default Country ID** field. If you want to promote your newsletter, set **1** or **2** in the **Show Newsletter Checkbox** field. Similarly, you can set **Customer Default Email Preference** to **1** =Text or **2** =HTML.

Some online shops require users to sign up before they can browse products and make purchases. If you want to do this, change the **Customer Shop Status – View Shop and Prices** field. You can set a value of **0** to **3**:

- If you want all visitors to be able to browse the products, but only require registration to place an order, then set its value to **0**.

- If you want only registered customers to be able to browse the products, then set its value to **1 =Must login to browse**.

- Setting it to 2 means everyone can browse the products but they cannot see the prices until they login to the shop.

- If you want to make it a showroom, so that nobody can place an order, set this field to **3 =Showroom only**.

Some of the other settings related to **Customer Authorization** are also on this screen. Default values will work for most of the shops.

You may want to track customer referrals, and provide a discount coupon up on signing up to your shop. In this case, you must define the necessary setting in the **Customer Referral Status** field. You may keep it off (0), use 1st Discount Coupon Code (1), or allow customer to type a coupon code during account creation (2). If you really want to give your customers a discount coupon on signing up, create a discount coupon via **Gift Certificates/Coupon | Coupon Admin first.** Then, select that coupon in the **New Signup Discount Coupon ID#** field from the **Configuration | GV Coupons** screen.

> Actual configuration of gift vouchers and discount coupons are discussed in detail in Chapter 6, *Promotion and Public Relations*. In that chapter you will learn how to configure and send discount coupons to customers on different occasions.

Product Listing

You can configure for how the product list and descriptions will be shown. From **Configuration | Product Listing**, you can define the fields that will be displayed on the product listing page. The first half of the options controls the fields that appear in the product listing, and their order. If you want an element to not appear on the page, give it a value of **0**. A non-zero value means the element will be shown, and the number defines the sort order for the field.

The **Display Product Listing Default Sort Order** setting on the same page depends on these settings. Settings with a value (that is, sort order) of **0** will be ignored, while the rest will be assigned an incrementing ID based on the sort order. For example, if you set **Display Product Name** to **1**, **Display Product Price/Add to Cart** to **3** and the rest to **0**, then **Display Product Name** is assigned an ID of **1** and **Display Product Price/Add to Cart** is assigned an ID of **2** (not **3**, which is the sort order).

You can also edit **Display Product Listing Default Sort Order**. This setting should contain two characters; the first character is the ID of the field which has already been discussed, and the second character should be the letter 'a' for ascending, or 'd' for descending. If you want to sort product field, in descending order, then use **2d**.

From this screen, you can also enable or disable display of product images, the add to cart box, product name, module, manufacturer, price, weight, quantity box, category, and so on.

Email Options

Several emails can be sent to your customers from your Zen Cart shop. Usually, customers who subscribe to newsletters and product notifications receive regular emails. However, whenever a customer registers or places an order, he or she receives an email. For some other reasons, you may also need to notify the customers from time to time. You can set various email configuration options via **Configuration | Email Options.** As a minimum, you have to configure the following options:

- **Email Transport method**: You must specify whether the server will use a local connection to send mail or use an **SMTP** connection via TCP/IP. Servers running on Windows and MacOS should change this settings to **SMTP. SMTPAUTH** should be used only when your server requires **SMTP** authorization to send messages. You must also configure your **SMTPAUTH** settings in the appropriate fields in this admin section. **Sendmail -f** is only for servers which require the use of the `-f` parameter to send email. This is a security setting often used to prevent spoofing. The default for this field is **sendmail**, and this will work fine with Linux servers.

- **Use MIME HTML When Sending Emails:** Set this to **true** if you want to send emails in HTML format. Otherwise keep the default value of **false**.

- **Send Copy of ***: There are several options such as **Send Copy of Order Confirmation Emails To**. Type an appropriate email address to which the notifications will be sent. If your store is small, and only one person handles all these, then set only one email address for all of the fields. But for large stores, you may assign several people to order tracking, gift voucher management, review management, and so on. In this case, you must provide email addresses of those persons or departments.

- **SMTP Email Account Mailbox**: If you have selected **SMTPAUTH** as the email transport mechanism, then type email account's SMTP mailbox name.

- **SMTP Email Account Password**: Here, enter the password for your SMTP mailbox. This field is required only if you are using SMTPAUTH as the email transport.

- **SMTP Email Mail Host**: Here, enter the DNS name of your SMTP mail server, for example, `mail.yourdomain.com`. This is required only if you are using SMTPAUTH as the email transport mechanism.

- **SMTP Email Mail Server Port**: Here, enter the IP port number, generally 25, that our SMTP mail server operates on. This is required only if you are using SMTPAUTH as email transport mechanism.

 When facing problems with email, always check these configurations first.

Logging

Logging is important for your online shop, especially when you face problems with your shop. You can set the options for controlling how events are logged via **Configuration | Logging**. The following are some of the options:

- **Store Page Parse Time**: Set this to **true** if you want to log the time it takes to parse a page. This information may be helpful to analyze your store's performance.

- **Log Destination**: Here, set the directory and filename of the page parse time log in this field. The default is `/var/log/www/zen/page_parse_time.log`. Change it to your required path.

- **Log Date Format**: Set the date format to be used in logging. The default format is **%d/%m/%Y %H:%M:%S**.

- **Display The Page Parse Time**: You can display the page parse time at the bottom of each page by setting this field to **true**. Otherwise, storing parse time in the log file will be a good choice.

- **Store Database Queries**: Storing database queries in the log file may help you troubleshoot query problems later. Set this value to **true** if you want to store the database queries in the page parse time log.

Log files are always helpful for troubleshooting. It is recommended that you enable logging for your online shop. This will give you the opportunity to analyze what happens in your shop. Also remember to manage the log file. You may need to clear the log file regularly to limit its growth.

Regulations

Every online store has some rules and regulations that must be followed by the customers. You must always provide the terms and conditions of purchasing products from your online shop, and obtain the customers' acceptance of these. You can set the terms and conditions for the customers in **Configuration | Regulations**.

If you set **Confirm Terms and Conditions During Checkout Procedure** to **true**, the **Terms and Conditions** page will be shown during the checkout procedure, and the customer must agree to them before they can complete their purchase. This is a good way of reminding the customer of the terms and conditions of purchasing products from your shop.

Nowadays, most of the customers are aware of their privacy. As you collect some private information from the customers, it would be good to show a privacy notice during account creation. Set **Confirm Privacy Notice During Account Creation Procedure** to **true** to show the privacy notice during the account creation procedure, which the customer must agree to before they can create their account.

[ You must develop your terms and conditions carefully. This should be legally correct and also acceptable to both parties. You will find some standard notices at Zen Cart website's download section.]

EZ Pages

EZ-pages in Zen Cart give us opportunities to easily create static pages. From the **Configuration | EZ Pages Settings** page, you can set various options to configure the EZ-Pages. Creation and editing of EZ-Pages is controlled via **Tools | EZ-Pages**.

You can set the elements of an EZ Page that will be shown – header, footer, left sidebar, right sidebar, Prev/Next buttons, table of contents, and so on. The default settings for these fields are suitable for most of online shops. However, you have the option of changing them to suit your requirements.

Images

A variety of images are shown in Zen Cart shop. You can configure the images and the way these images will be shown. Via **Configuration | Images**, you can set the options used to control the size of images on each page/for each type of content. Set these to the same size as the images you create. Otherwise, your images will appear distorted. There are some general options on how the images are handled, and a single option that controls the layout of additional product images on the **Product Info** page. You can set the options any way that you want them.

GZip Compression

From the **Configuration | GZip Compression** page, you can control the GZip compression settings for your online shop. Enabling **GZip Compression** means that all content from your store is compressed before it is downloaded to the user. The contents are then decompressed by the user's web browser. This compression and decompression is transparent to the user and significantly speeds up their browsing. It is therefore recommended that you turn this on if your webserver supports it.

Stock

You can set options to control various options regarding stock control via **Configuration | Stock**. There are also two Shopping Cart page layout options here. To get an updated stock level, enable **Check stock level** and **Subtract stock**. Specify a mark that will be shown when a product is out of stock. In **Show Sold Out Image in Place of Add to Cart** field, set **1** to show an image when a product is out of stock. You may set a **Stock Re-order Level** to a convenient value, instead of the default of **5**. If you want to show products that are out of stock, select **1** in the **Products status in Catalog when out of stock should be set to** field.

Shipping/Packaging

If you are selling physical products, then shipping and packaging options will be an important issue for your shop. You can set general shipping information including locations, and weight and size limits via **Configuration | Shipping/Packaging**. The following options needed to be configured:

- **Country of Origin**: The country of origin from which the products will be shipped. This will be used for calculating the shipping cost.

- **Postal Code**: Here, enter the postal code (ZIP code) of the store. This is to be used in the shipping quote.

- **Enter the Maximum Package Weight you will ship**: The shipping methods you are using may prohibit you from shipping a heavy package. Generally, carriers have a maximum weight limit for a single package. Set the maximum weight limit that can be shipped through all carriers.

- **Package Tare Small to Medium—added percentage:weight**: Here, you should define a percentage of the product weight as packaging. This is expressed as two numbers separated by a colon. The first number is a percentage of the weight of what will be our small package weight. The second is our small package weight maximum or upper limit.

- **Larger packages – added packaging percentage:weight**: Here, you should define a percentage of product weight as packaging. This is expressed as two numbers separated by a colon. The first number is a percentage of the weight of what will be our large package weight. The second is our large package weight average or maximum or upper limit.

- **Display Number of Boxes and Weight Status**: You must specify whether you want to show the number of boxes, the weight, or both the number of boxes and the weight during checkout. Set **0** to show none, **1** to show the number of boxes only, **2** to show the weight only, and **3** to show both the number of boxes and weight. The default is set to **3**.

- **Order Free Shipping 0 Weight Status**: For some products, the weight may be zero. In that case, calculating the shipping cost returns no value. You may consider such products as being eligible for free shipping. Set 1 to use free shipping for such products.

- **Shipping Estimator Display Settings for Shopping Cart**: You can show a link to the shipping estimator on our shopping cart. Set **1** to show it as a button, and **2** to show it as a link.

- **Shipping Estimator Display Settings for Shopping Cart**: You can show a link for the shipping estimator on your shopping cart. Set this filed to **1** to show it as a button, and **2** to show it as a link.

- **Display Order Comments on Admin Invoice**: For this option, there are again three options, **0= OFF** means that comments will not be displayed on the Admin Invoice. Option **1= First Comment by Customer only** will show the comments by the customes only. Option **2= All Comments for the Order** means that all of the comments for the order wll be displayed on the Admin Invoice.

- **Display Order Comments on Admin Packing Slip**: This is very much similar to the above option.

Attribute Settings

Via **Configuration | Attribute Settings**, you can set options for controlling which product attributes are maintained, and whether downloadable products are allowed, and how they are handled. For downloadable products, there are eight options. First, you have to set **Enable Downloads** to **true**. Then, you have options to set the following:

- Which method will be used for downloading – redirecting or streaming?
- After how many days will a download product expire?
- How many downloads are allowed per product?
- How will the download controller status be updated?

Other attribute settings are for pricing. You can enable price factors, quantity price discounts, attribute images, and text pricing by word or by letter.

Credit Cards

For online payments, you have the option to enable use of the credit cards. Via **Configuration | Credit Cards,** you can determine which credit cards can be accepted. However, this will not turn payment processing on. It will simply enable customers to use specific credit card, and display the credit card on the payment page. We can show the credit cards list as text or images. To show the image, set **2** in the **Credit Card Enabled - Show on Payment** field. You also need to upload the credit card images to the images directory and define these images in the language file. Editing the language file is discussed in Chapter 5, *Localization of Zen Cart.*

Product Info

From **Configuration | Product Info,** you can set some basic options for controlling the elements that are included on the **Product Info** page. You can also set some page layout options for the **Previous** and **Next** buttons. These settings will be applied to all product types.

You may define the product image, height and weight, previous and next buttons, previous and next bar position, and so on. From here, you can set the contents of the product information page.

Layout Settings

A wide range of options for controlling different layout options are available via **Configuration | Layout Settings**. These are global options that will appear on all pages, and there are also some options for individual sideboxes. From here, you can set column widths, breadcrumb positions and option, category display, banner display, and so on. Although you can change the width of the left and right columns, it would be wiser to look at your templates first. Changing these values may change your look and feel unexpectedly.

Zones, Currencies, and Taxes

The countries of the world can be divided into zones. These zones are useful for applying taxes and calculating shipping costs. Zen Cart can use multiple currencies in your shop. You can also use taxes specific to a zone. Zones, Currencies, and Taxes are managed from the **Locations/Taxes** menu. These are discussed in detail, in Chapter 5, *Localization of Zen Cart.*

Catalog

After configuring the shop, the shop owner's main task will be to manage the product catalog and orders. You can add and change products and categories from the **Catalog** Menu.

Product Types

Product Types in Zen Cart allow us to present different information for types of products in the shop (and possibly in a different format). If you are selling books, for example, you should show some special information, such as author name, edition, ISBN, number of pages, cover type, and so on. A product type, say a book, can collect this custom information in addition to other generic product information for that book. Similarly, a product type, say music, will collect different information (artist name, download size, mp3 clip) and will be displayed differently. **Catalog | Product Types** allows us to view and edit product types.

On the **Catalog | Product Types** page, you will see a listing of product types. For each product type, you can select the default settings, such as default tax class for the new products of that type. You can also set layout options by clicking on the **edit layout** button. You will see the layout options for the product type you have chosen.

When you are creating products via **Catalog | Categories/Products,** beside the **New Product** button you will see a pull-down menu for choosing a product type. The product type that you select from this menu is the type of product that you will create. The product creation form will be different depending on the product type you have chosen.

[ By default, the music product type is bundled with Zen Cart v 1.3.7.x. For earlier versions, there was a product type named book. I liked that for creating a book store. That add-on has been archived now.]

Manufacturers

Products should be cataloged according to manufacturer. This manufacturer information can also be displayed on the product details page. **Catalog | Manufacturers** allows us to view, add, edit, or delete manufacturer information.

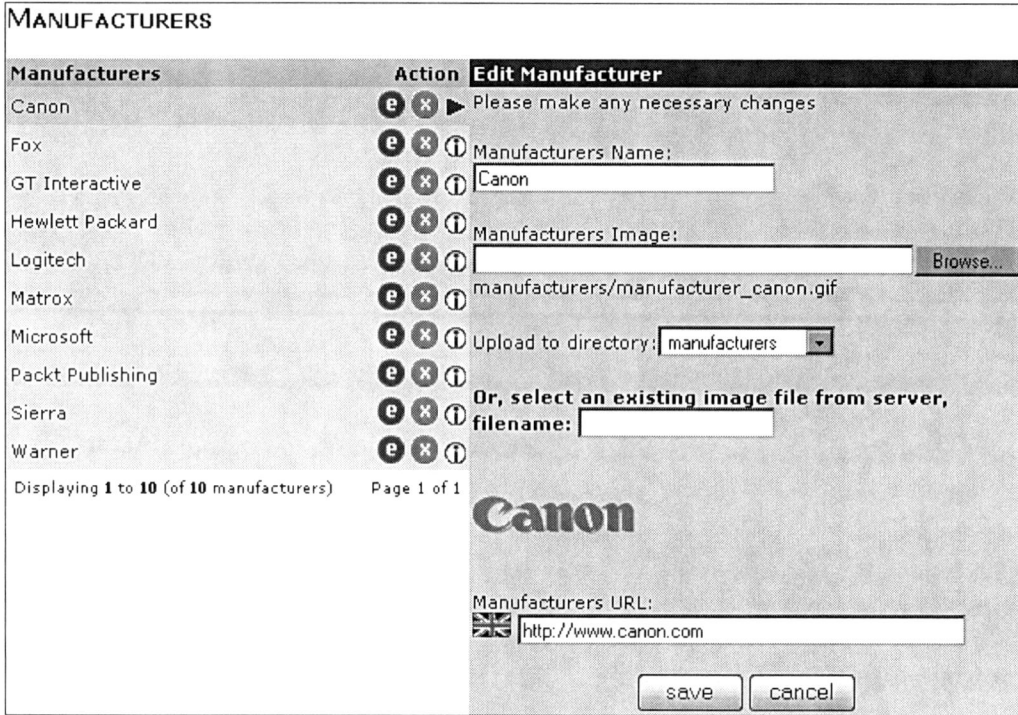

You can add a manufacturer by clicking on the **insert** button. This will display the new manufacturer screen (shown above). The following information should be provided on this screen:

- **Manufacturers name**: Here, enter the manufacturer name, for example, **Canon**.

- **Manufacturers Image**: Here, navigate to and select the product image on your computer. This image will be uploaded to your webserver.

- **Upload to directory**: Select the directory on the webserver to which the manufacturer's image will be uploaded. Alternatively, you can keep all of the manufacturers' images in one directory. Then, if you have already uploaded the image to that directory, you can select a folder and enter the image name in the **Or, select an existing image file from server, filename:** field.

- **Manufacturers URL**: Here, enter the URL for the manufacturer's website.

Categories/Products

Once you have added the product types and manufacturers, you can create the product categories and products. Create and edit your products and categories via **Catalog | Categories/Products**.

Managing Categories

In order to add products to your store, you need at least one category. Create a category by clicking the **new category** button. Products must be placed inside categories. Otherwise, Zen Cart may experience various problems. For example, it may not display the products, or searches may not work.

You can create multiple nested categories. For the new categories, you have to enter a name, description (in each active language), image to be uploaded for that category (or the filename of the image on the webserver), image upload directory, and sort order. To create a sub-category, click on the parent category and then click on the **new category** button.

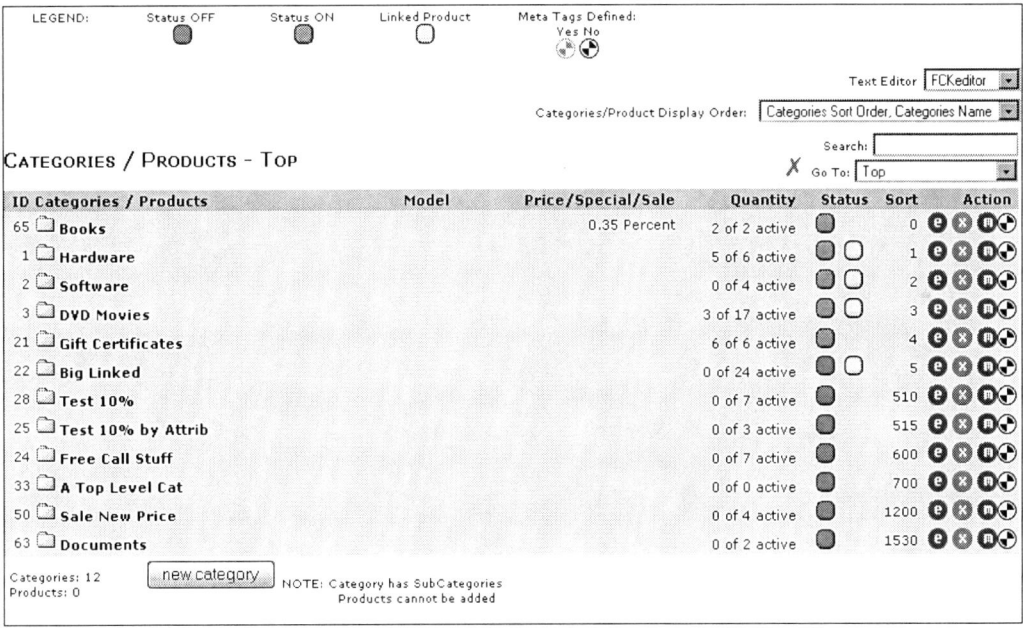

To edit a category, click on the edit icon on the right of the row for that category. From the edit screen, you can restrict that category (including sub-categories) to only contain a certain product type. For example, if you have a category named books, you can restrict this category to the book product type only. Similarly, the music category can be restricted to the music product type only. Select the appropriate product type in the **Restrict to Product Type** drop-down list and click on **Add include SubCategories** or **Add without SubCategories**.

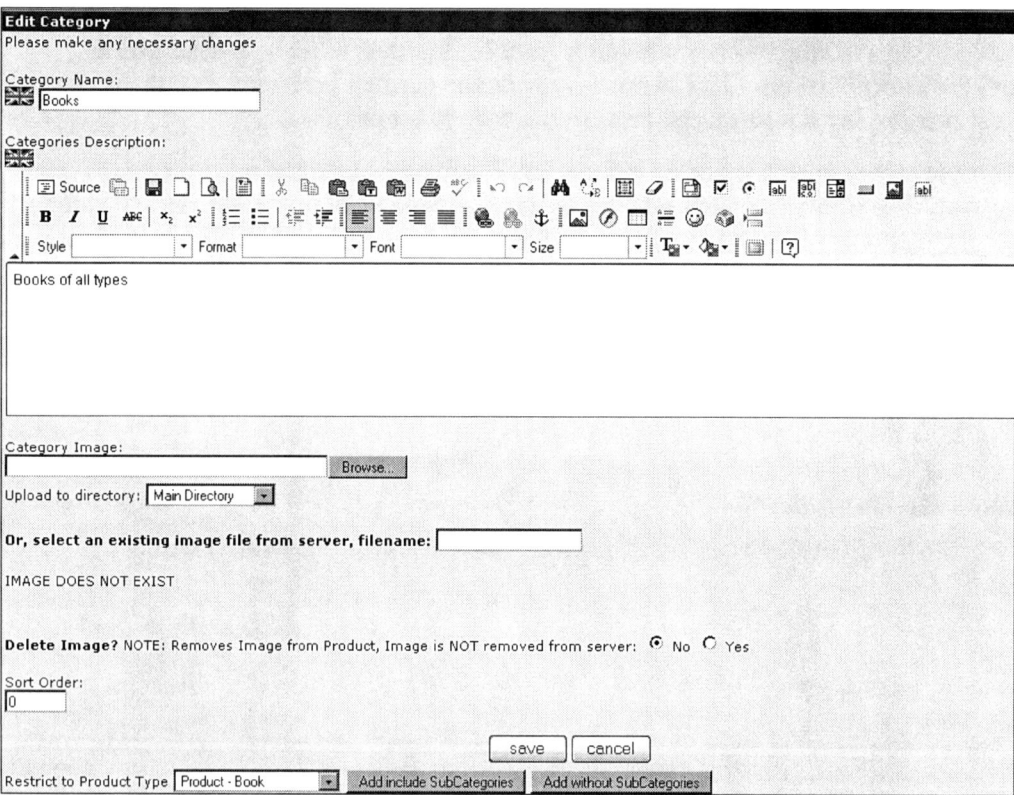

Each category may have multiple sub-categories, but it cannot contain both sub-categories and products. There is no restriction on the number of products or categories you can have in a category. Moreover, there is no restriction on the number of levels of subcategories. However, keep the nesting to a minimum for better management of the product catalog.

You can copy one category to another category and make it a sub-category. You can also delete a category, or a sub-category. Deleting a category does not automatically delete the products under it, but if the products lose their master category ID, they will no longer be shown in the catalog. Therefore, you must always move the products to another category before deleting their parent category.

Managing Products

Once you have created all of the categories and know which products to be included in each category, you can start adding products to these categories. For helping catalogers, you can prepare a guideline for choosing the appropriate categories. Restricting categories to specific product types will also help.

To add a product to a category, click on that category's icon. If that category has a sub-category, you will not see the **new product** button. So, click on the subcategories, until you see a **new product** button. Then, select the appropriate product type and click on the **new product** button. The following figure shows how a product is added:

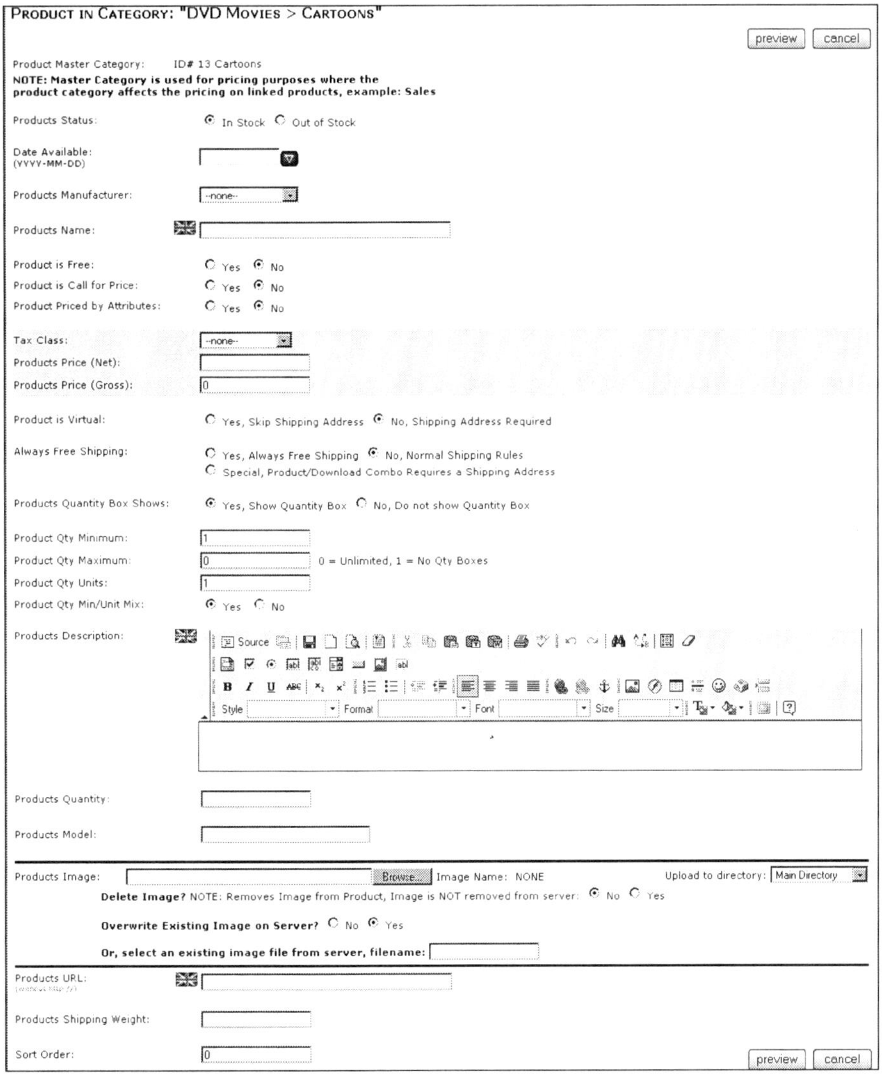

Based on the product type you have chosen, you will have to provide specific information about that product. Typical information that you may need to provide includes: product name, manufacturer name, stock status, availability date, tax class, net and gross price, minimum and maximum order quantity, product description, quantity, model, product image, URL, shipping weight, and sort order. If you are adding a product of music product type, you need to provide music genre, recording company, recording artist, and so on. For book type products, you need to add author(s) name, edition, number of pages, publisher, sub-title, subject, format, publication date, and so on.

Before adding a product to the catalog, you must prepare images for that product. Images for product should be high-quality but, at the same time, small in size. Although Zen Cart displays images according to the configured size, do not use very large images as these will take more webserver space and more time to load.

Products by Options/Attributes

You may sell products with options and attributes. For example, if you are selling T-shirts, you may offer four colors and four sizes S, M, L, and XL. For a change of color the price remains the same, but for a size change the price changes too. This type of product is appropriate for selling using attributes. We have to select **Yes** in the **Product Priced by Attributes** field while creating that product.

For using options and attributes with products, you have to create the options and values first, and then assign those option-value pairs to products through the attribute manager.

Option Name Manager

Before you can add attributes to your products in **Catalog | Attributes Controller**, you need to create option names and give them values wherever appropriate. **Catalog | Option Name Manager** allows us to view, edit, add, and delete option names.

Follow these steps to create an option:

1. In the first text box, **en:** type the name of your attribute option. This should be informative as it will appear in your shop.

2. In the second box, **Order:** type the sort order that you want the attribute to appear under the product.

3. In the drop-down box, select the type of attribute that you want.

- **Dropdown** box: Requires option values that you can set in **Catalog | Option Value Manager**.

- **Text**: A text area box that does not require option values.

- **Radio**: A button that allows customers to select an option value. The customer can only select a single value from the available options. This requires option values.

- **Checkbox**: A square box that allows customers to select an option value. The customer can select multiple values from the available options. This requires option values.

- **File**: This type of attribute allows customers to upload files. File extensions can be set via **Configuration | Maximum Values**, in **Allowed Filename Extensions**. This attribute does not require option values.

- **Read only**: These attributes are for display purposes only and are not part of a calculation. They also do not appear on the order page. It is an informational attribute that can be used with one or more products and then changed once to apply to all products to which the attribute has been assigned. However, this requires option values.

4. Click the **insert** button to save the option.

Once you have created an option, you can edit it by clicking **edit** next to the option name. Then, change the following settings:

- **Comments**: Specify the text that your customers will see above your option name. Make this informative so that customers know what they need to enter. For example, if the option name is to upload a file, you can tell your customer the file extensions that are allowed.

- **Rows**: The number of rows you want your input/text area box to have.

- **Display Size**: This is the size of the input/text area box your customers will see on the screen.

- **Maximum length**: This is the maximum number of characters including spaces, that your customer will be able to type into the input/text area box.

- **Attribute Images per Row**: The number of images and option values that you would like on each row.

- **Attribute Style for Radio Buttons/Checkbox**: If you choose your option as a radio box or checkbox, you can define how they will appear. The following number values can be used:

  ○ **0 = Images Below Option Names**

  ○ **1 = Element, Image and Option Value**

  ○ **2 = Element, Image and Option Name Below**

  ○ **3 = Option Name Below Element (check box/radio button) and image**

  ○ **4 = Element (check box/radio button) Below Image and Option Name**

  ○ **5 = Element Above Image and Option Name**

Option Value Manager

Once you have defined the option name, you can add values to it via **Catalog | Option Value Manager**. You will see the list of option names, values, and sort orders. At the bottom of the list, select the option name from the drop-down list, and then enter the value into the **en**: text box, and specify the sort order in **order** textbox. Now, click on **insert** to save it. Add all the other values for the same option name. Now, your option-value pairs are ready to be added in the attributes controller.

OPTION VALUES

<< | 1 | 2 | 3 | 4 | 5 | 6 | 7 | >>

ID	Option Name	Option Value	Default Order	Action	
6	Model	Premium	20	edit	delete
8	Model	PS/2	20	edit	delete
7	Model	Deluxe	30	edit	delete
67	Shipping	Free Shipping Included!	10	edit	delete
37	Size	Select from below ...	5	edit	delete
19	Size	X-Small	10	edit	delete
21	Size	Small	20	edit	delete
18	Size	Medium	30	edit	delete
20	Size	Large	40	edit	delete
68	Version	Book Hard Cover	5	edit	delete
69	Size ▼	en: [ ]	Order: [ ]	insert	

Attributes Controller

Once you have added option names and values using **Catalog | Option Name Manager** and **Catalog | Option Value Manager**, you can add these options to products via **Catalog | Attributes Controller**. You can also start attribute controller from product list by clicking on attribute controller icon (**A**).

To add an attribute to a product, you must follow these steps:

1. Go to the large gray box titled **Adding New Attributes**.
2. Select the option name that you want to add from the first scroll box .
3. Select a matching option value from the second scroll box, for example, select option name Size [dropdown] from the first box and Small [SIZE:] from the second box.
4. Click the **insert** button.

The price and weight of the product may vary depending on the product attributes. When adding attributes to a product, you can configure the price and weight changes. When selecting an option and a value, **Price** can be entered with a prefix of + (plus) or − (minus) or blank. '+' or blank means an increase, and '−' means a decrease. Generally, the price we enter here will be added to, or subtracted from, our base price based on the use of the + or − prefix. But when **Price by Attribute** is enabled, the price we enter here will be added to your base price regardless of the prefix.

Weight can optionally be entered if it affects the product weight. You can use a prefix of '+' or '−' or blank. Using '+' and blank will add the attribute weight, while '−' will subtract the attribute weight, from the product's base weight.

You can also define quantity discounts. Quantity discounts (**Attributes Qty Price Discount**) are useful when the entire group of products being ordered has a different price depending on the quantity purchased. You can also specify the quantity discounts as: 1:11, 5:10.00, 8:9.00,10:8.00,15:7.00,20:6.00, 50:5.00.

This can be best expressed as shown in the following table:

Size XL						
QTY 1	2-5	6-8	9-10	11-15	16-20	20+
PRICE $11.00	$10.00	$9.00	$8.00	$7.00	$6.00	$5.00

As you can see, definition consists of a number of quantity:price pairs. The first number in the pair is the minimum quantity that must be purchased, and the second number in the pair is the price that the customer will pay if they purchase (at least) that quantity. The quantity discount will be applied only to products with specific attributes (here, size XL).

One-time quantity discounts (**Onetime Attributes Qty Price Discount**) allow specific amounts to be applied to quantity discounts. For example, 400:5 will apply a one-time charge of $5 to an order with any number of items less than 400. Negative numbers work in these entries as well, creating a quantity discount. This is useful if you define a base price and would like to allow the user to have the discount off the base price.

Attribute flags

You can use flags for attributes to make these attributes special. These are used to define other features of the attribute, such as:

- **Used For Display Purposes Only**: Some attributes may be used for display purposes only, and cannot be selected and added to cart. For example, you may have a blue color t-shirt, and the color it has been expressed through an attribute. You don't want to give the option to the customers to choose a color. In this case, you can set this attribute to be display only.

- **Attribute is Free When product is Free**: Select this to make the attribute free when the product is free. Otherwise, selecting the attribute will add the price to the free product.

- **Default Attribute to be Marked Selected**: Selecting this will set a default value for attribute. A default value needs to be selected.

- **Apply Discounts Used by Product Special/Sale:** This will apply the same type of discount that the product is getting from the products' price against the special or sale price.

- **Include in Base Price When Priced by Attributes**: When products are priced by attributes, selecting this flag will add the lowest-priced attribute to the base price of the product.

- **Attribute Required for Text**: This means that the customer must fill in this field before adding it to the cart.

Attribute Images

Images can be attached to attributes. To add an image to each attribute, you can either type the filename of the image file into the **Attributes Image Swatch** text box, or click **Browse** and select the image from your computer. You also need to select the directory where the image will be uploaded. If you enter the filename, then you will need to upload it to your server yourself and select the **No** radio button under **Overwrite Existing Image?**. Click on the **insert** button to upload the image.

Downloadable Products as Attributes

You can set a product as downloadable, so that customers can download. To add the downloadable attribute to a product, enter in the filename of the file that will be downloaded. Then, type the number of days after which the download will expire, and the maximum number of downloads that can be made. Click **insert** to save the attribute.

Copying Attributes to Other Products or Categories

One easy way to use attributes on a group of products is to copy the attributes from one product to another, or to every product in a category. The attribute images and any other attribute options for price or weight also get copied and can be edited once copied.

At the top of the attributes controller are several self-explanatory buttons that link to other sections of the admin panel. The last two are both **copy to** — the first is to a product, the second to a category.

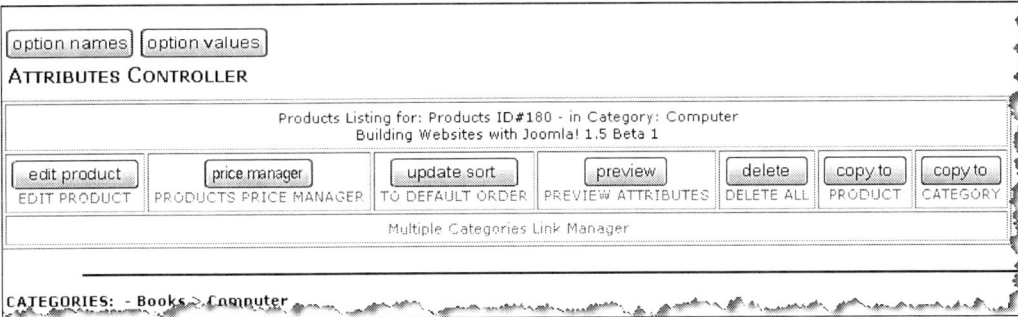

Click **copy to** (product or category depending on our preference), and in the large scroll box choose the category or product to which you want to copy the selected product attributes.

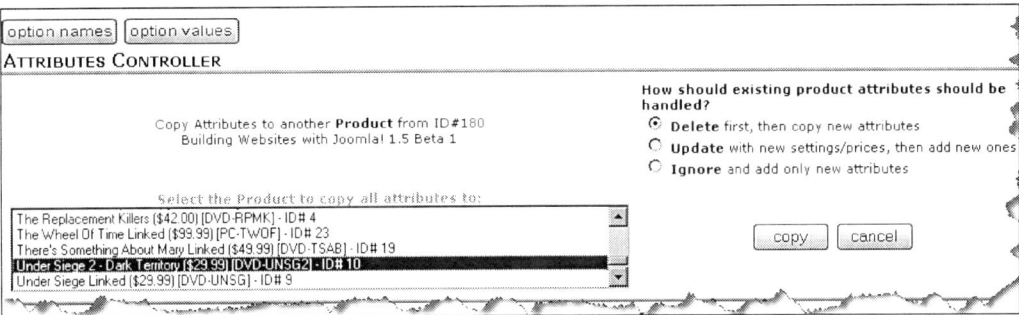

Then, you have three options:

1. **Delete first, then copy new attributes:** This will delete any existing attributes that are attached to the products to which you are copying the new attributes. New attributes are then added to the products.

2. **Update with new attribute settings/prices, then add new ones:** If the product you are copying to already has the same attributes, the values of those existing attributes will be updated. Then, the new attributes will be added to that product.

3. **Ignore and add only new attributes:** This will not alter any existing attributes, but will only add new ones.

You select one of the above options and click the **copy** button. You will then be notified about the success of copying the attributes. You can copy the attributes of the product to a category in similar way. In that case, the attributes will be applied to all of the products in that category.

Option Name and Value Sorter

Although, you can edit the sort order via **Catalog | Option Name manager**, it is easier to edit the sort order via **Catalog | Option Name Sorter**. You can then assign the sort order of each option and click on the **Update Sort Order** button to update the sort order. You need to do this for each language.

Similarly, you can manage option values easily via **Catalog | Option Value Sorter**. Select an option and click on **edit** to get the list of values for that option. Then enter the new sort orders and click on **Update Sort Order** button to update it.

Downloads Manager

Products for downloads can be managed via **Catalog | Downloads Manager**. You will see a list of all downloadable products, along with the associated product ID and name. You will also see the names of the files to be downloaded. A red icon in the **Filename** column indicates that the file is not on the webserver. A green icon means that the file is available on the webserver. For a red icon, upload the file to Zen Cart's download directory or, if the file is named differently, change the filename via the attribute controller. You can also do this by clicking on the **edit** button.

1088 ms_word_sample.zip

edit   Attribute Controller

Attr ID	Prod ID	Product Name	Model	Option Name	Option Value Name	Filename	Days	Count	
					● Missing filename ○ Valid filename				
1107	180	Building Websites with Joomla! 1.5 Beta 1		Ebook	PDF Format	○ ecommerceguide.pdf 7	5		①
1106	180	Building Websites with Joomla! 1.5 Beta 1		Ebook	MS Word (.doc)	● ecommerceguide.doc 7	5		①
1088	171	Sample of Document Product Type	DPT	Documentation	MS Word - English	○ ms_word_sample.zip 7	5		▶
1089	171	Sample of Document Product Type	DPT	Documentation	PDF - English	○ pdf_sample.zip	7	5	①
26	22	Unreal Tournament Linked	PC-UNTM Version		Download: Windows - English	○ unreal.zip	7	3	①

DOWNLOADS MANAGER — Search: [ ]

Product: Sample of Document Product Type
Model: DPT
Filename: ms_word_sample.zip
Max Days: 7
Max Downloads: 5

Displaying 1 to 5 (of 5 downloads)   Page 1 of 1

Prices

The **Catalog | Products Price Manager** menu allows us to edit product pricing by category. You can change the price, availability date, in stock / out of stock setting, quantity minimum (qty min), quantity units (qty units), quantity maximum (qty max), quantity minimum, and unit mix (qty min/unit mix), and whether the product is free, call for price, or priced by attributes, all from the products price manager. You can also edit special product and featured product information from this screen.

Bulk Import/Export of Products

For building a catalogue, it will be useful if you could bulk import/export products from, the catalog. If you have an existing shop, then bulk import may help. Bulk export may help you when moving the catalog to another shop. It may also help if you want to build the catalog offline, and then upload it to the online shop. You may ask the manufacturers to send their catalog in a specified format and upload that to the webserver. By default, Zen Cart has no feature to bulk import/export products. However, some third party add-ons are available for this.

One of the easiest bulk import tools for Zen Cart is EasyPopulate by Langer (www.modhole.com). You can download it from the Zen Cart website's download section. Once downloaded, you just have to unzip it and upload the files, keeping the directory structure intact. EasyPopulate does not overwrite any core files. Apply the install_sql.sql file via **Tools | Install SQL Patches**. This will give you options for configuration.

To configure Easy Populate, select **Configuration | Easy Populate**. You will see only one option to configure—**Uploads Directory**. The default is temp/. You change it to be any path you choose. You may create a directory named ep in the Zen Cart directory and enter the path of that directory in this field. Then all Easy Populate files will be created in this directory. You must also remember to set the file permission on this directory to 777.

```
EASY POPULATE 1.2.5.4

Upload EP File
[                              ]  [ Browse... ]  [ Insert into db ]
Split EP File
[                              ]  [ Browse... ]  [ Split file ]
Import from Temp Dir (pub/)
[                              ]  [ Insert into db ]

Download EP and Froogle Files

Download Complete tab-delimited .txt file to edit (Attributes Not Included)
Download Model/Price/Qty tab-delimited .txt file to edit
Download Model/Category tab-delimited .txt file to edit
Download Froogle tab-delimited .txt file
Download Model/Attributes tab-delimited .txt file

Create EP and Froogle Files in Temp Dir (pub/)

Create Complete tab-delimited .txt file in temp dir (Attributes Not Included)
Create Model/Price/Qty tab-delimited .txt file in temp dir
Create Model/Category tab-delimited .txt file in temp dir
Create Froogle tab-delimited .txt file in temp dir
Create Model/Attributes tab-delimited .txt file in temp dir
```

After uploading the files and configuring the Upload Directory, select **Tools | Easy Populate**. Here, you will see some links to download and create Easy Populate and Froogle files. Click on the **Download Complete tab-delimited .txt file to edit (Attributes Not Included)** link. This will download a tab-delimited text file, which can be opened using Microsoft Excel or the OpenOffice.org Calc spreadsheet program. If you want to build your own catalog based on this file, you must only keep the header row and delete/overwrite all other rows. You should type only the necessary information in these rows and save it. Once the file is ready, select **Tools | Easy Populate** and click on **browse** to select the file to upload in the **Upload EP file** field. Then, click on the **Insert into db** button. New product information will be added to catalog.

Similarly, you can download template for model/category, model/price/quantity, and prepare your file for uploading. In all of these cases, keep the header row intact. Otherwise, bulk import will not work.

Modules

Modules are functional add-ons for Zen Cart. You can have payment modules, shipping modules, or order total modules. Each type of module performs a different task for the shopping cart. For example, payment modules process payment through different payment gateways, while shipping modules are used to calculate shipping cost based on the destination and the carrier.

Installing/Uninstalling Modules

Modules in Zen Cart are automatically added to the shopping cart system when you put the module files in the appropriate directories. All of the modules in Zen Cart are located in the `includes/modules` directory. Under this directory, there are at least three subdirectories: `payment`, `shipping` and `order_total`. Once we put the files in these directories, we will find the module listed in the respective configuration screens, that is, **Modules | Payment**, **Modules | Shipping**, or **Modules | Order Total** screen. When you select that module for the first time you will see the **install** button on the right. You can install the module by clicking on this button.

Payment Modules

Payment modules are for processing payment through a payment processing gateway. For example, you may use the Authorize.net payment module to receive payment through the Authorize.net gateway. By default, there are about nine payment modules installed. The functions and configuration of each payment module are described below:

Authorize.net

If you have an Authorize.net merchant account, you can use this payment gateway. You can accept credit cards and electronic checks through Authorize.net. You can create an account at `www.authorize.net`.

There are two modules for Authorize.net: **Authorize.net SIM** and **Authorize.net AIM**. Authorize.net AIM is the preferred method for connecting a shop to the Authorize.net Payment Gateway. AIM allows merchants to customize their own payment forms (the web page that collects the customer's payment information) and receipt page, as well as submit transactions over an end-to-end Secure Sockets Layer (SSL) connection. On the other hand, Authorize.net SIM is a Payment Gateway connection method that allows merchants to post transactions directly to the payment gateway's secure server and requires transaction-unique encryption for transaction authentication. SIM provides merchants with a hosted payment form and a hosted receipt page.

Install either of the two modules. Both modules need some configuration values. Let's see how to configure the Authorize.net AIM module.

For the Authorize.net AIM module, you have to configure the following values:

- **Enable Authorize.net Transaction (AIM) Module**: If you want to process transactions through Authorize.net using the AIM method, select **True**.
- **Login ID**: Type the login username for you Authorize.net account.

- **Transaction Key**: A transaction key is used for encrypting transaction processing data. You can get this code from your **Authorizenet Account | Security Settings | API Login ID** and **Transaction Key**.

- **MD5 Hash**: This will be encryption key used for validating received transaction data (MAX 20 CHARACTERS). This hash value needs to be set in Authorize.net admin section.

- **Transaction mode**: Transaction mode can be set to **Test** or **Production**. You can use **Test** mode only for testing your configuration, but always keep it in the **Production** mode when your shop is live.

- **Authorization Type:** If you want to authorize only the submitted credit card number, select **Authorize** only. Selecting **Authorize + Capture** will also record the credit card number.

- **Enable Database Storage**: To save the gateway data in your database, select **True**.

- **Customer Notifications**: If you select **True** in this field, for every transaction, Authorize.net will send a receipt to the customer.

- **Merchant Notifications**: If you select **True** in this field, for any transaction, Authorize.Net will send a receipt to the merchant.

- **Request CVV Number**: If you want customers to provide card's CVV number, select **True** in this field.

- **Sort Order of Display**: Enter a sort order for displaying the Authorize.Net payment method. The lowest sort order will be displayed first.

- **Payment Zone**: Certain payment methods may be applicable only for certain zones. For example, you may use **Check/Money Order payment** only inside your country. For each payment method, you can specify a Payment Zone from this drop-down list.

- **Set Completed Order Status**: Here, you can select the order status upon successful transaction using this payment method. As authorize.Net is an online payment processor, you may set the order status to Processing.

- **Set Refunded Order Status**: Here you set the status of refunded orders to this value. You can select either of the following: **default, Pending[1], Processing[2], Delivered[3]**, or **Update[4]**.

- **Debug Mode**: Enable the debug mode as this will help us know why a transaction has failed. In this case, select **Log** only, or **Log** and **Email**. If you select **Log** and **Email** for each failed transaction, the debug info will be written into the log, and an email will be sent to the administrator.

Configuration of the Authorize.net SIM module is almost similar, but has fewer options. It has a different configuration option, **Transaction Method**, where you can define what you want to accept **Credit Card** or **eCheck**.

Credit Card

The Credit Card module is not for instant online payment. Instead, credit card information is collected through this module, and we can charge it to that credit card using our credit card processing terminal.

To use the Credit Card module, you click on this, and install it. Then, you click on **edit** to change the following options. Set **Enable Credit Card Module, Collect & Store the CVV Number** to **True**, and select **Store the Credit Card Number**. Credit card numbers will be stored partially in the database. Then, you have to type an email address, usually the administrator's email address, to which part of the credit card number will be sent. You may keep **Payment Zone** blank. Set the **Order Status** field to **Pending**, as credit cards are not authorized instantly.

When customers use this module, they will provide their credit card information during check-out. You can see the order in **Customers | Orders** screen. If you click on that order, you will see the details. Their credit card numbers will be displayed, but with the middle eight digits masked with XXXXXXXX.

Check your email for a message related to the order number that you have on your screen. You will find the blacked out eight digits in the email. Now, you can assemble the credit card number and enter it into your merchant terminal to process the credit card transaction. If the credit card purchase is approved by your merchant, you can mark the order status as **Processing**. It is better to add the authorization number to the Comments field before you save the new order status. Select the **notify customer** box to let the customer know that the payment has been approved. Finally, when you ship the order, you will update the order status to **Delivered** and notify customer again.

Customer credit card numbers are not allowed to be stored in a retrieval system. So, if you do store them, and your system is hacked and your customer's credit card info stolen and used fraudulently, you will be liable for all unauthorized purchases made using those credit cards. Hence, to protect yourself and your customers, the full numbers are not stored in Zen Cart, but are split up into two separate mechanisms for safety. However, if you have other payment methods, such as PayPal online payment, try to avoid using this simple credit card module.

Cash on Delivery

For some products, or in some areas, your payment option may be **pay by cash** when the product is delivered. As for Bangladesh, we have no online transaction facility. So cash on delivery may be a suitable payment method.

If you want to use this module, then click on it to install it. Then, change its configuration. It has very few options: enable the module, set the **Payment Zone**, **Order Status** and **Sort order of display.**

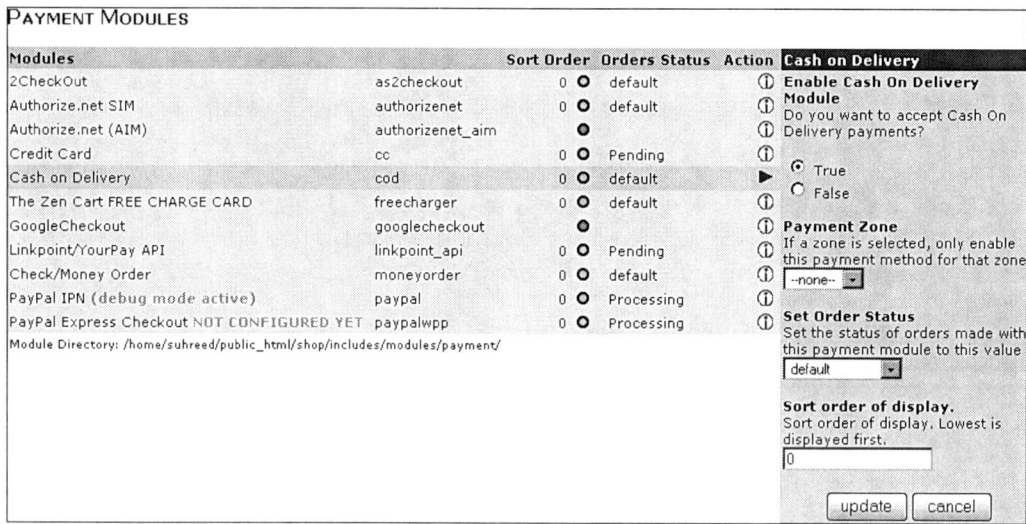

Zen Cart Free Charge Card

You may be wondering whether this really involves payment. Actually, this module is used when you do not have to pay for a product. When checking out a free product, this payment module will be used. If you have free products in your shop, you can install and enable this module.

LinkPoint/YourPay API

If you have a LinkPoint or YourPay account for online payment, you may use this module. If you have no account at LinkPoint or YouPay, simply click on the link provided on the right side box to Sign Up for an account.

Before installing this module, check that your system fulfills all of the requirements. You should have **CURL** enabled to be able to use this module. You also need to have **Port 1129** to be configured for bidirectional communication, and a PEM RSA Key digital certificate. Instructions for getting this key are given in the box on the right most side of the screen:

1. First, install the module and enable it.
2. Then, type your LinkPoint/YouPay merchant ID.

3. Select **LinkPoint Transaction Mode** as **LIVE:Production**, **TESTING: Successful** or **TESTING:Decline**. This must be **LIVE:Production** for live shops.

4. In the **Authorization Type** field, select either **Authorize only**, or **Immediate Charge/Capture**.

5. Then, select **Order Status**, **Payment Zone**, **Sort Order**.

6. If you want to be notified of any fraudulent credit card activity by email, select **Yes** in the **Fraud Alerts** field.

7. Select **True** in **Enable Database Storage** field to store logs of all credit card activities. It is a good idea to log all credit card activities into the database, so that you can analyze this log in case of any fraudulent activity.

Cheque/Money Order

If you want to allow payment via Cheques and Money Order, install and enable this module. The configuration is simple. Set the **Payment Zone**, **Order Status** and **Sort Order**. Then, type the name of the person to whom the cheque or money order will be issued. The store address will automatically be shown as the address to which the money order or cheque will be sent to. As you do not receive the cheque or the money order instantly, set the order status to **Pending**. When you receive the cheque or money order, change the order status and notify the customer. It is better to record the cheque number in the comments field when you update the order status.

PayPal

If you are starting an online shop, you may already know about PayPal. PayPal is a popular online transaction network through which you can pay to other PayPal account holders and others with your credit cards. It supports major credit cards and several types of accounts. For more information, you can visit www.paypal.com. If you don't have a PayPal account, you can create one to start accepting PayPal at your store.

By default, you will get three PayPal modules installed in Zen Cart: **PayPal IPN-Websites Payments Standard**, **PayPal Website Payments Pro**, and **PayPal Express Checkout**. Either can be used depending on your PayPal account type. The following sections describe the configuration of these two modules.

PayPal IPN Websites Payments Standard

The PayPal IPN module is the easiest way to use PayPal for your site. Instant Payment Notification (IPN) is PayPal's interface for handling real-time purchase confirmation and server-to-server communications. Whenever a transaction occurs, IPN delivers immediate notification and confirmation of PayPal payments, and provides the status and additional data on pending, cancelled, or failed transactions.

Checkout using the PayPal IPN module consists of the following six steps:

1. Customers select the products they want to purchase and choose to pay with PayPal.

2. Customers are transferred to PayPal's secure site via an HTML redirect.

3. Customers log in to their account and review their shipping and billing information. Customers then click **Pay** to make their payment, which is processed instantly.

4. Customers review their payment confirmation at PayPal.

5. Customers are automatically redirected back to your site via an HTML redirect.

6. Customers arrive at the order confirmation screen on your website. Shop owners are notified of a successful payment via email, Instant Payment Notification, or Payment Data Transfer.

Note that payment information, PayPal account and credit card, are entered on PayPal's site, not on your shop's checkout page. PayPal just notifies you whether the transaction has been successful or not. The transaction amount automatically goes to your PayPal account.

To use the PayPal IPN module, install and enable it from the **Modules | Payment** screen. If you don't have a PayPal account, create one and configure your profile. In the profile settings, type `http://www.yourdomain.com/shop/ipn_main_handler.` `php` as **Instant Payment Notification Preferences URL**, and in the **Automatic Return URL** field under **Website Payments Preferences,** type `http://www.yourdomain.` `com/shop/index.php?main_page=checkout_process.` These URLs will be shown in the box on the rightmost side of the screen, when you click on the module.

You have to configure the following options for your PayPal IPN module:

- **Enable PayPal Module**: Here, select **True** to enable and use this module.

- **Business ID**: Here, type your PayPal account's primary email address. Check with your PayPal account if you have any doubts about the email addresses used for the account.

- **PDT Token (Payment Data Transfer)**: Enter your PDT Token value here to activate transactions immediately after processing (if they pass validation). You will get a token when you enable Payment Data Transfer under Website Transaction Preferences in your PayPal Profile.

- **Transaction Currency**: Here, select the currency that you want to use with PayPal. If an unsupported currency format is sent to PayPal, it will automatically be converted into USD.

- **Payment Zone**: Here, select the payment zone in which this module can be used. You can leave it blank to make it available in all zones.

- **Set Pending Notification Status**: Here, select the order status for the pending transactions. The default is **Pending**.

- **Set Order Status**: Here, select the order status of a successful PayPal transaction. The default is Processing, and it is fine to leave this as it is.

- **Set Refund Order Status**: Here, select the order status for a refund request. The default is **Pending**, and it is fine to leave this as it is.

- **Sort Order of Display**: Here, enter a number for the display order of the module in the checkout's payment options list. An option with a lower value will be placed first.

- **Page Style**: If you have created a custom page style in your PayPal account profile, then type the name of that page style in this field. If you would like to always reference your Primary style, set it to **primary**. If you would like to reference the default PayPal page style, then set this to **paypal**.

- **Mode for PayPal web services**: Here, specify the paypal processing URL. The default is `www.paypal.com/cgi-bin/webscr`. Alternatively, you can use `www.paypal.com/us/cgi-bin/webscr` for the US and `www.paypal.com/uk/cgi-bin/webscr` for the UK.

- **Debug Mode**: Here, enable debug mode to collect information about failed transactions. You may choose **Off**, **Log** or **Log and Email**. Transaction logs are written in the `/includes/modules/payment/paypal/logs` file.

Once these options are configured, click on the **update** button to save the settings. Now, customers will see the PayPal IPN payment option during checkout. When they select this option, they are redirected to the PayPal page, where they can pay from their PayPal account or credit cards. When the transaction is successful, they will be redirected to the page specified in **Automatic Return URL** (that is, the checkout page of our shop).

PayPal Express

We may use the PayPal Express module to enable the PayPal express checkout. Express Checkout allows customers to complete transactions in very few steps. It allows them to use shipping and billing information stored securely in PayPal to check out, so that they don't have to re-enter it on our site.

Express checkout works in the following way:

- After selecting the products to purchase, customers click Checkout with PayPal on our website.

- They are transferred to PayPal, where they select their payment method, as well as the correct shipping and billing address. Then, they are returned to your website to complete their purchases.

- PayPal automatically gives you the shipping address, email, and other customer information needed to fulfill your order.

With Express Checkout, your buyers finish their orders on your website, and not on PayPal's. So, you can get real-time notification of successful payments.

To use PayPal Express Checkout, install and enable this module. This module requires PayPal API credentials and CURL enabled on your server. First, request an API key in your PayPal profile and keep the credentials at hand, and then check that CURL is enabled on your server. If your server uses a CURL proxy, get that proxy address. Also ensure that the IPN is enabled, and the IPN URL is provided in your PayPal profile.

In addition to the settings for the PayPal IPN module, the following are needed for PayPal Express module:

- **Express Checkout: Require Confirmed Address**: If you want customers to provide a confirmed address for shipping, select **Yes** in this field.

- **Express Checkout: Select Cheapest Shipping Automatically**: To make the checkout process faster, you may want to automatically select the cheapest shipping method when the customer returns from PayPal, and thus skip the shipping page. To do this, select **Yes**.

- **Express Checkout: Skip Payment Page**: You may want to skip the checkout payment page when the customer is checking out with Express Checkout. Select **Yes** if you do not want to display the payment page. Note that enabling this will not give the customers options to use their coupons or gift certificates, as the Payment Page will be skipped.

- **Payment Action**: Here, select the **Final Payment** in order to get the payment at the end of the transaction. Alternatively, you can select **Auth** only to receive payments upon authorization only. The default is Final Payment.

- **API Signature — Username**: Enter the API Username from your PayPal API Signature settings under API Access. This value typically looks like an email address and is case-sensitive.

- **API Signature — Password**: Here, enter the API Password from your PayPal API Signature settings under API Access. This value is a 16-character code, and is case-sensitive.

- **API Signature — Signature Code**: Here, enter API Signature from your PayPal API Signature settings under API Access. This value is a 56-character code, and is case-sensitive.

- **Live or Sandbox**: If you are using the module for testing purposes, select **Sandbox**. But for live shops, to receive payment through PayPal, you must select **Live**.

Once these configurations are saved by pressing the **update** button, you are ready to use PayPal Express checkout.

PayPal Website Payments Pro

You can also use PayPal Website Payment Pro module for processing payment in Zen Cart. Website Payments Pro module gives some extra benefits than other two PayPal modules. However, for using this module you must have PayPal Express Checkout module installed and configured. Most of the configuration options are same as other two modules. Only new setting you have to configure in this module is PayPal Mode. This setting has the following options:

- **PayPal**: If you have US Paypal account and want to use that for Website Payments Pro service, select this option. However, for using this you must have configured **API Settings** in PayPal Express Checkout module.

- **Payflow-UK**: This option will allow you to use Payflow-UK payment processing gateway. You need a Payflow-UK account for using this option.

- **Payflow-US**: For using Payflow-US payment processing gateway, select this option. You need a Payflow-US account for using this option.

 For more information on PayPal's merchant solutions like Express Checkout, Website Payments Pro, Payflow and other, please visit www.paypal.com and consult **Business** section.

Other Payment Modules

There are a lot of payment modules that can be downloaded from the Zen Cart website and used for processing payments using other payment processor gateways. The configurations differ depending upon the gateways used. Here, you are going to learn about two popular payment modules that you may like to use for your shop.

WorldPay

WorldPay is a popular payment processor for online merchants. We can use WorldPay as payment processor by adding the third-party module, WorldPay for Zen Cart 1.3.x, available from the Zen Cart website's downloads section. After downloading the package, extract it and copy the files to your web server's Zen Cart directory, maintaining folder structure.

Once you have uploaded the files, you can see the new module **Credit Card via WorldPay** in the **Modules | Payments** screen in the Zen Cart administration area. Click on the module, and click the **install** button to install it. After installation, the configuration screen will be displayed. This module has the following configuration options:

- **Enable WorldPay Module**: Select **True** to enable this module.
- **WorldPay Installation ID**: When you sign up for the WorldPay services, you get the installation ID. Enter that ID in this field.
- **Transaction Mode**: Set the transaction mode in this field. There are three options — **100** = Test Mode Accept, **101** = Test Mode Decline, and **0** = Live. Select one of these.
- **Use MD5**: Select **True** to enable MD5 encryption for transactions.
- **MD5 secret key**: You must enter your MD5 secret key if you want to use MD5 encryption. This key also needs to be entered into the WorldPay installation configuration.
- **Use Pre-Authorization?**: If pre-authorization in your WorldPay account is enabled, and you want to use that pre-authorization with Zen Cart payments, select True.
- **Set Order Status**: Select the status of orders made with this payment module.
- **Pre-Auth**: For pre-authorization, select a mode from the following available options: **A**= Pay Now, **E**= Pre Auth. Settings in this option is ignored if **Use Pre-Authorization** is **False**.
- **Payment Zone**: Select the zone in which this payment method will be allowed.

WorldPay module for Zen Cart comes with a sidebox that shows the credit cards accepted by WorldPay. Enable this sidebox via **Tools | Layout Boxes Controller**.

Google Checkout

Google Checkout is a new checkout method for online merchants. It provides sellers with checkout facilities similar to those provided by PayPal. As an owner/administrator of Zen Cart shop, you can use Google Checkout as a payment method. To use Google Checkout with Zen Cart, you need to install the Google Checkout module from Zen Cart's website , and then configure it. The module comes with detailed documentation on installation and configuration.

To use the **Google Checkout** module, you first need to sign-up for Google Checkout. Once you have an account, you can install and configure the Google Checkout module as follows:

1. Download Google Checkout from Zen Cart's website.
2. Extract the Zip file on your computer. Upload the files to your web server's Zen Cart directory, maintaining the folder structure. Uploading will not overwrite any file.
3. Log in to your shop's administration area and select **Modules | Payment**.
4. From the list of payment modules, click on **Google Checkout** and click the **install** button.
5. Once Google Checkout module is installed, you will see the configuration form for it. The following configuration options are used for this module:

   - **Google Checkout module version**: This option will display the Google module version you are using. If you have installed more than one version, you can select the version that is to be used.

   - **Enable Google Checkout module**: You can enable or disable this module by selecting **True** or **False** here.

   - **Select mode of operation**: You can select development mode or production mode. Before using this module in production, you should try first using the development mode. Select `https://sandbox.google.com/checkout/` to use the development mode, and for live mode, select `https://checkout.google.com/`.

   - **Production merchant ID**: To use this module in the production environment, you need to enter a Production merchant ID. You can find this ID on the **integration** page under the **settings** tab on your Google Checkout account page.

   - **Production Merchant Key**: You must provide the merchant key, which is also available on the **integration** page under the **settings** tab on your Google Checkout account page.

   - **Sandbox merchant ID**: Enter the merchant ID, which can be found on the **integration** page under the **settings** tab of our Google Merchant account page.

   - **Sandbox Merchant Key**: Enter the merchant key, which can be found on the **integration** page under the **settings** tab of your Google Merchant account page.

- **.htaccess Basic Authentication Mode**: When using PHP over CGI, PHP basic authentication is not compatible with Google Checkout responses. Therefore, you need to enable this option by selecting **True** and configuring the .htaccess file. After enabling this option, click on the link shown and configure your .htaccess file for Google Checkout module.

- **Select Merchant Calculation Mode of Operation**: This option allows you to select an http or https URL for merchant calculation. This only applies for the sandbox environment. The production environment checkout always uses an https URL.

- **Disable Google Checkout for Virtual Products**: For virtual products you may not need checkout. In that case, enable this option by selecting **True**. Once enabled, this Google Checkout button will be displayed disabled for virtual products.

- **Allow US PO Box Shipping**: If you want to allow shipping to United States Post Box numbers, then select **True** here.

- **Default Values for Realtime Shipping Rates**: Usually, shipping rates are taken from the shipping providers' web services. Sometimes, these web services may fail to provide shipping rates, so as a fallback you need to provide default shipping rates. You can click the `shipping generator` link and add your default rates for each provider.

Shipping Methods generator

Domestic Shipping address		Int'l Shipping address	
Country:	US	Country:	GB
City:	Miami	City:	Glasgow
Region:	FL	Region:	LANARKSHIRE
Postal Code:	33102	Postal Code:	G42 8RB

Cart Description	
Weight:	7
Quantity:	1
Total Price:	30

Get Shipping Methods

- **GoogleCheckout Carrier Calculated Shipping**: For Google Checkout, you may also use calculated shipping. This calculated shipping can also be used for Flat Rate Shipping, but merchant calculation cannot be used. Once you enable it by selecting **True** in this option, you also need to configure calculated shipping in the next option.

- **Carrier Calculated Shipping Configuration**: For each type of shipping, you need to specify the rates. For each shipping method, rates can either be fixed or variable.

Carrier Calculater Shipping Configuration
Set Default Values, Fix and Variable charge
Set **Def. Value** to **0** to disable the method

FedEx
   domestic_types

Def. Value	Fix Charge	Variable	Method Name
USD: 1.00	USD: 0	0	% Ground
USD: 1.00	USD: 0	0	% Home Delivery
USD: 1.00	USD: 0	0	% Express Saver
USD: 1.00	USD: 0	0	% 2Day
USD: 1.00	USD: 0	0	% Standard

Overnight

USD: 1.00	USD: 0	0	% Priority Overnight
USD: 1.00	USD: 0	0	% First Overnight

UPS
   domestic_types

Def. Value	Fix Charge	Variable	Method Name
USD: 1.00	USD: 0	0	% Ground
USD: 1.00	USD: 0	0	% 3 Day Select
USD: 1.00	USD: 0	0	% 2nd Day Air
USD: 1.00	USD: 0	0	% Next Day Air Saver
USD: 1.00	USD: 0	0	% Next Day Air
USD: 1.00	USD: 0	0	% Next Day Air Early

AM

USPS
   domestic_types

Def. Value	Fix Charge	Variable	Method Name
USD: 1.00	USD: 0	0	% Media Mail
USD: 1.00	USD: 0	0	% Parcel Post
USD: 1.00	USD: 0	0	% Express Mail

- **Rounding Policy Mode**: In this option, you have to specify the rounding policy for shipping charges. The options are similar to the rounding options in Google Checkout. Details of these options are available through the links to the Google Checkout website.

- **Rounding Policy Rule**: This configuration option determines how rounding is to be applied — either per line of monetary values, or to the total order only.

- **Cart Expiration Time (Minutes)**: Here, specify the time in minutes after which the cart will expire (and everything in it is deleted). Type **NONE** if you don't want to apply expiration to the cart.

- **Also send notifications with Zen Cart**: Usually, Google Checkout will send notifications to customers. If you want to send notifications to customers from Zen Cart too, select **True** here.

- **Google Analytics ID**: If you want to integrate the Google Checkout module with Google Analytics, enter your **Google analytic ID** in this field. To disable the use of Google Analytics, enter **NONE** in this field. The use of Google analytics enables you to monitor how customers interact with our site.

- **3rd Party Tracking**: Similar to Google Analytics, you can also integrate the Google Checkout module with aother, third-party tracking system. If so, enter the URL of the tracker or enter **NONE** to disable third-party tracking.

- **Google Checkout restricted product categories**: Some of the products, such as bulk marketing, alcohol, weapons, and so on, are restricted on Google Checkout. A full list of these products and categories can be found on the Google Checkout help page. However, you can restrict these product categories by typing the product categories, in comma separated list, in this option box. Enter **NONE** to exclude no product or category.

- **Continue Shopping URL**: In this option, you have to specify the name of the page to which the customers will be redirected when checkout is completed. The default is suitable for use with Zen Cart. Please type the exact name of the `checkout_success` page if you have modified it in Zen Cart.

Once these settings have been saved, your Google Checkout module is ready for use. For troubleshooting and other resources, please read the documentation that accompanied the module package.

2CO Payment Module

2CO is a popular online payment processing service provider. You may obtain an account at 2co.com for a very low price. Please check www.2co.com for details of their services.

If you are a user of 2CO, you can use that for Zen Cart shop by using 2CO Payment Module, developed by Absolute Solutions and available from the Zen Cart website's download section. Upload the files in this package, and install the SQL patch file update_database.sql via **Tools | Install SQL Patches**.

The configuration options are almost the same as for PayPal and other modules. You have to enable it and provide the **Login/Store Number,** which is used for 2Checkout.com (2CO) login. Then, set the currency, order status, transaction mode, merchant notifications, payment zone, and the secret word. If you have more than one currency in your store, only one currency will be sent to 2Checkout. Select **Yes** in the **Currency Converter** option whenever you want to enable automatic currency conversion. Another important thing is that 2Checkout has a policy as to which products can be sold from your store. If you want to send your product information to 2Checkout, then select **Enabled** in **Product Integration**.

MoneyBooker Module

MoneyBooker (www.moneybooker.com) is an online wallet where registered users can upload their money and use it for purchases whenever needed. Online payments can be made using MoneyBooker. If you have an account with MoneyBooker, you can receive payments to that account.

Installation and configuration of the MoneyBooker payement module is straightforward. Download the module from the Zen Cart website's download section, unzip it, and upload all files. No file will be overwritten by this payment module.

Once the upload is complete, go to **Modules | Payment**. You will see the MoneyBooker listed as an available payment module. Install it and click **edit** to configure it. First, enable this payment method, provide the email address used for your MoneyBooker account, select **Transaction Currency**, **Payment Zone**, **Set Order Status**, and set **Sort Order of Display.** Your MoneyBooker payment module is now ready for use.

During checkout, the moneybooker.com payment option will be shown. On confirming the order, the customer will be redirected to the moneybooker.com site. The customer needs to log in to moneybooker.com using his or her account name and password, and make payment from his or her balance at moneybooker.com.

Shipping Modules

Shipping is one of the important features of your online shop. You have to give customers a choice of shipping options. Several modules are used to provide shipping options to the customers. Shipping modules are administered from the **Modules | Shipping** screen.

Flat Rate

A flat rate shipping charge is simple to use and is the most straight-forward method. If you use flat rate shipping for all products, you charge the same shipping fee. To use a flat rate for shipping, enable this module and enter the shipping cost for all orders in the **Shipping cost** field. You may also define the **Tax Class**, **Tax Basis**, **Shipping Zone**, and **Sort Order** for this module.

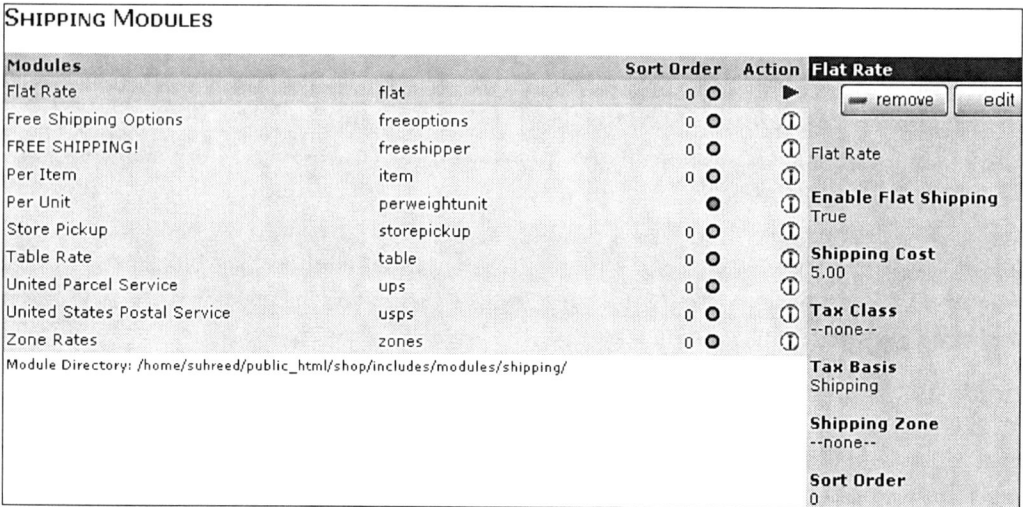

Free shipping

Here, you can use the **FREE SHIPPING! (freeshipper)** and **Free Shipping Options (freeoptions)** modules if you want to offer free shipping for some or all products. In this case, you have to enable these modules and configure both the modules.

Free Options is used to display a **Free Shipping** option when other shipping modules are displayed. It can be based on: Always show, Order Total, Order Weight, or Order Item Count. For example, you may offer free shipping for an order of more than USD 200. However, the Free Options module will not be shown when Free Shipper is displayed.

Setting Total to >= 0.00 and <= nothing (leave blank) will activate this module to show with all shipping modules, except for Free Shipping. Leaving all settings for Total, Weight and Item Count blank will deactivate this module.

Free Shipping Options do not get displayed if Free Shipping is used, based on zero weight for Free Shipping. In Free Shipping Options configuration, you can define the total order, weight, and item count for which free shipping will be applicable, and the minimum cost and handling fee for free shipping.

The Free Shipping option is shown when a product is always shipped for free. But conditional free shipping, that is, for purchases above a total price or size, and so on, is handled by the Free Shipping Options module. If you have some products marked for free shipping, enable the Free Shipping module, and specify the minimum shipping and handling charges when free shipping is used.

You may be wondering when to configure the Free Shipping Options and Free Shipping modules. Here, you have to specify the shipping charge and handling charges. If you charge for this, then it is not completely free shipping. So, remember that free shipping does not always mean absolutely FREE! You may need to pay something for Free Shipping!

Per Item and Per Unit

Depending on your products, you may choose either per item, or per unit shipping costs. For example, for each shipping box you may charge USD 2.50, and for each book in your store, you may charge USD 1.00. These types of shipping are handled by the Per Item and Per Unit modules.

The main configuration for the Per Item shipping module is Shipping Cost per Item. Specify a cost here. When calculating the total shipping cost, this amount will be multiplied by the number of items in the order. In addition to per item costs, you may also specify a handling cost per shipping method. Then, the total cost of shipping will be:

Total Shipping Cost = (No. of Items × per item shipping cost) + Handling fee

If you ship your products in a box or other package, you may use the Per Unit shipping module. Similarly, you have to configure the per unit shipping cost and the handling fee. When using the per unit shipping method, you need to specify the shipping unit (box, packet) when adding a product to the catalog. Otherwise, this module cannot calculate the shipping cost.

Store Pickup

Store Pickup is a shipping method wherein the store owner does not ship the products to the customer. Instead, the customer visits the physical store and picks up the products. This may sound good, and you may think that there is no cost involved, but, you may also charge a nominal fee for packaging the products. In fact, for the Store Pickup module you can configure this fee in the Shipping Cost field. Configuring Shipping Zone is important for this module as you cannot provide store pickup options for customers all over the world. For example, if your shop is in Bangladesh and you provide the store pickup option to customers in America, it would be weird!

Table Rate

You may calculate the shipping cost from a cost table where you can see the total price or the weight and determine the shipping cost. If you know the shipping cost for a region by weight, you can use the **Table Rate** module. In this module, you have to build a table for weight: cost or price:cost. In the **Shipping Table** field, you can provide shipping cost based on total cost, weight, or the number of items. This is denoted as 10:2.5, 20:4.5, and so on. In the **Table Method**, select the criteria on which you are calculating the cost—weight, price or items. If you select **weight**, then 10:2.5 means for 10 Kg you are charging USD 2.5; if you select price then 10:2.5 would mean that for every USD 10.00 spent, the shipping charge is USD 2.50; and when you select **items**, 10:2.5 means mean you will charge USD 2.5 per 10 purchased.

United Parcel Service

United Parcel Service (UPS) is a reputed worldwide parcel delivery service. You may like to use UPS as a shipping method. To use the UPS shipping method, install and enable the United Parcel Service shipping module and configure the following:

- **UPS Pickup Method**: Specify how your packages will be handed over to UPS. You may take them to a **UPS Customer Counter (CC)**, tell UPS to regularly pick the packages up from your store (RDP), ask for UPS to make a **one-time pickup (OTP)**, send the packages to a **letter centre** (LC) or use **On Call Air (OCA)**. You have to type the code, as indicated, for the different pickup methods.

- **UPS Packaging?**: Specify the type of packaging that will be used for your parcel. You may use your **own packaging (CP)** or UPS packaging such as **UPS Letter (ULE), UPS Tube (UTE), UPS Express Box (UBE)**. Enter the codes in this field.

- **Residential Delivery?**: Indicate whether the delivery will be **Residential (RES)** or **Commercial (COM)**. As you are normally shipping to individual customers, Residential delivery is recommended.

- **Shipping Methods**: Choose the shipping methods to be used by UPS. A brief explanation of all methods are available on the page for this module in Zen Cart. For more information you may check the UPS website at www.ups.com.

You can also configure other generic options such as **Shipping Zone**, **Handling Fee**, **Tax Class** and **Tax Basis**.

United States Postal Service

You can use the United States Postal Service (USPS) for shipping your products. Zen Cart has a built-in USPS shipping module, which can be installed and configured for this purpose. Before using this module, you need to register at www.usps.com for a USPS web tools User ID. Install and enable this module and configure the following options:

- **Enable USPS Shipping**: Do you want to offer USPS shipping? You have two options here: select **True** in order to enable it, or select **False** to disable it.

- **USPS Web Tools User ID**: Enter the Web Tools user ID that you have received from USPS after registration.

- **Which server to use**: Initially, you should use the testing server. Once you are satisfied that it is working, set it to **production**. It must be production for live shops. But before setting it to **production**, you have to mail to icustomercare@usps.com to activate it for the Production server. Once you have received a confirmation email from USPS, you can set this option to the **Production** server.

- **All Packages are machinable**: Here, specify whether all packages will be considered machinable (processable by a machine - for example with a barcoded ZIP code on the address label). Machinable packages have lower charges. But packages more than 35 lbs or less than 6 ounces will automatically be considered as non-machinable.

- **USPS Options**: Select the information that will be shown in the USPS shipping option during checkout. It may show the weight and transit time, along with the shipping cost.

- **Domestic Shipping Methods**: Select the domestic services that will be used. Options available are: Express, Priority, First Class, Parcel Media, BPM, and Library.

- **International Shipping Methods**: Select the international shipping methods that will be used. Available options are: **Global Express**, **Global Express Non-Doc Rect**, **Global Express Non-Doc Non-Rect**, **Express Mail Int**, **Express Mail Int Flat Rate Env**, **Priority Mail International**, **Priority Mail Int Flat Rate Env**, **Priority Mail Int Flat Rate Box**, and **First-Class Mail Int**.
- **Debug Mode**: Turn the debug mode on to have a complete detailed log of USPS quote results emailed to the store owner.

You can also configure other generic options, such as **Shipping Zone**, **Handling Fee**, **Tax Class**, and **Tax Basis**.

Zone Rates

You may use one shipping rate for each zone. Although **Table Rate** allows us to apply a rate table for a specific zone, you can use multiple zones by using **Zone Rates**. First, you have to define which countries are in which zones. Then, define the shipping rates for each zone. The rates may be based on weight, price, or number of items.

As with the Table Rate shipping method, you have to indicate, in the **Calculation Method** field, the basis on which shipping cost will be calculated. Then, define Zone 1, Zone 2, and Zone 3 countries by entering the two-letter ISO codes for the countries that are to be assigned to each zone, separated by commas (,). Type the rates in Zone 1 Shipping Table, Zone 2 Shipping Table and Zone 3 Shipping Table field. The rates should be in the format: 10:2.5, 15:4.5, 20:6.5, and so on. If you select weight as a calculation method, then an entry of 10:2.5 in the Zone 1 Shipping Table means that for Zone 1 Countries, customers have to pay 2.5 USD per 10 Kg weight. For each zone, you can also specify a handling fee.

Order Total Modules

Order Total modules are used to calculate the total cost due during checkout. You can see the list of Order Total modules on the **Modules | Order Total** screen. These modules are located in the `includes/modules/order_total/` directory. The following list shows the default Order Total modules:

- **COD Fee:** If you want to enable Cash on Delivery as a payment option, then you may also charge a fee for using this payment method. The **COD Fee** (ot_cod_fee) module will add this COD fee to the subtotal of the product prices during checkout. You have to specify the COD fee for each shipping method used.

- **Discount Coupon**: If a customer is using a discount coupon, this module's task is to deduct the discount coupon amount from the total amount due. In other words, this module actually provides the discounts to the customers. Here you have to configure how the discount will be granted. If you want to give a discount on total including shipping cost, select **true** in the **Include Shipping** field. If you want to give a discount on the total including tax, then select **true** in **Include Tax** field. Specify how to recalculate the tax. The three options available are **None**, **Standard**, and **Credit Note**.

- **Group Discount**: This module deducts group discounts for eligible customers. Settings for this module are the same as for the Discount Coupon module.

- **Gift Certificates**: This module is used to redeem gift certificates and allow gift certificates as a payment option. During checkout, payments made by gift certificates are deducted by this module. Settings for this module are the same as for the Discount Coupon module.

- **Low Order Fee**: If the order amount is lower than a threshold value, then you may charge a low order fee. This module adds the low order fee to the order total. To charge a low order fee, enable low order fee through this module and specify the threshold value below which the low order will be charged. Also, specify the value of the low order fee in the **Order Fee** field. You can specify the fee as a percentage of the order total, or as an absolute amount. You may exempt the low order fee for the national orders, international orders, gift vouchers, or virtual products, individually.

- **Shipping**: This module adds shipping cost to the order total. In the settings for this module, you can enable free shipping. Select **true** in the **Allow Free Shipping** field and specify the order amount over which an order will be eligible for free shipping. You can also enable free shipping for national, international, or both types of orders.

- **Sub-Total**: This module shows the order sub-total, based on what discounts or other charges have to be applied. You need to simply enable this module; there is no option to configure.

- **Tax**: This module adds taxes to order sub-total, to calculate the order total. You need to simply enable this module; there is no option to configure.

- **Total**: This module calculates the total amount to be paid for the order. It must be enabled, and it has no configuration options.

These are the default Order Total modules. If you install other modules, you may find some other order total module in the **Modules | Order Total** screen. For example, installing Better Together module (which we will discuss in Chapter 6) will show the Better Together Discount moduel in this list.

Customers

Managing customers will be one of your tasks as a shop owner or administrator of Zen Cart. Customer Management includes customer registration, retrieval of forgotten passwords, informing customers about site update or maintenance, or any other important issues.

Registration/Authentication of Customers

Generally, users need to register with the Zen Cart shop before shopping. An unregistered customer may add items to the shopping cart, but before checking out, he or she needs to register. A customer can always register by clicking on the **Log In** link on the home page. You may specify the required fields for user registration via **Configuration | Customer Details**.

Once registered, a confirmation email containing a verification code is sent to the customer. The customer clicks on the link provided to visit your shop and enter the verification code. This way, the customer is verified. Once a customer is verified, he or she can place orders in the shop.

Customers can retrieve their forgotten password by clicking on the **Forgot your password?** link on the Login page. Administrators can change customer information (but not the password) on the **Customers | Customers** screen.

Managing Customers

All customer accounts are listed on the **Customers | Customers** screen. Select a customer name and you will see some command buttons in the right side box. Click on **edit** to change a customer's information. Although you can change any information in the customer's profile, it is not wise to change their address or other personal information. However, you may change the customer's authorization status, if you need to disable a customer for some reason.

We can see a customer's orders by clicking the **orders** button. A summary of the customer's activities will be shown in the right-side box.

Communicating with Customers

You may need to communicate with the customers to clarify some order, items or any other reason. In this case, select that customer and click on the **email** button shown in the right-side box. E-mail screen will be shown, where you can type the email subject and message, and can send it by clicking on the **send** button. From this screen you can also send mails to a group of customers.

Order Fulfilment and Inventory

After opening the shop in production, your main task will be to manage orders and fulfill these in a timely manner. You can see the list of all orders on the **Customers | Orders** screen. From this screen, you can edit or delete an order, or print invoice and packing slip for that order.

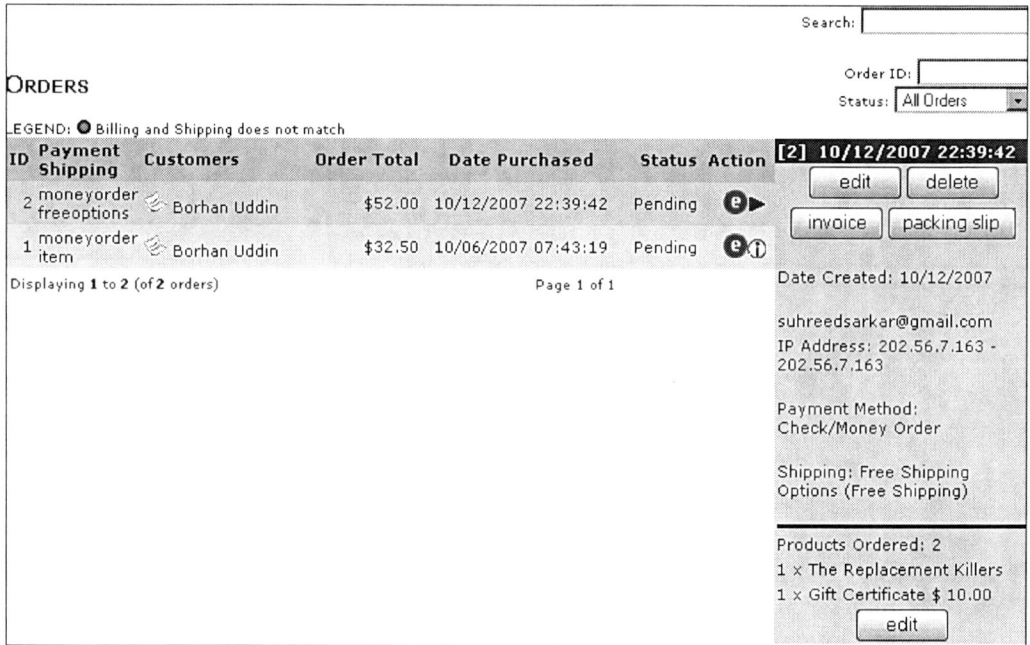

Order Statistics

Order statistics can be seen from dashboard. In the orders section, you can see the order status, which shows the pending orders, orders being processed, orders delivered, and orders that have been updated. In the new orders section, you will find all new orders. The list of products sold can be seen on the **Reports | Products Purchased** screen.

Managing Inventory

Managing inventory includes knowing the stock levels of all products and adding products to the catalog as and when necessary. You can identify products with low stock from the **Reports | Products Low Stock** screen. The screen will show the products that need immediate repletion.

Group Pricing

Group pricing can be used to provide a discount to a group of customers. You can manage group pricings from **Customers | Group Pricing**. To create a new group price, click on the **insert** button. Enter a group name and a discount percentage. Save the group. Now add customers to that group by editing the customer's profiles. From the **Customers | Customers** screen, select a customer and click on the **edit** button. In the options section, select the appropriate group in **Discount Pricing Group** field.

Order Status

You need to update the order status manually. When an order is shipped or delivered, you need to change the order status. For managing an order, select that order from the list and click on the **edit** button. Now, change the **Status** field, for example, to **Processing**. You can also add a comment and select the **Notify Customer** and **Append Comments** checkboxes. You click on the **update** button to update the status. An email will be sent to the customer notifying them of the status of this order. When you have shipped the product, update the status to **Shipped**, and notify the customer. Again, you will need to update the status when the product is delivered.

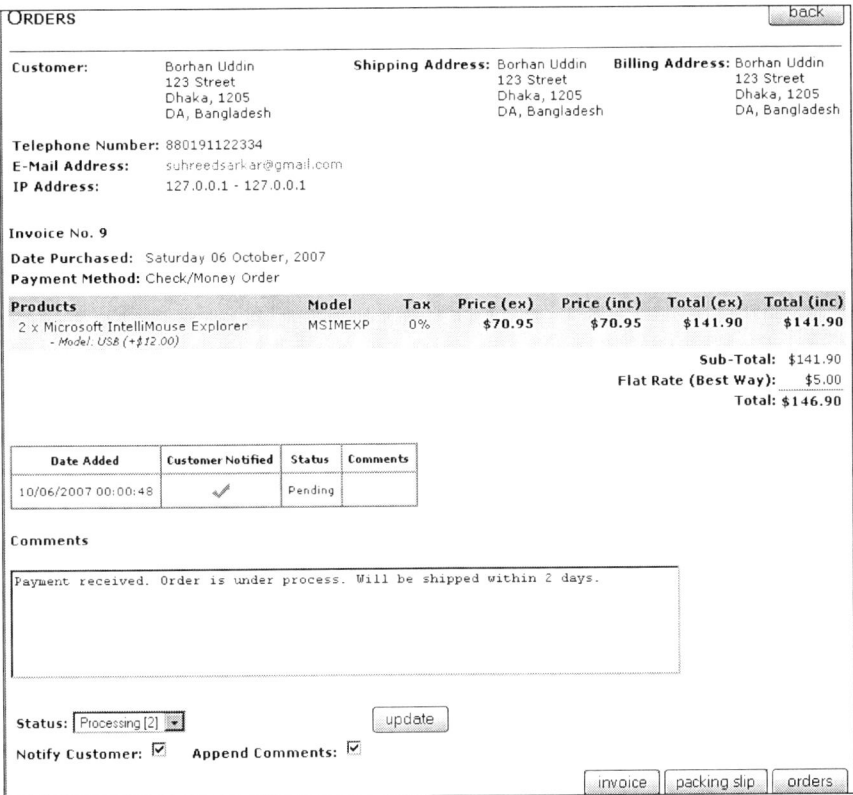

When shipping products, you need to enclose an invoice. This invoice can be generated by clicking on the **invoice** button. You can also generate a packing slip by clicking on the **packing slip** button. The difference between an invoice and a packing slip is that the invoice includes the prices of the products, whereas a packing slip only lists the products.

Summary

In this chapter, we have discussed different configuration options for Zen Cart shop. First, we learned how to set global configuration options from the **Configuration** menu in the **Administration** area. Then we discussed the configuration of the available modules. We also learned how to enable and configure online payment methods using payment modules. Further, we discussed configuration of our shop for using several shipping methods, including Universal Parcel Service and the United States Postal Service. The use of Order Totals modules was also discussed. After examining how to configure these, we learned how to manage the product catalog by maintaining categories, products, and attributes. We are now also familiar with customer and order management. With all of this information, we now know how to configure a Zen Cart store.

Although we have learned how to configure the store, we have still not configured the look and feel of the store. In the next chapter, we are going to learn about customizing the look and feel of a Zen Cart store.

Customizing Look and Feel

4

One of the good features of Zen Cart is that, with some knowledge in HTML, CSS, and PHP, users can customize its look and feel. As an administrator, you can customize its look and feel through the administration panel. But for further customization and matching it to your own style, you need to edit template files. This chapter is going to show you how to customize the look and feel of a Zen Cart shop.

On completion of this chapter, you will be able to:

- Configure the look and feel through the administration panel
- Apply different templates to your Zen Cart store
- Change the texts and graphics displayed in the store front-end
- Customize the look and feel by editing files
- Understand the override system
- Modify templates to suit your needs
- Create new templates for the front-end
- Modify templates for sending mails to customers

Each of these topics will be discussed to enable you to perform the tasks of customizing the look and feel of your store.

Configuring Look and Feel

Zen Cart templates define the look and feel of the store through different graphics, colors, and fonts. By default, only the Classic template is shipped with Zen Cart version 1.3.8.x. However, you have the liberty to download and install new templates from the Internet and also develop your own look and feel of a Zen Cart store and configure it through the administration panel.

Zen Cart provides great design flexibility. You can see the design showcase on the Zen Cart website www.zen-cart.com. The website lists Zen Cart shops throughout the world. Visiting these shops will give you an idea about the extent to which you can change the design of a Zen Cart shop.

> You can download lots of templates from the Zen Cart website: www.zen-cart.com. There are some other sites from which you can download Zen Cart templates, free of charge. http://www.zencarttemplates.info allows us to preview and download free templates. However, professional looking Zen Cart templates are also available from some other template stores such as www.templatemonster.com. You can use Google to find such templates.
>
> For the exercise in this book, you are going to design a template that will look like www.packtpub.com. You will use the same logo and design scheme.

Zen Cart templates reside in the /includes/templates directory. Before applying any template, you need to copy the template files to the /includes/templates directory under your Zen Cart installation root directory.

To start building your customized template, copy the /includes/templates/ classic folder to a new folder of /includes/templates/packt. Now, open the /includes/templates/packt/template_info.php file in your favorite text editor and change it as follows:

```
$template_name = 'PACKT Publishing';

$template_version = 'Version 1.0';

$template_author = 'Suhreed Sarkar (c) 2008';

$template_description = 'This template set is designed for packtpub.
com, as an illustartion of Zen Cart template design procedures.';

$template_screenshot = 'scr_template_packt.jpg';
```

Save the file when you have made these changes. Now, your template is ready for use in your Zen Cart shop.

Note that the template is not complete yet. You have only created a skeleton. While going through the following sections, you will gradually customize this template.

Applying a Template

Generally, you need to set the template for each language. You can change the template used by your shop via **Tools | Template Selection** in the administration panel. The screen lists the installed templates. The template in use is selected by default.

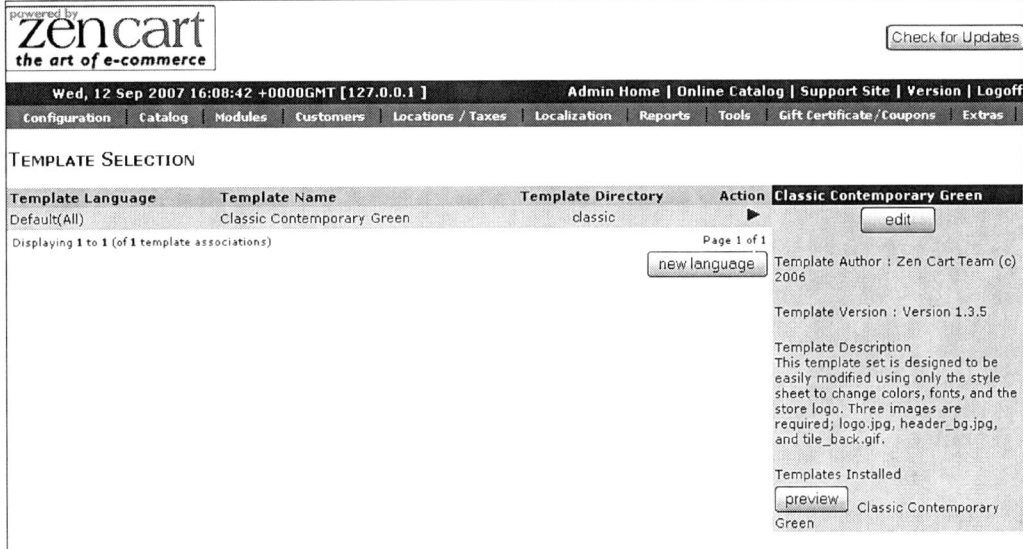

To change the template for a language, click on that language. Then, you see a right-arrow in the action column for that language. On the right, information about the selected template is shown. To apply the template, click on the **edit** button, select the template of your choice from the drop-down list, and then click on the **update** button.

To apply your newly created template, select **PACKT Publishing** from the drop-down list, and click **update**. Your new template will be applied. As you have still not changed much in the template, it will look similar to the previous, classic, template.

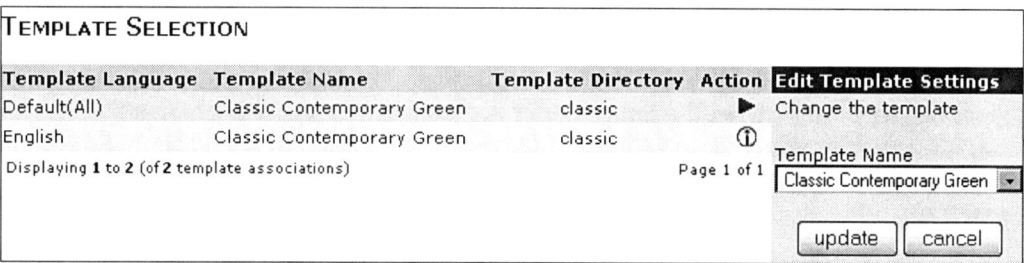

If the language for which you want to assign a template, is not available in the list, click on the **New Language** button. Then, select the template name and language from the drop-down list. If the preferred language is not available in the drop-down list, you will need to add it via **Localization | Languages**.

Any template that you have copied to the `includes/templates/` directory is generally displayed in the drop-down list accessible via **Tools | Template Selection**. If the template is not displayed in the drop-down list, it means that something is wrong with the template files. Check that all of the files have been copied to the templates directory, and ensure that the `template_info.php` file is in that template directory.

Controlling Layouts

A Zen Cart shop layout consists of left and right column sideboxes, a header, a footer, and the main content in the middle column. You can define which sideboxes will be shown where. You can also choose the width of the left and right column sideboxes. The following sections will show us how to do this.

Layout Settings

A wide variety of layout settings can be defined via **Configuration | Layout Settings**. The screen provides an array of configuration options for defining the column widths and other layout characteristics.

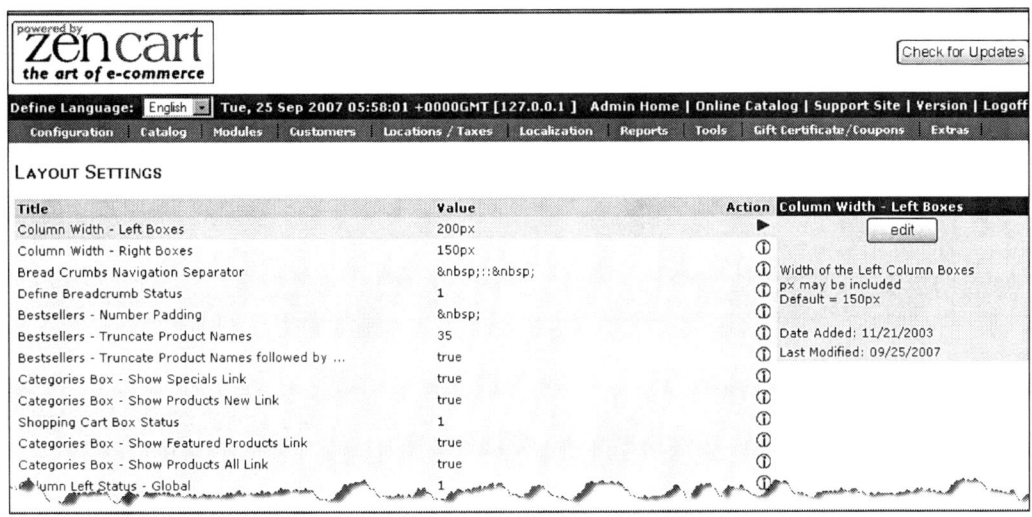

The column width for the left and right boxes can be defined in the **Column Width – Left Boxes** and **Column Width – Right Boxes** fields respectively. The default width of these boxes is **150px**. You can extend this setting to whatever width you prefer, for example **200px**, based on the availability of screen space.

Breadcrumbs (showing our current location) status can be specified in the **Define Breadcrumb Status** field. Although the default value is **1**, you may set this value to **2**, which will show the breadcrumb on all pages except the homepage. In fact, showing **Home** on the homepage looks odd, so this should be turned off for the homepage. You can also set the breadcrumb separator in the **Bread Crumbs Navigation Separator** field.

You can hide the left or right column by setting the **Column Left Status – Global** and **Column Right Status – Global** fields to 0.

If you want to show the categories on the homepage, you must change the **Categories - Always Show on Main Page** field's value to **1**. To speed up the page loading, you may also be tempted to use CSS buttons, instead of gif or jpg image buttons, to speed up the page loading. Set the **CSS Buttons** field's value to **Yes** to use the CSS buttons.

Showing/Hiding Sideboxes

The layout of the store front-end can be defined via **Tools | Layout Box Controller**. Clicking on this, you will see the boxes and names of the files that can be assigned to the left, right or center position in the front-end.

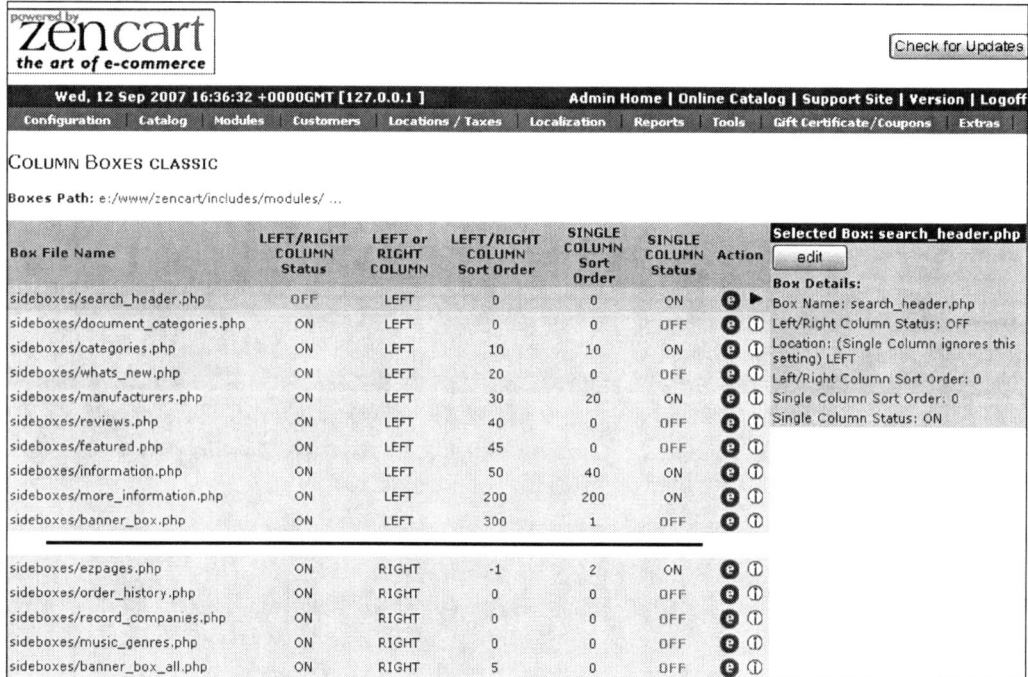

Sideboxes are generally located in the `includes/modules/sideboxes` directory. All the files in this directory will be shown in the **Tools | Layout Boxes Controller** screen. You will find five fields to the right of each sidebox. You can change the value of these fields by selecting the sidebox and then clicking on the **edit** button to the right of the fields.

COLUMN BOXES CLASSIC

Boxes Path: e:/www/zencart/includes/modules/ ...

Box File Name	LEFT/RIGHT COLUMN Status	LEFT or RIGHT COLUMN	LEFT/RIGHT COLUMN Sort Order	SINGLE COLUMN Sort Order	SINGLE COLUMN Status	Action	Edit Box
sideboxes/search_header.php	OFF	LEFT	0	0	ON	⊙ ①	Please make any necessary changes Box Name: document_categories.php
sideboxes/document_categories.php	ON	LEFT	0	0	OFF	⊙ ▶	Left/Right Column Status:
sideboxes/categories.php	ON	LEFT	10	10	ON	⊙ ①	⊙ ON ○ OFF
sideboxes/whats_new.php	ON	LEFT	20	0	OFF	⊙ ①	Location: (Single Column ignores
sideboxes/manufacturers.php	ON	LEFT	30	20	ON	⊙ ①	this setting)
sideboxes/reviews.php	ON	LEFT	40	0	OFF	⊙ ①	⊙ LEFT ○ RIGHT
sideboxes/featured.php	ON	LEFT	45	0	OFF	⊙ ①	Left/Right Column Sort Order:
sideboxes/information.php	ON	LEFT	50	40	ON	⊙ ①	0
sideboxes/more_information.php	ON	LEFT	200	200	ON	⊙ ①	
sideboxes/banner_box.php	ON	LEFT	300	1	OFF	⊙ ①	Single Column Sort Order: 0
sideboxes/ezpages.php	ON	RIGHT	-1	2	ON	⊙ ①	Single Column Status:
sideboxes/order_history.php	ON	RIGHT	0	0	OFF	⊙ ①	○ ON ⊙ OFF
sideboxes/record_companies.php	ON	RIGHT	0	0	OFF	⊙ ①	
sideboxes/music_genres.php	ON	RIGHT	0	0	OFF	⊙ ①	update cancel
sideboxes/banner_box_all.php	ON	RIGHT	5	0	OFF	⊙ ①	

The configuration options are available for each sidebox:

- **Left/Right Column Status**: If you need to show a sidebox in the left or right column on the store front-end, select **ON** in this field. It is displayed on the left or right column, as you indicate in the **Location** field.

- **Location**: Once the **Left/Right Column Status** is indicated here, you have to indicate the column in which you would want to show the sidebox, whether left or right. For sideboxes with the **Single Column Status ON**, this selection will not be effective.

- **Left/Right Column Sort Order**: This field indicates the order in which the sideboxes will be shown in the left or the right column. A lower value indicates a position nearer the top, and a higher value moves it down.

- **Single Column Sort order**: This field indicates the order of the Single Column sideboxes. A lower value puts the sidebox nearer the top.

- **Single Column Status**: If you want to show a sidebox in the center column, you select **ON** in this field.

You can customize the location and order of the sideboxes through this screen. You can also hide or show the sideboxes in the left and right columns from here.

Another way of hiding some sideboxes from a page is to edit the page's template file. For example, if you want to hide the right column sideboxes on the Privacy Policy page, follow the instructions given here:

1. Open the file `includes/templates/template_default/common/tpl_main_page.php` in your favorite text editor.

2. Find the line which reads as:

    ```
    if (in_array($current_page_base,explode(",",'list_pages_to_skip_
    all_right_sideboxes_on_here,separated_by_commas,and_no_spaces')) )
    {
        $flag_disable_right = true;
            }
    ```

3. Change the above line to:

    ```
    if (in_array($current_page_base,explode(",",'privacy,
      contact_us,shippinginfo')) ) {
        $flag_disable_right = true;
    }
    ```

    Note that the names of three pages have been entered here. For these pages, the right column sideboxes will not be shown. You can add more page names here separating them with a comma (,).

4. Save the file as `includes/templates/packt/common/tpl_main_page.php`.

5. Open your browser and point it to `http://yourdomain.com/index.php?main_page=privacy`. The page will now look like the following screenshot:

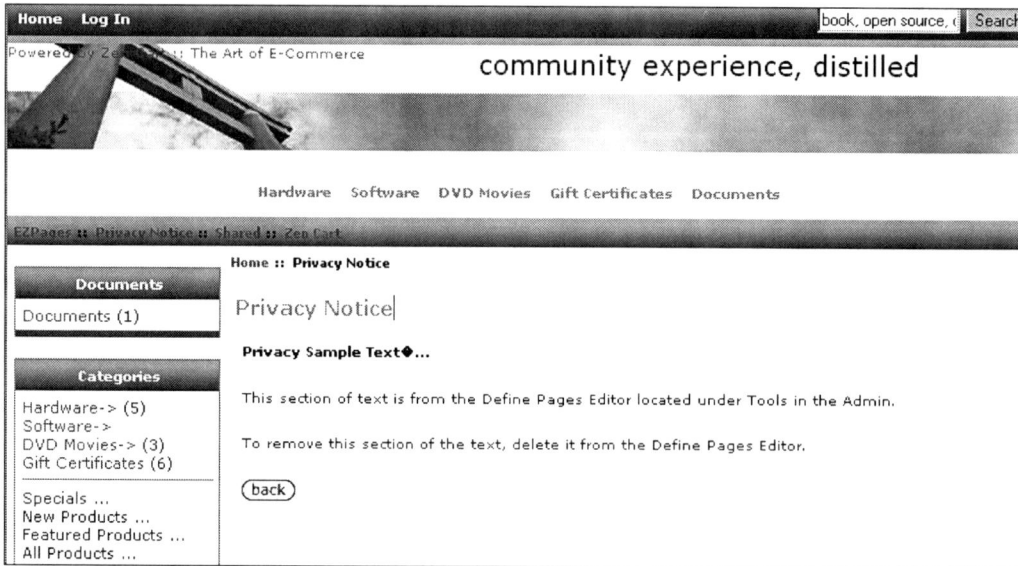

Understanding Zen Cart Templates

Designing a template for the first time is not an easy job. But once you have understood the basics and worked out some hacks, the process will be much easier. Getting to understand the logic behind Zen Cart templates is the first step towards developing templates for Zen Cart.

A Zen Cart template consists of a set of PHP files containing HTML and PHP codes. Each page consists of a header, a footer and sideboxes. While you are designing any page or module, you should keep in mind where you are going to show that page or module.

Whereas HTML and PHP codes give the structure of the page, CSS styles control the presentation of the page components. You need to edit the respective CSS to get the appropriate look and feel of a page.

While tweaking the Zen Cart template, you will often have to change the layouts and try them on the local server. Upload the tweaked or new template files to the production server only when you are fully satisfied with their output.

 Remember how Zen Cart handles images. There are two ways of inserting images into the page output. You can use a relative path to the images directory, or use PHP variables to declare the images in the template. Also remember that there will be shops using https server, and if you use relative image paths, it is likely that the https server will throw up warnings about insecure items. One solution to this is to keep a copy of the images inside the images directory at the https installation directory. To be on the safer side, I recommend you always use PHP variables for images.

In this section, you are going to understand how Zen Cart templates work, and what you need to change to get your desired look and feel.

Template Files Structure

The Zen Cart templates are located in the `includes/templates` directory. The typical structure of the templates directory is shown in the following figure. Note that by default there is a default template named `template_default`. This template contains most of the files needed for any template, and can be used as a base for all new templates. Therefore, it is wise not to modify or replace any file in this template directory. Instead, create the new template in a separate directory and apply the template override. Through this template override, all new changes will be applied along with this default template.

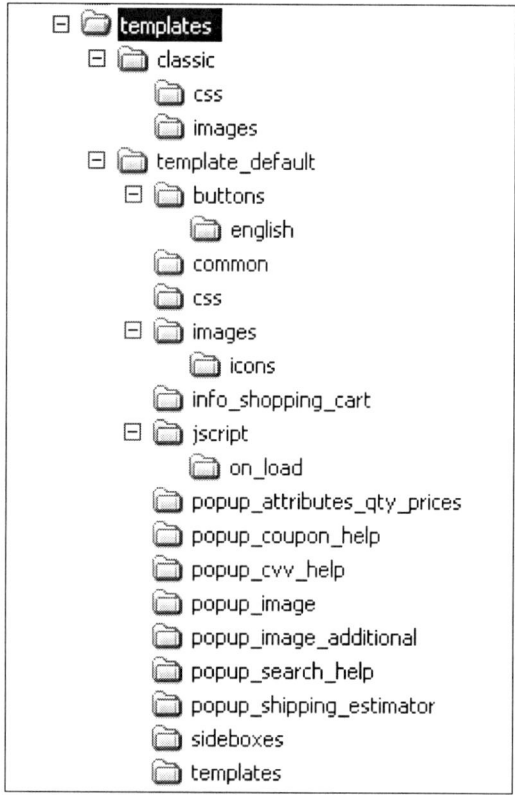

The template files used in Zen Cart provide the structure and layout of the various pages of your cart. They make use of the definitions from your language files.

The template files of Zen Cart are located in the `includes/templates/template_default` directory under the installation root of the shop. Template files have a `tpl` prefix (for example, `tpl_filename.php`). They provide the structure and layout of the various pages of a Zen Cart shop.

You will find three types of template files:

- **Common**: These template files are located in the `includes/templates/template_default/common` directory. These are common to every page used in Zen Cart. Generally, these files consist of the main page, header, footer and box files for the sideboxes.

- **Specific pages**: There are some template files specific to certain pages. These are located in the `includes/templates/template_default/templates` directory. For example, the display for the Login page is defined by the `tpl_login_default.php` file. If you want to change the display of a particular page, change the respective template file in this directory.

- **Sideboxes**: Display of the contents in the sideboxes is defined in the sideboxes template files. You will find these files in the `includes/templates/template_default/sideboxes` directory.

Besides these three types of template files, there are also CSS stylesheets and graphics files in the template directory. Editing the template and CSS files will not be too hard as most of the sections in those files are commented for your understanding.

CSS in Zen Cart Template

Zen Cart uses CSS for layout and display of the store's front-end. There are several CSS stylesheets for different purposes. Generally, CSS stylesheets are located in the CSS folder within the template directory. You can change most of the layout and display characteristics, such as color, font, and so on, by editing these stylesheets.

The names of the stylesheets and their descriptions are given in the following table.

CSS file Naming	Purpose
`style*.css`	These stylesheets load at the very beginning and define site-wide properties.
`language_stylesheet.css`	These files are for language-specific properties. For each language, you may need to define a separate stylesheet. For example, while using the Bangla language, you need to use the appropriate fonts, instead of default Arial or Helvetica. In this case, you have to define Bangla language-specific style properties in the bangla_stylesheet.css file. On selecting the Bangla language from the front-end, language-specific style information will be used from the bangla_stylesheet.css file.
`page_name.css`	These files are for page-specific styles. You can define different style properties for each page through these stylesheets.

CSS file Naming	Purpose
`language_page_name.css`	These are language-specific style definitions for a specific page. When a page's language changes, the style definitions from these stylesheets are used to display that page in the selected language.
`c_??_??.css`	These files are for a specific category. On changing the category, the style information from these pages is used.
`language_c_??_??.css`	These files contain language-specific style information for each category.
`m_??.css`	These files define style properties specific to a manufacturer.
`language_m_??.css`	These files contain language-specific style properties for a manufacturer.
`p_??.css`	These files define style properties for a specific product's info page. By adding these stylesheets, you can display the product information pages differently for each manufacturer.
`language_p_??.css`	These files define the language-specific style properties for a product's info page.
`print*.css`	These files contain site-wide style properties for generating printer-friendly pages.

The stylesheets mentioned above are listed in the order in which they load. `stylesheet.css` always loads first, and should contain the majority of your CSS selectors. Files loaded later takes priority over previously loaded file(s).

 You can speed up loading time by including only new selectors or selectors whose properties you wish to change in the optional CSS files. You can also have different overrides for the same page, in different languages, because the two would never be called at the same time.

Language-specific stylesheets are of great use while considering the localization of your store. As you know, fonts may need to be different for different languages. Fonts used for English will not be enough to display the contents in Bangla or in Hindi. For these languages, you need to define the `bangla_stylesheet.css` or `hindi_stylesheet.css` files. These files should contain only the site-wide changes that you want to make to `stylesheet.css`. For example, you may only need to change the `background-image` and `font-family` for Bangla or Hindi.

You can also set different stylesheets for different pages. For example, you may set a different `background-image` for different pages.

 Although you have the flexibility to add new stylesheets and selectors, it is better to use existing CSS files and the standard tags as much as possible. Only change their properties when needed. It is also suggested that you do not change the core code. Use the existing CSS files to do the work for you. Keeping your custom design in custom CSS files will later help you upgrade Zen Cart easily.

Understanding Overrides

One of the useful features of Zen Cart is its override system. This feature allows template designers to use existing templates as a base, and apply new or modified designs to the template system on an incremental basis. Overrides also allow you to make and save changes to your cart without the fear of losing them when upgrades and patches are released.

The override system is applicable to:

- Language Files (`includes/languages`)
- Module Files (`includes/modules`)
- Template Files (`includes/templates/template_default`)
- Extra Definitions (`includes/languages/language_name/ extra_definitions`)
- Extra Data Files (`includes/extra_datafiles`)

This means, that you can customize these files without modifying them directly. Creating some new files and adding modifications to the new files will help you achieve the desired customization. All of these new modified files can be saved in the `custom_folder`, say `my_mods`.

Overriding Language Files

Let us consider an example for modifying a language file. Generally Zen Cart uses the language strings from the `includes/languages/english.php` file. You can make site-wide changes to this file. For example, you may want to adapt the language to suit a book store. As you sell only books, you can use 'Books' instead of 'Products', and also 'Publishers' instead of 'Manufacturers'. You can also change languages for specific pages. For example, you can change the language for the Featured Products page (`featured_products.php`) by applying overrides as follow:

1. Create a new directory `/includes/languages/english/packt`

2. Copy `includes/languages/english/featured_products.php` to this new directory. You now have `/includes/languages/english/packt/featured_products.php`

3. Open the file `featured_products.php` in a text editor, then find the following lines of code to modify:

   ```
   define('NAVBAR_TITLE', 'Featured Products');
   define('HEADING_TITLE', 'Featured Products');

   define('TEXT_DATE_ADDED', 'Date Added:');
   define('TEXT_MANUFACTURER', 'Manufacturer:');
   define('TEXT_PRICE', 'Price:');
   ```

   Replace 'Manufacturer' with 'Publisher' and 'Products' with 'Books'. Now the above lines will look like:

   ```
   define('NAVBAR_TITLE', 'Featured Books');
   define('HEADING_TITLE', 'Featured Books');
   define('TEXT_DATE_ADDED', 'Date Added:');
   define('TEXT_MANUFACTURER', 'Publisher:');
   define('TEXT_PRICE', 'Price:');
   ```

4. Save the file.

Similarly, open the `/includes/languages/english/index.php` file and replace all instances of **products** with **books** and all instances of **manufacturers** with **publishers**. Also, replace all instances of **models** with **edition**.

Now, the Featured Products page of your Zen Cart shop will look like the following screenshot. Note that 'Books' is shown instead of 'Products'.

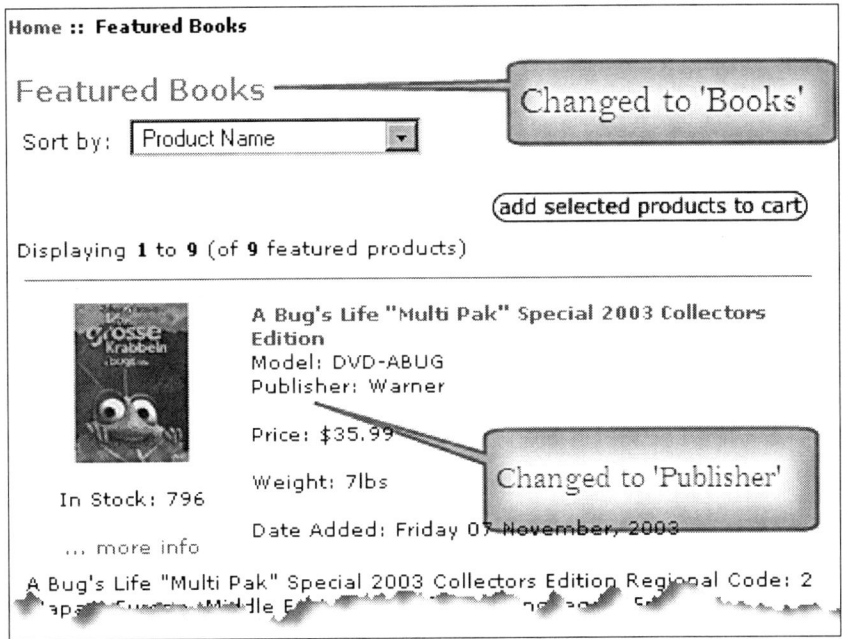

Overriding Module Files

As with Language overrides, you can apply overrides to module files located in `/includes/modules/sideboxes/`. Each `.php` file in this folder represents a sidebox. If you want to make changes to a sidebox, the best way is to use an override. For example, in your book shop you may want to use a custom Information sidebox. Instead of modifying `information.php`, you can use an override. Follow the given instructions:

1. Create a new directory, `includes/modules/sideboxes/packt`.
2. Copy `includes/modules/sideboxes/information.php` to this new folder.
3. Now, open the file `includes/modules/sideboxes/packt/information.php` in your favorite text editor.
4. Modify the file to suit your needs.
5. Save the file.

Whenever you develop a new module for this bookshop, you can put it in this directory. The module will override the modules in the other directories, when you apply the Packt publishing template.

Overriding Template Files

Overrides can also be used for page-specific template files. Page-specific templates are located in the `includes/templates/template_default/templates/tpl_*.php` files. If you need to modify some part of a page-specific template, for example `tpl_product_reviews_default.php`, follow the given instructions:

1. Create the directory, `includes/templates/packt/templates`.
2. Copy `includes/templates/template_default/templates/ tpl_product_reviews_default.php` to the above directory.
3. Open the file in your favorite text editor.
3. Find the appropriate sections and modify them to suit your needs.
4. Save the file.

The changes you have made to `tpl_product_reviews_default.php` will now override the previous design.

Using Your Own Definitions

You may need to include additional definitions during customization of your Zen Cart. Additional definitions are generally kept in the `includes/languages/english/extra_definitions/` folder. To add your own definitions, open your favorite text editor, create a definition file named `my_own_definition.php` and save it in an appropriate folder. Write all of the definitions that are needed for customization of your Zen Cart shop in this file.

Using Extra Data Files

Sometimes, you may also need to create extra data files for some modules or for customizing your Zen Cart shop. Follow the same method used for creating your own definition file. You can define extra data files and save these in the `includes/extra_datafiles/` folder. For example, you have created a custom page (about_us) and need to reference the filename. You can do this by creating a new file (`about_us_filenames.php`) which will include the following:

```php
<?php
// About Us Filename Define
define('FILENAME_ABOUT_US', 'about_us');
?>
```

Now, save the file as `/includes/extra_datafiles/about_us_filenames.php`.

Zen Cart Upgrades and Overrides

One of the benefits of using the override system is that you don't have to worry about over-writing your custom files when you upgrade to a later version, because all of your modified files are in the custom directories. If you do not use override, but directly modify the core files, it will be difficult to save or recreate your changes during an upgrade.

For safety, wherever you see a `classic` folder, you can add another `custom` folder, where `custom` is the name of your customized template. You can do all the changes in this `custom` folder, keeping the original files intact. This will help when you are upgrading to later versions.

Customizing Zen Cart Templates

The preferred way to customize the look of a page is to do so with a stylesheet. It is much easier to keep track of a stylesheet than hacks in the source code.

When Zen Cart loads a page, it first looks for a stylesheet with the same name as your page. You can see what Zen Cart calls each page by looking at your URL. It should be something like `your_domain/index.php?main_page=index.main_page`. It tells the cart which page to display. For example, if you want to hide the breadcrumbs on your homepage, you can do so by adding the following stylesheet:

- Create a new stylesheet (`.css` file) in your templates CSS directory named `index_home.css`.

- Add the styles for your homepage. The style required to hide the breadcrumbs is:

  `#navBreadCrumb{ display: none; }`

- Save the changes to the file.

Now, refresh your browser to your shop's homepage. If the new style is not applied, try emptying your browser cache. The homepage will be shown without the breadcrumb.

Another example of using a page-specific stylesheet may be for the Privacy page. Suppose that you want to show the heading of the privacy notice in red, and the background of the notice in silver. For this, you can create a stylesheet named `privacy.css` and place the following style declaration in that file:

```
#privacyDefaultHeading {
 font-family: Arial;
 color: red;
 text-transform: uppercase;

}


#privacyDefaultMainContent {
  color: red;
  background-color: silver;
}
```

In this way, you can create stylesheets for each page. However, it is convenient to add only those style declarations that are unique to that specific page.

Changing Logos and Texts

After installation of Zen Cart you will find the Zen Cart logo in the header of the store front-end. In the main body, you will see **'Congratulations! You have successfully installed your Zen Cart E-commerce Solution'**. An advertisement for the Zen Cart manual follows that. You have to customize this page before starting your online shop. In fact, the first step towards customizing your look and feel will be to change these texts and the logo of the store.

Changing Default Texts

The first thing that you may want to change is the statement **'Congratulations! You have successfully installed your Zen Cart™; E-Commerce Solution'**. To remove this statement, open the `includes/languages/english/index.php` file in your favorite text editor and find the following code:

```
/*Replace this text with the headline you would like for your shop.
For example: 'Welcome to My SHOP!'*/
define('HEADING_TITLE', 'Congratulations! You have successfully
installed  your Zen Cart&trade; E-Commerce Solution.');
} elseif ($category_depth == 'nested') {
  // This section deals with displaying a subcategory
 /*  Replace this line with the headline you would like for your shop.
For example: 'Welcome to My SHOP!' */
define('HEADING_TITLE', 'Congratulations! You have successfully
installed your Zen Cart&trade; E-Commerce Solution.');
```

In the highlighted lines in the preceding code, replace the text starting 'Congratulations...' with your own text. Make sure that the single quote marks are not deleted. You may put a welcome message here, say, 'Welcome to Packt Publishing'. However, if you do not want to show anything, just delete the default words and keep one space. Then save the file as `includes/languages/english/packt/index.php`, to use the overrides.

Another default text you need to change is **'Sales Message Goes Here'**. You may also need to change the **'Tagline Here'**. To do so, open the `includes/languages/english/header.php` file in your favorite text editor and find the following line of code:

```
define('HEADER_SALES_TEXT', 'Tagline Here');
```

Replace **'Tagline Here'** with your own text, such as **'community experience, distilled!'**. Make sure that the single quotes are not deleted and the text you specify remains inside the quotes. Save the file as `includes/languages/english/packt/header.php`.

If you see **'Zen Cart!, The Art of E-Commerce'** on your browser title bar, you need to edit another file `includes/languages/english/meta_tags.php`. Open it in your text editor and find the following lines of code:

```
// page title
define('TITLE', 'Zen Cart!');

// Site Tagline
define('SITE_TAGLINE', 'The Art of E-commerce');
```

Replace the title and tagline texts with your own texts, making sure that the single quote marks are not left out, and new quote marks are not added. Save the edited file as `includes/languages/english/packt/meta_tags.php`.

Note that after changing the above texts, the advertisement placed on the homepage is still visible. This is defined in the `/includes/languages/english/html_includes/classic/define_main_page.php` file. Open the file in the text editor and delete all of the contents of file. To be safe, you may apply override by creating a file named `/includes/languages/english/html_includes/packt/define_main_page.php`. Enter your desired text in this file using HTML markup, or keep it blank to show nothing.

You may use the pages in the `/includes/languages/english/html_includes/` folder more intelligently. You can add any HTML content to any page by creating a `define_page_name.php` page in this folder and sub-folder. For example, the texts to be displayed in the **Privacy** page can be put in `define_privacy.php` file in the HTML format. Similarly, `define_checkout_success.php`, `define_conditions.php`, `define_contact_us.php`, `define_page_not_found.php`, and `define_discount_coupon.php` can be of great use if you want to display related information as nicely-formatted text.

Changing the Header Image

The header image of Zen Cart is one of the first things you will want to change. By default, Zen Cart uses a graphic named `header_bg.jpg` for its header, but you have the freedom to change its name as you wish. To do this, create a new background graphic using an image editor—GIMP or Adobe Photoshop—and save that image as `includes/templates/packt/images/header_bg.jpg`.

> For Zen Cart customization, it is better not to change the original files. Zen Cart uses an override system which can be used to add customization to templates, modules, sideboxes, and so on. Let us start using the override system for the following exercises.

From Zen Cart 1.3.7.x, stylesheets are used to define the background image for the header. Therefore, you need to edit the stylesheet. Open the `stylesheet.css` and find the following lines:

```
#logoWrapper {
  width:760px;
  height:110px;
  background-image:url(../images/header_bg.jpg);
  background-repeat:no-repeat;
}
```

In the highlighted line above, specify the name of your header background image, for example, `my_header_bg.jpg`. Save the file as `includes/templates/packt/css/stylesheet.css`.

As Packt website does not use a header image, you can remove this as well. To do this, change the preceding code block to be as follows:

```
#logoWrapper {
  width:90%;
  height:110px;
  background-color:#ffffff;
}
```

As www.packtpub.com uses a fluid design, you have to make it much more flexible by defining the width as a percentage. Instead of the background header, display a white background. Now, your store will look as shown in the following screenshot:

Before using any new image as background , make sure you resize its height and width to fit the header region. Also note that you can specify its height and width from this style declaration.

Adding a New Logo

You need to change the logo of your store to make it branded. One easy way to do this is to replace the includes/templates/template_default/images/logo.gif file with another logo.gif file of the same dimension. But often, you would want to do more by creating your own image of different sizes and in different image formats (that is, .jpg, .png). You may also want to change their position. Now, you are going to learn how to do this.

First, prepare your logo using an image editor of your choice. Save the image to includes/templates/packt/images/packt_logo.png.

Now, you need to adjust the height, width and logo name in the language file. To do this, open includes/languages/english/header.php and find the following lines:

```
define('HEADER_LOGO_WIDTH', '192px');
define('HEADER_LOGO_HEIGHT', '64px');
define('HEADER_LOGO_IMAGE', 'logo.gif');
```

Make appropriate changes to these lines and save the file as `includes/languages/english/packt/header.php`. You have to do it for each language. For example, for the Bangla language, you have to copy `header.php` file to `includes/languages/bangla/packt/header.php`.

By default, the logo is left-aligned. This alignment is defined in `includes/templates/template_default/css/stylesheet.css`. Open the file and find the following:

```
#logo, .centerBoxContents, .specialsListBoxContents,
    .categoryListBoxContents, .centerBoxContentsAlsoPurch,
    .attribImg {float: left;}
```

Because this is a collection of several selectors (`#logo`, `.centerBoxContents` and so on), split this into two separate statements as shown here, so as not to interfere with the layout of the other sections:

```
.centerBoxContents, .specialsListBoxContents,
.categoryListBoxContents, .centerBoxContentsAlsoPurch,
.attribImg {float: left;}

#logo {float: left;}
```

To center the logo, use **text-align: center**; or to align it to the right, use **float: right**;

Save the files as `includes/templates/packt/css/stylesheet.css`. After adding the logo, the logo area will appear as follows:

Changing Colors and Fonts

If you open any page of your Zen Cart in a text editor, you will find that the page is broken into smaller pieces called 'classes'. The style for each class is defined in the `stylesheet.css` file. You can control the look of your shop by changing the fonts, colors, text sizes, borders, background images, and so on, by changing the class styles. You can change the colors by using standard HTML color numbers for the text and background colors. You can also change the text size by increasing or decreasing the size, and change the typeface by using a different font name.

For example, you want to change the font size and the color of the Tag Line. If you view the source code, you will find the tag line in following code:

```
<div id="tagline">community experience, distilled</div>
```

If you want to change its style—font, color, and so on—you have to change the style definition of your tagline ID in `stylesheet.css`.

To do this, open the `includes/templates/packt/css/stylesheet.css` file in your favorite text editor, and find the following lines:

```
#tagline {
    color:#000000;
    font-size: 2em;
    text-align : center;
    vertical-align: middle;
    }
```

Let us change its color and font as follows:

```
#tagline {
    color:#6600FF;
    font-size:3em;
    font-style:italic;
    text-align : center;
    vertical-align: middle;
    }
```

Now, reload the homepage in your browser. You will see the difference in the display of your tagline.

You have the freedom to edit the stylesheet. You can remove a CSS element, such as a border, simply by commenting out the line with a "/*" (slash, asterisk) at the beginning of the line and "*/" (asterisk, slash) at the end of the line. You can add new style properties and make your Zen Cart shop more attractive. But what you need to know to do this is how CSS works.

The Web Developer Toolbar extension for Mozilla Firefox may be of great help to you while editing stylesheets for Zen Cart. This will help you identify classes and IDs for HTML elements, and show you associated style declarations and stylesheets in use. It will also help you see the source code and identify document object models.

As you want to make the site similar to www.packtpub.com, you have to change its look and feel by changing its fonts and colors by editing stylesheets. The following changes are to be made to /includes/templates/packt/css/stylesheet.css:

```css
#mainWrapper {
...
    width: 90%; /* instead of 750px, we make it fluid */
...
    }

#logoWrapper{
    /* background-image: url(..);
    background-repeat: repeat-x; */
    background-color: #ffffff;
    height:100px;
    }
#navMainWrapper, #navSuppWrapper, #navCatTabsWrapper {
    ...
    background-image: url(../images/tile_back.png);
    ...
    }

#navCatTabs li {
    ...
        background:url("../images/tableftI.gif") no-repeat left top;
    ...
    }

#navCatTabs a {
    ...
        background:url("../images/tabrightI.gif") no-repeat right top;
    ...
    }
```

```
#navCatTabs a.category-top {
      ...
      background:url("../images/tabrightI.gif") no-repeat right top;
      ...
      }

#navEZPagesTop {
   background-color: #abbbd3;
   background-image: url(../images/tile_back.png);
   ...
   }

h3.leftBoxHeading, h3.leftBoxHeading a,
h3.rightBoxHeading, h3.rightBoxHeading a {
   font-size: 1.2em;
   color: #cd6601; /* for Packt */
   }


.leftBoxHeading, .centerBoxHeading, .rightBoxHeading {
   ...
   /* background-image: url(../images/tile_back.png); */ /*for packt
*/
   ...

   }

A.category-top, A.category-top:visited {
   color: #008ccf; /* packt */
   text-decoration: none;
   }

.productListing-rowheading {
   background-color: #abbbd3;
   background-image: url(../images/tile_back.png);
   ...
   }
```

After all of these changes have been made for the two image files, `tile_back.png` and `tabrightI.gif`, and these images are added to `/includes/templates/packt/images` directory, the site now looks quite similar to www.packtpub.com, though it may need some more tweaking. Look at the following screenshot:

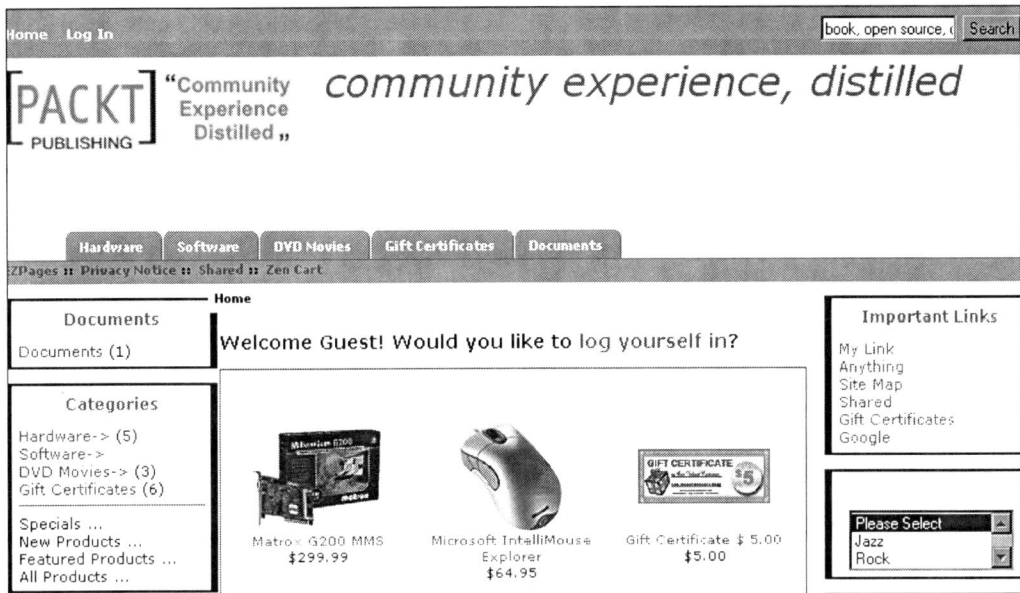

Note that now the color scheme has been changed to look similar to Packt's website. The borders of the sideboxes also look similar to Packt's boxes. You may try to fine-tune its design after learning more about changing buttons and page layouts.

Changing Buttons and Icons

You can change the buttons and icons used in your Zen Cart shop. This will help you customize the Zen Cart shop as you wish. In Zen Cart, the buttons and icons are generally located in the following places:

- `/images` folder: This is where your product images are kept. Whenever you upload a product image, it goes into this folder. This folder may have subfolders to contain product images by manufacturers and/or types.

- `/includes/languages/english/images` folder: The language icon (icon.gif) is located in this folder. For each language, create such a folder and put your language flag there.

- `/includes/templates/template_default/buttons/english` folder: This folder contains the buttons used by the Cart. You need to add buttons for each language. First, generate the buttons in your language, and then put them in the appropriate folders. For example, the buttons for the Bangla language should be in either the `includes/templates/template_default/buttons/bangla` folder or the `includes/templates/packt/buttons/bangla` folder.

- `/includes/templates/template_default/images` folder: This folder contains `header_bg.jpg`, `logo.gif`, and other images required by the template. Your template-specific image files should be put in the images folder under your template directory, for example, `includes/templates/packt/images`.

- `/includes/templates/template_default/images/icons` folder: This folder contains additional images used by Zen Cart. The delete icon, warning icon, and so on can be found in this folder. Put your template-specific icons in the `includes/templates/packt/images/icons` folder.

Once you have generated the custom buttons and icons for your template, the names of these buttons need to be defined in `includes/language/english/button_names.php`. For each language, you need to set the names in this file. For example, the names of buttons specific to the Bangla language should be defined in the `includes/languages/bangla/button_names.php` file.

The editing of `button_names.php` will be straightforward. It has two sections: one for defining the button image files, another for defining `alt` text for those images. The following is a code snippet from `button_names.php`:

```
/** define the button images used in the project */
define('BUTTON_IMAGE_ADD_TO_CART', 'button_add_to_cart.gif');
define('BUTTON_IMAGE_ADD_ADDRESS', 'button_add_address.gif');
define('BUTTON_IMAGE_ADD_PRODUCTS_TO_CART','button_add_selected.gif');
define('BUTTON_IMAGE_BACK', 'button_back.gif');
define('BUTTON_IMAGE_BUY_NOW', 'button_buy_now.gif');
. . .


/* ALT tags used for buttons */

define('BUTTON_CREATE_ACCOUNT_ALT', 'Sign Up');
define('BUTTON_LOG_OFF_ALT', 'Log Off');
define('BUTTON_ADD_TO_CART_ALT', 'Add This to My Cart');
define('BUTTON_ADD_ADDRESS_ALT', 'Add Address');
...
```

You can use your favorite image editor for creating the buttons in your language. The buttons may be saved as GIF, JPG or PNG, but if you are not using the same format and names as the original buttons, you need to edit the button_names.php file to reflect the new names of the buttons, and save this edited file in your language override directory.

There are some online tools which can be used to generate buttons for the Zen Cart store, simply by specifying the background and foreground color, font, language and button template. One such tool is available at http://www.advancewebsoft.com/downloads/free-scripts/free-oscommerce-cre-loaded-zen-cart-oscmax-button-generator-p.html. This online tool can generate buttons for Zen Cart, osCommerce, CRE-Loaded, and oscMax.

Changing Layout of a Template

Changing the layout of a template mainly involves changing its width and showing/hiding sideboxes. You have already learned about showing or hiding sideboxes. Now, you will learn how to change the width of a template.

In Zen Cart version 1.3.x, CSS are used for layout, instead of tables. Therefore, you only need to edit the main stylesheet for that template. When changing the width of a template, it is better to use an override. Open the /includes/templates/packt/css/stylesheet.css file and find the following style declaration:

```
#mainWrapper {
 background-color: #ffffff;
 text-align: left;
 width: 750px;
 vertical-align: top;
}
```

The highlighted line specifies the width of the page. To make the template fluid, that is, fit it in the available browser window space, change its value to 100%. You could also choose any other desired value.

In Zen Cart version prior to 1.3.x, changing the width was tricky. For such a template open the stylesheet.css file for editing, and find the .centershop, TABLE.header, .main_page, and TD.headerNavigation declarations. In all the declarations, you will find a line saying, width: 750px !important;. Change the width in this line. Remember that all four instances need to be changed.

Modifying a Page Template

Page-specific templates are located in the `/includes/templates/template_default/templates/` directory. For each page there is a `tpl_*.php` page. The layout of the page is defined in its related `tpl` file. You can change the template for each file by editing these files and applying overrides. For example, you may want to change the layout of the Product Information page. Information regarding a product is shown in this page when you click a product link. By default, this page looks like the following screenshot:

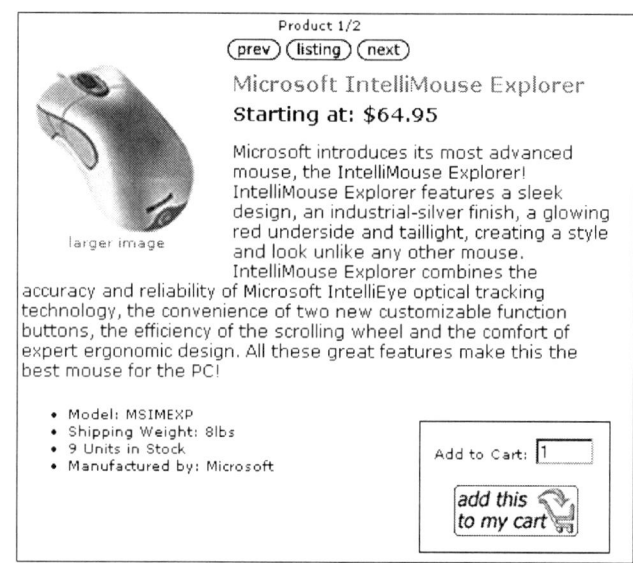

Note that the **Add to Cart** block is shown after the product description. You may opt to put this just after the product name to persuade customers to buy it. To do this, you need to edit the `tpl_product_info_display.php` file. Open it in your favorite text editor, and find the following block:

```
<!--bof Add to Cart Box -->
.....

<!--eof Add to Cart Box-->
```

Select the whole block and cut it. Now, locate the following block:

```
<!--bof Product Name-->
<h1 id="productName" class="productGeneral">
    <?php echo $products_name; ?>
</h1>
<!--eof Product Name-->
```

Paste the `<!—bof Add to Cart Box -->` block just after `<!—eof Product Name -->`. Now save the file in your override directory `/includes/templates/packt/templates/`.

Refresh the page in your browser. Now, you will see the **Add to Cart** block just after the product name. You can edit other files in the same way.

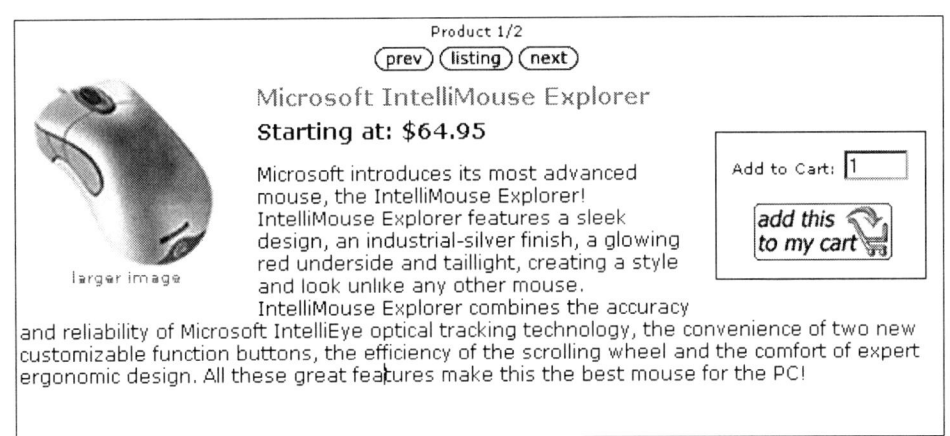

Using EZ pages

The product catalogue in the Zen Cart shop consists of dynamically-generated pages. Of course, the product catalogue is the core of an online shop. However, besides product catalogs, a good shop also needs to have some static pages that describe such things as privacy policy, shipping & return policy, frequently asked questions, and so on. These pages generally do not change frequently and need to be linked to the homepage so that customers can access these pages whenever necessary.

A feature called EZ-Pages provides the flexibility of adding static pages to a Zen Cart shop in a fast and easy way. It also helps create links to other internal and external pages. You can also create related links to form a group or a chapter.

EZ-Page can be added to your store via **Tools | EZ-Pages | New File** in the Administration Panel. Options for creating an EZ-Page are shown in the following table:

Option	Description
Page Title	Type the name of the page in this field. The page or link you are creating will be referred to by this page title. Page Title is mandatory, and all EZ-Pages and links need it in order to function.
Open New Window	Selecting 'Yes' for this field will open the page or link in a new window when on in the Header, Footer or Sidebox.
Page is SSL	Select 'Yes' to indicate that the page or link is using Secure Socket Layer (SSL).
Link placement locations	Although you have the option of adding additional links to the Header, Footer and Sidebox with EZ-Pages, you are not limited to only these three link locations. Links can be placed in one or more locations simply by enabling the Order for the Location(s) where the Link should appear. The Link Location Status for the Header, Footer and Sidebox is controlled simply by setting these to 'Yes' or 'No' for each setting. Then, set the order in which the Link should appear for each location.
Chapter and TOC	The Chapter and TOC, or Table of Contents, are a unique method of building Multiple Links that interact together. While these links still follow the rules of the Header, Footer and Sidebox placement, the difference is that only one of the links, the main link, needs to be displayed anywhere on the site.
HTML Content	Add HTML content that will be shown on the page in this text area. HTML editors will often add the opening and closing tags for sections such as `<html>`, `<head>` and `<body>` to the file you are working on. You need to remove these when copying from another HTML page, as these are already added to the pages via EZ-Pages.
Internal Link URL	Internal Link URLs are links to internal pages within your shop. These can be to any valid URL, but should be written as relative links such as `index.php?main_page=index&cPath=21`. It is convenient to write it as a Relative Link so that after changing domains, the link still remain valid.
External Link URL	External Link URLs are links to pages outside your shop. These can be to any valid URL such as: `http://www.zen-cart.com`. For an external link, you need to include the full URL. You can also mark these to open in a New Window or the Same Window.

After typing a page title, if you provide an internal or external link, it will be considered as a link, and not a page. In that case, the text you have typed in the HTML Content box will be ignored.

Creating A New Template

Creating a new template for Zen Cart is fun. You have already learned the basics of how a Zen Cart template works. Prior to version 1.3.x of Zen Cart, some HTML tables were used for layout. But in version 1.3.x onwards, Zen Cart has fully abandoned the use of HTML tables for layout, using a CSS-based layout instead.

Creating A File System

Let us start building a new template for Zen Cart by creating a new folder under `includes/templates/`. Let us name it Packt (or whatever you like). But remember to use underscore instead of spaces in a long name. Avoid using `Book Shop`. Instead, use `book_shop` or `BookShop`.

Under the `packt` template folder, create the following folders:

- `images`: this folder will contain all the images needed for the template.
- `css`: this folder will contain all the CSS files for the template. It's better to copy all the files from the `includes/templates/template_default/css` directory to this `css` folder.
- `common`: this folder will contain the common files for the template. You may copy the files from the `includes/templates/template_default/common` folder, and edit those to suit your needs.
- `sideboxes`: this folder will contain module-specific sideboxes. Here, you can add new sideboxes, which you are going to use.
- `templates`: this folder contains page-specific templates. Whenever you want to change a page's layout, copy the template for that page to this directory and modify it as required.

Information regarding a template is located in the `template_info.php` file. You need to create a new `template_info.php` file for the new template. Copy the file called `includes/templates/template_default/template_info.php` into the new template folder, and then open the `template_info.php` file in your favorite text editor.

Change the text between each set of single quotes to suit your new template.

```php
<?php
$template_name = 'Packt Publishing';
$template_version = 'Version 1.0';
$template_author = 'Suhreed Sarkar';
$template_description = 'This template is designed for Packt
Publishing';
$template_screenshot = '';
?>
```

Remember to keep the single quotes. Your template name does not need to be identical to your folder name, and you can use spaces to make it read well, but it is best to keep them similar. Leave the space between the quotes for the template screenshot field empty for now, as you don't have one yet.

When you've finished, your new file structure should appear as follows:

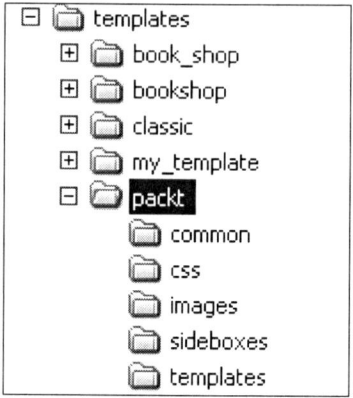

Open your Admin panel and navigate to **Tools | Template Selection**. Click the **Edit** button, then choose **Packt Publishing** from the drop-down menu and click the **Update** button. Now, navigate to **Tools | Layout boxes controller**, and click the **Reset** button at the bottom of the page.

Your new template is now enabled and ready to be customized.

Using Overrides

When building a new template for Zen Cart, you can use its powerful overriding feature. Overriding means using some template as the base and extending it by adding different properties through separate templates. For example, you may want to make some modifications to the default template, `template_default`. You could modify the files in the `template_default` directory to do this. But due to its overriding character, you can add the changes in the new template, say `packt`, which will apply the changes to the shop.

In fact, you can override any file in the path `includes/templates/template_default`. Files in this directory generally determine the layout and the HTML formatting of your web pages. By default, Zen Cart has two standard templates: `template_default` and `classic`, both of which are located in the `includes/templates/` folder.

Out of these two standard templates, only `template_default` contains a full set of files. Every other template contains only the files that differ from `template_default`. If your template does not contain a particular file, Zen Cart will pull that file from `template_default`.

Graphics

You need to add your templates graphics to the appropriate folders as discussed previously in the section on Changing Buttons and Icons. The header image, logo, background image, background image for sidebox headings, and so on should be placed in the images directory under your template directory. If you want to change the buttons and icons, create the graphic files in the GIF, JPG or PNG format and put them in the `/includes/templates/template_name/buttons/language_name` folder. Then, update the `button_names.php` file to define the button image file name, and the ALT texts for those images.

Sideboxes

You do not need to copy existing sideboxes from the `template_default` directory, as these will automatically be displayed. If you are planning to develop a new sidebox, put the template for that sidebox in the **sideboxes** folder under your template directory.

A sidebox consists of three files, which are located in the includes directory:

- `modules/sideboxes/template_name/name_of_sidebox.php`
- `languages/english/extra_definitions/template_name/name_of_sidebox_defines.php`
- `templates/template_name/sideboxes/tpl_name_of_sidebox.php`

You need to replace `template_name` and `name_of_sidebox` with you template name and the sidebox name respectively. For example, let us build a sidebox named `my_sidebox`. Then, `my_sidebox.php` file will read like this:

```php
<?php
$show_my_sidebox = true;
if ($show_my_sidebox == true){
require($template->get_template_dir('tpl_my_sidebox.php',
  DIR_WS_TEMPLATE, $current_page_base,'sideboxes').
  '/tpl_my_sidebox.php');
$title =  BOX_HEADING_MY_SIDEBOX;
$left_corner = false;
$right_corner = false;
$right_arrow = false;
require($template->get_template_dir($column_box_default,
  DIR_WS_TEMPLATE, $current_page_base,'common') .
  '/' . $column_box_default);
  }
?>
```

This page actually defines what is to be shown in that sidebox. Note that this page also includes the corresponding template file. Here, we have used a constant `BOX_HEADING_MY_SIDEBOX`. You need to define this in the `includes/languages/english/extra_definitions/packt/my_sidebox_defines.php` file. This file will look like this:

```php
<?php
  define('BOX_HEADING_MY_SIDEBOX', 'My Sidebox');
?>
```

Now, you have to build its template file `includes/templates/packt/sideboxes/tpl_my_sidebox.php`, which will read as:

```php
<?php
  $content = "This is my first Sidebox. I have created it in 5
minutes. Although it is not of practical use yet, I hope I can
eventually build a good sidebox.";
?>
```

If you have created these files for the `packt` template, you can try it by going to **Tools | Layout Boxes Controller** in the administration panel. From here, turn the sidebox **ON** and set it up to display in the left or the right side column. This sidebox will look like the following figure.

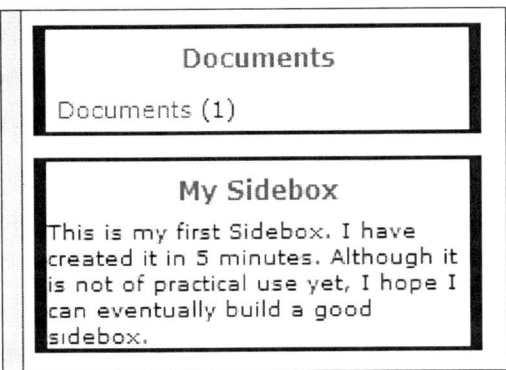

Stylesheets

All stylesheets for your new template should be placed in the `/includes/templates/template_name/css` folder. You should follow stylesheet naming conventions as discussed earlier in this chapter. It is a good idea to copy an old stylesheet and then modify it to suit your needs. As discussed earlier, you can have multiple stylesheets for your shop –you can even add a stylesheet for each page.

As a design rule, try to keep the declarations minimal, simple, and self explanatory. Try to restrain yourself from changing the class and ID names in the core files.

Creating and Modifying Email Templates

As a store owner, you need to send several mails to your existing and potential customers. You will learn about promotion and public relations activities available in Zen Cart in Chapter 6. All these emails use some templates that reside in the `/email` folder under the Zen Cart installation directory. To change these emails to your style, you may edit these templates.

The email's structure is determined in one of two ways. If you are sending plain text emails, the email structure is determined by the way you put together the various items (customer greeting, order number, link to detailed invoice, and so on) in a string variable that is then passed to the `zen_mail()` function. If you are sending HTML emails, the structure is determined by the template you use.

Text Email Template

You can rearrange, add, or delete items in a plain text email. To do so, you will need to edit the Zen Cart files where the email is created. For example, if you want to edit the order confirmation email, you will need to edit the file includes/classes/ order.php.

In your example, open up includes/classes/order.php and scroll down to the bottom of the file, in the function send_order_email(). There, you will see the lines that construct the plain text email message:

```
[Line 827]
$email_order = EMAIL_TEXT_HEADER . EMAIL_TEXT_FROM . STORE_NAME . "\n\
n" . $this->customer['firstname'] . ' ' . $this->customer['lastname']
. "\n\n" . EMAIL_THANKS_FOR_SHOPPING . "\n" . EMAIL_DETAILS_FOLLOW
. "\n" . EMAIL_SEPARATOR . "\n" . EMAIL_TEXT_ORDER_NUMBER . ' ' .
$zf_insert_id . "\n" . EMAIL_TEXT_DATE_ORDERED . ' ' . strftime(DATE_
FORMAT_LONG) . "\n" . EMAIL_TEXT_INVOICE_URL . ' ' . zen_href_
link(FILENAME_ACCOUNT_HISTORY_INFO, 'order_id=' . $zf_insert_id, 'SSL'

[Line 848]
$email_order .= zen_db_output($this->info['comments']) . "\n\n";

[Line 855]
$email_order .= EMAIL_TEXT_PRODUCTS . "\n" .
                EMAIL_SEPARATOR . "\n" .
                $this->products_ordered .
                EMAIL_SEPARATOR . "\n";
```

In this file, the variable that holds the plain text email message is called $email_order. It generally has a different name in each file, such as $email or $email_text. Whatever its name, this is the place where you will make your changes. You can add, delete, and rearrange the order of the items to suit your wishes.

HTML Email Templates

HTML Email templates have two parts: embedded CSS and HTML codes. You may be surprised to see the embedded stylesheet in each mail template and may want to know why linked stylesheets have not been used. One reason for not using the linked stylesheet is that you may not know how the email clients will behave. Most email clients used today can handle HTML emails and stylesheets to some extent. But there is no guarantee that every customer will have an email client that can retrieve linked stylesheets and render the emails in the desired format.

Stylesheet

The first portion of the email template is devoted to defining styles for different parts of the mail. Open the `/email/email_template_welcome.html` file in your favorite text editor to examine the stylesheet in an email template. The stylesheet in this template will appear as follows:

```
<style type="text/css">
.body {background-color:#ffffff; color:#000000; font-family:Verdana,
Arial, Helvetica, sans-serif;}
...
.header {font-size:10px; padding:0px; width:550px;}
.content {font-size:10px; padding:5px; width:550px;}
.content-line {padding:5px;}
.coupon-block { padding: 5px; border: 1px #cccccc solid; background-
color: #FFFF99; }
...
.disclaimer1 a:link {color:#666666;}
.disclaimer1 a:visited {color:#666666;}
.disclaimer2 { color: #666666; padding: 5px; }
.copyright { border-bottom: 0px #9a9a9a solid; padding: 5px; }
</style>
```

Style declarations in this stylesheet are straight-forward. First, it has defined style for the body and hyperlinks. Then, it defines the content and email related styles. Most of the style names are self-explanatory. You will find the HTML blocks with these names in the template.

HTML with variables

The main part of the email template is the HTML code with style classes and variables. The following are some of the variables used to construct content for the email:

- $EMAIL_GREETING
- $EMAIL_WELCOME
- $COUPON_BLOCK
- $GV_BLOCK
- $EMAIL_MESSAGE_HTML
- $EMAIL_CONTACT_OWNER
- $EMAIL_CLOSURE
- $EMAIL_FOOTER_COPYRIGHT

- `$EMAIL_DISCLAIMER`
- `$EMAIL_SPAM_DISCLAIMER`
- `$EXTRA_INFO`

These variables are defined in several PHP files, such as `create_account.php`. Once you have found the files that need to be edited, you may want to add a definition for your new HTML item to each one. For example, you have added an item called `$EMAIL_HOURS_OF_OPERATION` to the `email_template_order_status.html` template. One of the files that you will need to edit is `admin/orders.php`. Find the part of that file where the email message is being constructed. In this case, it begins around line 100.

You can see that the HTML message is constructed with several statements such as:

```
$html_msg['EMAIL_CUSTOMERS_NAME'] = $check_status->fields['customers_
name'];
$html_msg['EMAIL_TEXT_ORDER_NUMBER'] = EMAIL_TEXT_ORDER_NUMBER . ' ' .
$oID;
```

All you need to do is add a new statement under all of these, to define your new item:

```
$html_msg['EMAIL_HOURS_OF_OPERATION'] = 'We are open from 9 AM to 5 PM
every day of the week.';
```

 Use a `$` in front of the name of your new item in the HTML template, but do not use the `$` where you define it.

To change the text displayed in your emails, edit the corresponding language file. You can change an existing text, or add a new one (if you've added it to your email structure). You add or change text values using the `define()` statements:

```
define(EMAIL_LOVELY_YOU_DROPPED_BY,'We are just so immeasurably
delighted that you stopped by our store today!');
```

There is another language file you need to modify when altering text for your emails, `includes/languages/english/email_extras.php`. This file contains several text strings common to all emails sent from your store.

Summary

In this chapter, we have learned about customizing the look and feel of a Zen Cart Shop. You have seen how Zen Cart templates can be used to change the look and feel, and have also understood how the template override system works. We have discussed assigning template to a Zen Cart shop, changing default text and logos, changing fonts, colors and other styles. We have also discussed customizing Zen Cart template by editing template files and using overrides. Then, we learned how to create a new template based on an existing template. We have also learned about using side-boxes and customizing email templates.

With this knowledge, you are now ready to move forward to next chapter, which will discuss localization of the Zen Cart shop.

Localization of Zen Cart

Localization is one of the important features of Zen Cart. Although our online shop serves globally, it can also be localized to a specific community or customer niche. For example, when customers from Bangladesh connect to the online shop, the language of the shop could be changed to Bangla, and customers from France may have French as the store's front-end language.

This chapter discusses the localization features of Zen Cart. After finishing this chapter, you will know:

- Why localization is necessary
- How to localize regions and taxes
- How to use multiple currencies for a store
- How to add a new language
- How to translate the front-end into another language
- How to modify or add order status to suit your need

Most of the tasks discussed in this chapter need to be completed before opening the shop for online selling.

The Need for Localization

As opposed to globalization, localization is the process of customizing software and documentation for a particular country. Localization includes the translation of menus and messages into the native spoken language as well as changes in the user interface to accommodate different alphabets and cultures. It also includes using appropriate locales (for example, date and time formats.) for that country or region. For example, for customers from Bangladesh, an online store's front-end language may be changed to Bangla, but only changing the language will not be enough for localization. For successful localization, appropriate locales—including currency, date formats, time-zone, and so on—for Bangladesh will also be used. So, a localization attempt for Bangladesh will automatically translate the website interface. The prices will be shown in Bangladeshi Taka (with a symbol ৳), and the date will be shown in the dd/mm/yyyy format.

Localization plays an important role in attracting customers — especially for a niche market. When a store is localized, customers from the niche market are easily attracted to that store, because they think that it is their 'own' store. Localization also helps in understanding the content of the store in a better manner. As for Bangla, customers speaking Bangla will be more comfortable reading the product description in Bangla.

Countries and Zones

The first step in localization of the Zen cart shop is to define the zones and zone-specific taxes. As you may know, sales taxes vary across countries, and also across regions. If the shop can be adapted to the customers' regions, and can appropriately calculate the taxes based on the tax rates applicable to their regions, it will be of great help to the customers. They will also think that you, the shop owners, are more responsive to their needs.

Countries

Locations can be configured into two entities: Countries and Zones. The first identifier for a location is a country. You can see the list of countries from the **Locations/Taxes | Countries** screen.

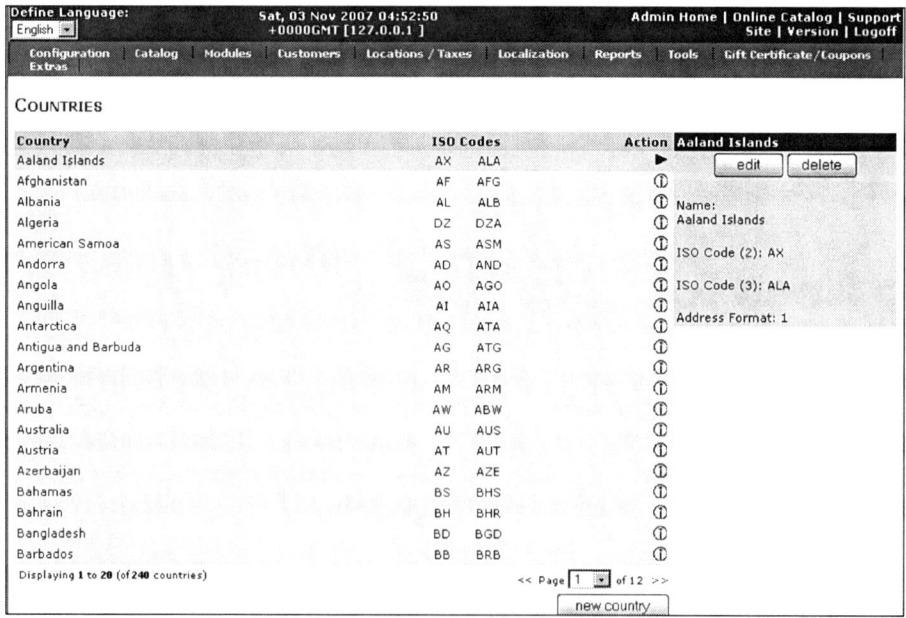

Each country has a name, a two-letter ISO Code and another three-letter ISO Code. For example, **Bangladesh** has two ISO country codes: **BD** and **BGD**. These **ISO codes** are based on globally accepted standards. Another field associated with each country is the address format. These address formats are also based on the ISO standard formats for addresses. These range from 1 to 5. If you explore a little bit, you will find that most of countries is use address format 1.

The five formats are as following:

Format 1	Format 2
Firstname Lastname	Firstname Lastname
Address line 1	Address line 1
<optional second address line>	<optional second address line>
City, Postcode	City, State Postcode
State, Country	Country

Format 3	Format 4
Firstname Lastname	Firstname Lastname
Address line 1	Address line 1
<optional second address line>	<optional second address line>
City	City (Postcode)
Postcode - State, Country	Country

Format 5

Firstname Lastname
Address line 1
<optional second address line>
Postcode City
Country

You need to choose an appropriate format for the country. For Bangladesh, an appropriate address may be format 4, as state names are not used in addresses in Bangladesh.

Adding a New Country

Usually, all countries are listed with their associated **ISO Codes**. However, if you want to add a new country, you can do so clicking on the **new country** button. For each country, you need to enter the name, and the ISO-3166 codes (two and three digits) for that country. You also have to select an address format used for that country.

Editing a Country

Rarely do you need to edit country information. However, you may like to change the address format for countries. In that case, select the country from the list, and click on the **edit** button. Then change the country information—**Name, ISO Code (2), ISO Code (3)** and **Address format**—as appropriate. Click on the **update** button to save your changes.

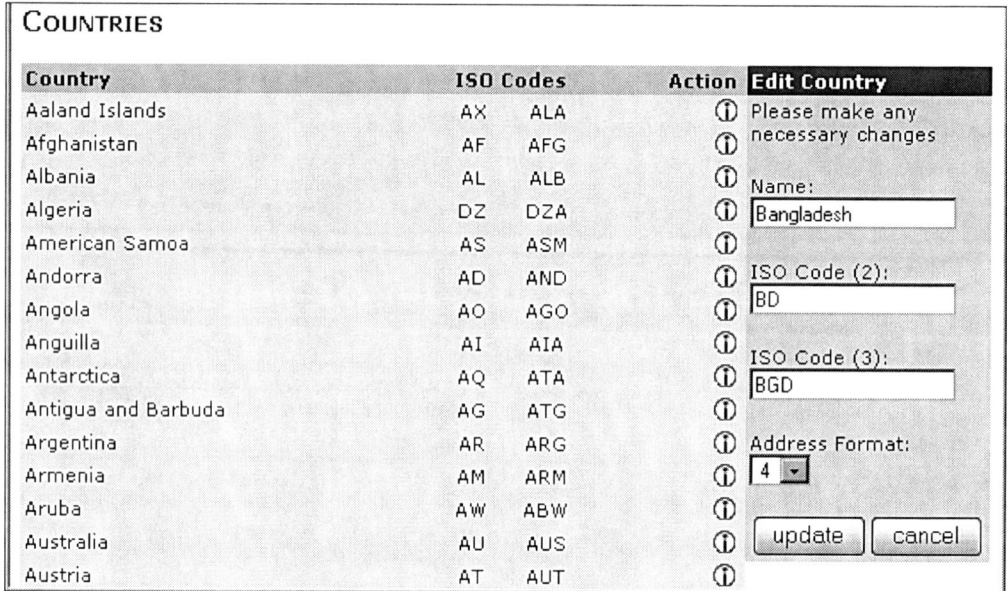

Deleting a Country

Generally, all countries are listed in the **Location/Taxes | Countries** screen. If you are sure that you do not need a country, you can delete it from the database. Remember that once you delete a country, it will not be shown in the **Country** drop-down list during account creation. You can delete a country easily by selecting it and clicking on the **delete** button. A confirmation dialog will be displayed to check whether you really want to delete the country. Confirm the deletion by clicking on the **delete** button.

Zones

You may need zones in order to calculate shipping costs, taxes, payment methods and discounts. There may be multiple zones in a country. By default, there are two kinds of zones in Zen Cart: zones and zones definitions (sometimes referred to as geo zones). Zones are local; that is, zones can be defined for countries or provinces within a larger entity such as a state or a country.

For example, you can have a zone defined as SAARC, for all the countries in the SAARC region, that is, Bangladesh, India, Pakistan, Nepal, Maldives, Sri Lanka and Bhutan. Then you can define zones for each of these countries, containing the provinces for that country. In Bangladesh, there are six divisions, which can be defined as six zones.

You always have to define at least one zone, and every location (country or state) in which you plan to sell should be included in your zone definitions. However, unless you have to distinguish between provinces or countries (for taxes, or shipping, for example), you don't really need to define additional zones.

The zones and zone definitions (geo_zones) are used to tie Tax Rates and Tax Classes to geographic locations. For example, you may ship to all of the states in the USA, but if your store is located in Florida, you only need to charge sales tax to the customers in Florida. You can define two zones, one containing all the states except Florida, and one containing only Florida. Then, you can specify the Tax Rate that the Florida zone should use.

Now, if your state has separate tax rates for different cities or countries (say California), then you need to establish one for each city or country in order to account for sales across cities, or countries, according to your sales tax return.

Some Shipping Modules (such as the zones shipping module) also work with geographic zones. These zones are specified in the module itself, and are independent of the zone definitions you make. This means that you can specify different shipping rates, for example, for countries in the same zone definition.

Creating a Zone

You can create a zone via menu option **Locations/Taxes | Zones**. Click on the **new zone** button. In the **Zones Name** box, type the name of the zone, enter a code in the **Zones Code** field, and select the country in which the zone is situated. For example, you may type a district name, assign a code to it, and select Bangladesh as the country. After typing this information, click on the **insert** button to save the zone.

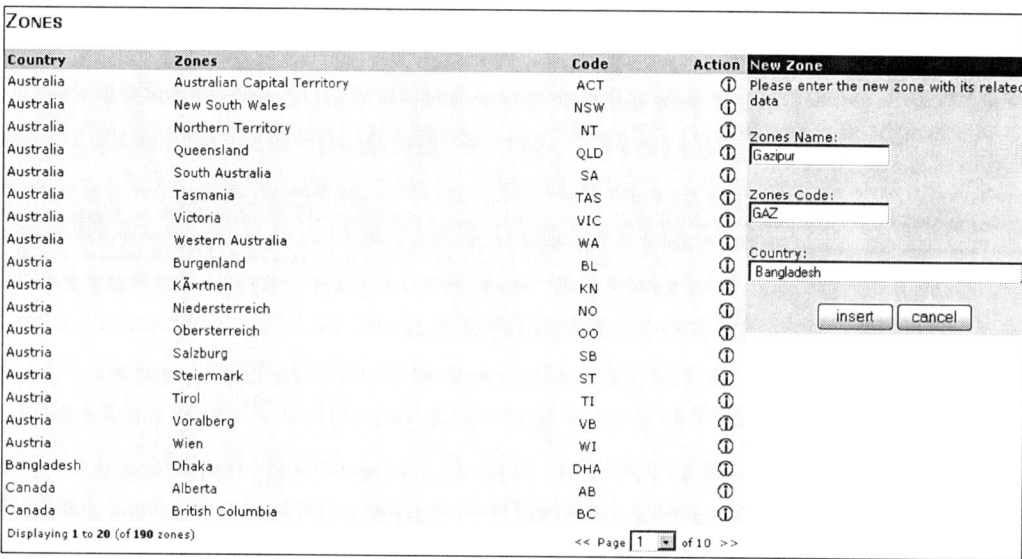

You can create as many zones as you need. For example, you may create 64 zones for 64 districts in Bangladesh. These zones can be used for calculating shipping costs by courier service. Remember that creating a zone alone will have no effect on the shipping costs or taxes until you use the zones for those purposes. The uses of these zones are defined via menu option **Locations/Taxes | Zone definitions**.

Zone Definitions

Zone definitions are zones used for shipping, payment and taxes. To create and use a zone definition, you first have to create geo zones in the **Locations/Taxes | Zones** screen, as described earlier. Then, you can use the zones in zone definitions.

By default, you will see one zone definition—**Florida**, which is used to ascertain local taxes. You can create new zones from the **Locations/Taxes | Zone definitions** screen. You will see a list of **Zone Definitions** in this screen with three status indications: **Taxes & Zones Defined** (green), **Zones Defined but not Taxes** (yellow), and **Not Configured** (red).

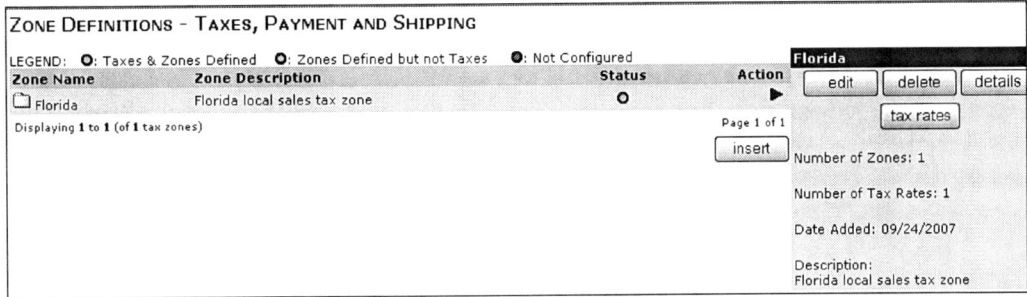

To create a new zone definition, click on the **insert** button. Then, type the zone name and a description of the zone. In **Description**, indicate the purpose for which you have created the zone, for example, for shipping to the Dhaka division. Click on the **insert** button to save the zone.

The status of the zone will be shown as **Not Configured** (red) after creating the zone definition. You need to configure it by adding geo zones to it. Select the zone, and click on the **details** button to list the geo zones under this zone definition.

Click on the **insert** button to add a new geo zone to the zone definition. A New Sub Zone box will be shown. Select the country and the zone from the drop-down list, and click on the **insert** button. The zones must be defined beforehand. You can add multiple geo zones from multiple countries. For example, you may create a Zero Tax zone and include all geo zones where you don't need to add taxes.

Taxes

As discussed earlier, taxes can be applied to a specific zone definition. Therefore, first create a zone definition for tax purposes. **Tax Classes** are typically used to differentiate between the types of tax calculations that apply to a given product. Typical tax classes would include: **Taxable Goods**, **Non-Taxable Goods**, **GST-Only**, and so on. You can see a list of tax classes via **Locations/Taxes | Tax Classes**.

Creating a Tax Class

To create a tax class, go to **Locations/Taxes | Tax Classes**, and click on the **new tax class** button. Now, enter a title and description for this tax class. Click **insert** to save the tax class.

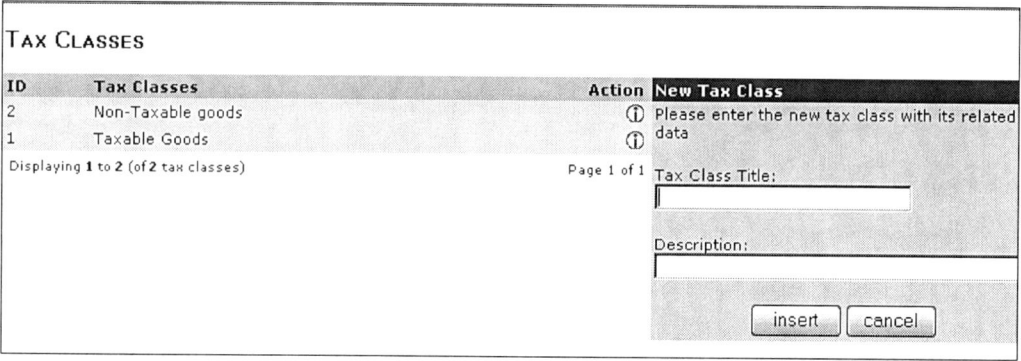

Assigning Tax Classes

When entering new products via **Catalog | Categories/Products**, it is necessary to select the appropriate tax class for that product. Otherwise, taxes won't be calculated appropriately during checkout. To assign a tax class, select the appropriate tax class from the **Tax Class** drop-down list. The result of changing the tax class is immediately reflected in the **Products Price (Gross)** field.

Instead of assigning a tax class for each product, you can assign a default tax class for a product type. This will apply a consistent tax class to all the products of the same type. For example, Music may be tax free. So, it will be wise to set the default tax class as **Non-Taxable Goods** for **Music** product type.

Before assigning a default tax class to a product type you need to identify the Tax Class ID number. To identify the Tax class ID, do the following:

1. From **Locations/Taxes | Tax Classes**, select a tax class and click **edit**.
2. Now, look at the URL in the browser address bar. You will find something that looks like: `&tID=2`, which mean Tax class ID number is 2.

Once you get the Tax class ID, it is time to set that ID in the product type's default tax class field. To do this:

1. Go to **Catalog | Product Types**.
2. Select the product type from the list, for example **Product – Music**, and click on **Edit Layout**.
3. Click on **Product Price Tax Class Default - When adding new products?**
4. Enter the number of the tax class ID determined above (that is, 2).
5. Click on the **update** button to save the setting.

PRODUCT TYPE INFO PAGE LAYOUT OPTIONS :: PRODUCT - MUSIC

Title	Value	Action	Product Price Tax Class Default - When adding new products?
Show Model Number	1	ⓘ	Please make any necessary changes
Show Weight	0	ⓘ	
Show Attribute Weight	1	ⓘ	**Product Price Tax Class Default - When adding**
Show Artist	1	ⓘ	**new products?**
Show Music Genre	1	ⓘ	What should the Product Price Tax Class Default ID be when adding new products?
Show Record Company	1	ⓘ	
Show Quantity in Shopping Cart	1	ⓘ	2
Show Quantity in Stock	0	ⓘ	
Show Product Reviews Count	1	ⓘ	update cancel
Show Product Reviews Button	1	ⓘ	
Show Date Available	1	ⓘ	

Creating a Tax Rate

Creating a tax class will not automatically add taxes to the products sold. You have to create tax rates for the specific zones.

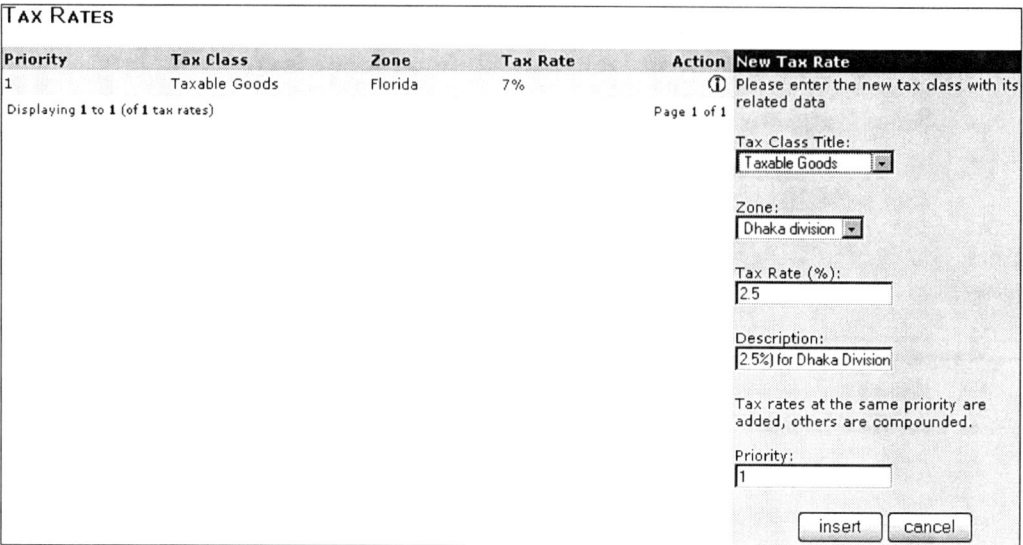

You can create a tax rate for a zone, for example Dhaka, via **Locations/Taxes | Tax Rates** and clicking on the **new tax rate** button. You have to define the following information in the **New Tax Rate** box:

- **Tax Class Title**: Select a tax class from the drop-down list. The tax classes you have defined earlier will be shown in this list. If you do not find an appropriate tax class, go back to the **Locations/Taxes | Tax Classes** page, and define a new tax class.

- **Zone**: Select a zone from this drop-down list. Zones you have defined earlier will be listed here. The Tax Rate you are defining will be applicable for the zone you select in this drop-down list.

- **Tax Rate (%)**: Define the Tax Rate percentage that will be applied to the products.

- **Description**: Type a description of the Tax Rate in this field. This will explain why it was created and where it will be used.

- **Priority**: Set a priority for Tax Rate. You may have several tax rates for a zone. In that case, tax rates with the same priority will be added to the product price. On the other hand, tax rates with different priorities will be compounded. That means a lower numbered tax rate will be applied first, then the next priority tax rate will be applied to the resulting amount.

Once you have entered all required, click on the **insert** button to save your changes. This tax rate will be automatically applied based on the shipping or billing address zone.

Using Multiple Currencies

Localization | Currencies screen allows us to add new currencies or edit existing ones. The predefined currencies in this module are **U.S. Dollar (default)**, **Euro**, **GB Pound**, **Australian Dollar** and **Canadian Dollar**. You can add a new currency, or edit an existing one.

Adding a New Currency

By default, only five currencies are defined in Zen Cart. You may need to add other currencies, if you want to trade in those currencies, or want to show prices in those currencies. To add a new currency, click on the **new currency** button in the **Localization | Currencies** screen.

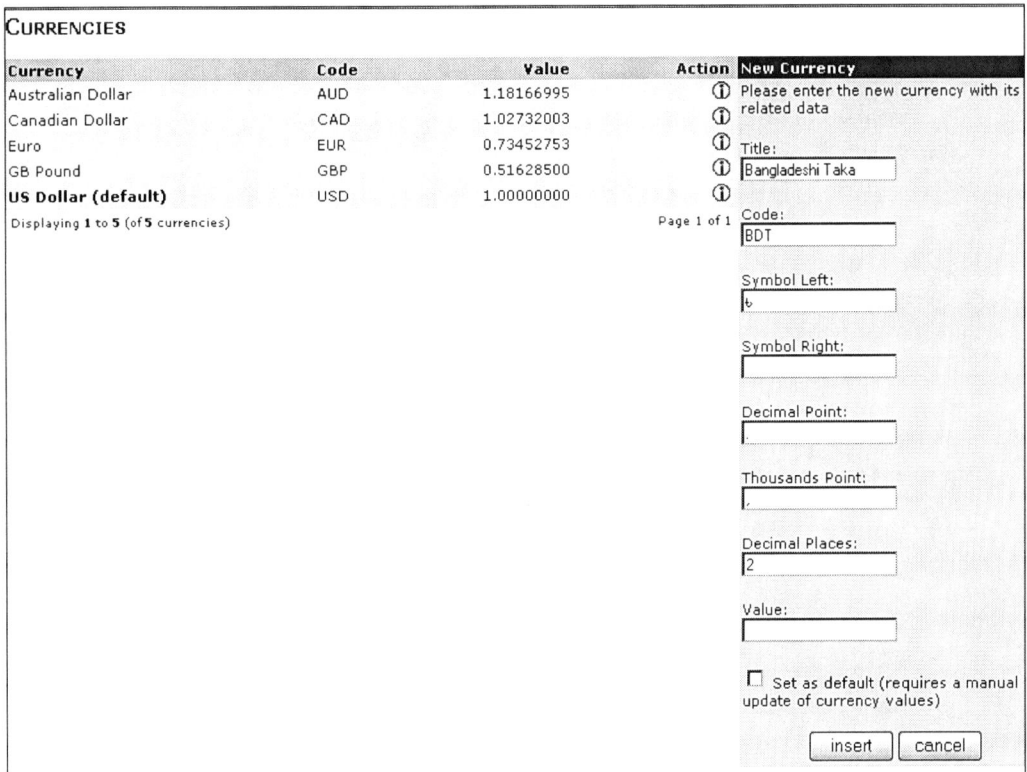

In the new currency screen, you need to enter the following information:

- **Title**: This is the name of the new currency, as in Canadian Dollar, Mexican Peso or Bangladeshi Taka.

- **Code:** This is the three-character ISO 4217 international name for the currency –CAD for Canadian Dollar, MXN for Mexican Peso, USD for US Dollar, JPY for Japanese Yen, BDT for Bangladeshi Taka, and so on. Note that to use the automated currency conversion feature, this code must be correct.

- **Symbol Left** and **Symbol Right:** If you need to display some symbol to the left or the right side of the currency amount, you need to type that symbol in this box. If no symbol appears before or after the amount (as in CA$ for Canadian Dollar), leave these fields blank.

- **Decimal Point**: This is where you indicate the symbol that appears between the whole and fractional amounts of a currency. For U.S. and Canadian dollars, this is a period; in some countries it is a comma.

- **Thousands Point**: This is where you indicate the symbol that appears between the figures of a currency, in thousands. For U.S. and Canadian dollars, this is a comma; in some countries it is a period.

- **Decimal Places**: This indicates the number of decimal places that appear to the right for this currency. The U.S. and Canadian dollars have two digits after the decimal point. Some currencies may have others, such as zero, four or six.

- **Value**: This is the value of the other currency relative to the default currency of our store. Our default currency should have a value of exactly **1**. If you are going to use the automatic conversion feature (see the **update currencies** button below), then you can simply leave this field blank (or enter zero, both are the same) and let the website update the value.

- **Set as default (requires a manual update of currency values)**: If this is the default currency for this store, you need to check this box. Note that this may require some manual changes, as indicated in the box. Thus, you might want to set this before loading any pricing data.

After you finish entering the new information, click on the **insert** button to save this new currency entry.

Currency Conversion

Zen Cart has a built-in facility to update currency exchange rates from the exchange rate server. For this to work, all currencies defined in our shop must use the correct ISO 4217 codes in the **code** column.

To update currencies, click on the **update currencies** button. The site will request current exchange rate values from various conversion sites on the Internet for all of the currencies that have a correct ISO 4217 code. Within a few seconds, your shop will obtain current values, and automatically update the exchange rates.

Rates that are correctly converted will be listed with a green background at the top of the page. Rates that were not correctly converted will be listed with a red background. Zen Cart shop will try more than one converter if it has failed in converting a particular currency. If you see a red item after updating currencies, you have to pay attention to it. It may be caused by misspelling the ISO 4217 code for that currency. Currencies that were not correctly updated because of the unavailability of exchange rates at the exchange rate server will have to be manually updated using the edit feature.

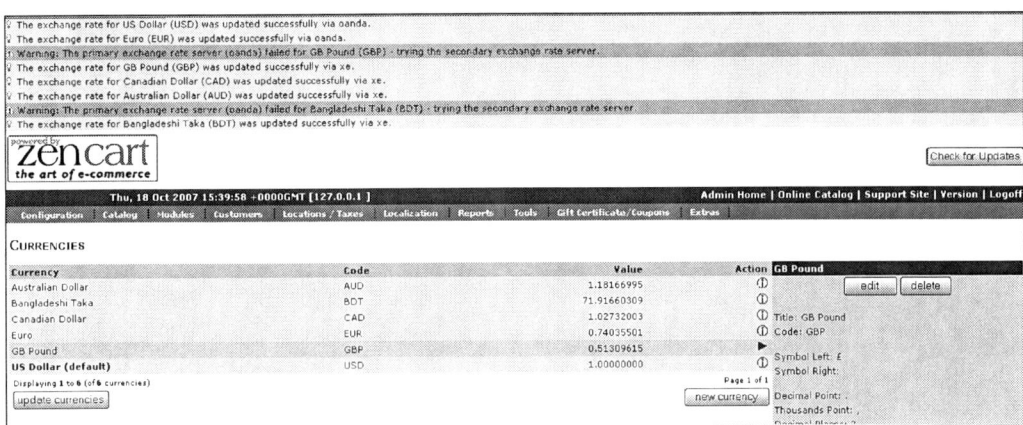

If you do not wish to use the automatic conversion feature, you can set the conversion rate manually by selecting the currency and clicking **edit** button. From **Localization | Currencies screen**, you can see the sample conversion rates. Note that these are sample values; you need to know the exact conversion rate at a given point in time, as currency conversion rates can fluctuate.

Editing a Currency

If you only need to correct the exchange rate, you can use the **update currencies** button to change all the conversions on our website. If, however the automatic conversion does not work for some reason (for example, you entered Russian Rubles using code RUS instead of RUB), you would need to change that. To do this:

1. Click on the line showing the currency that you want to change.
   A right-arrow will appear in the action column.

2. Now click on the **edit** button. A series of entry fields, the same as provided for the **add new currency** button, will appear, but this time those fields will be loaded with their current values.

3. Change any field as required.

4. Once you have finished, click on the **update** button to save your changes.

5. If you decide not to save the changes, click on **cancel** to keep the original values intact.

Deleting an Existing Currency

If you no longer want a particular currency, you can delete the currency as follows:

1. Click on the line showing the currency you want to delete. A right-arrow will appear in the action column.

2. Click on the **delete** button. You will be asked to confirm if you want to delete the currency.

3. Click on the **delete** button again to delete the currency, or click the **cancel** button if you do not wish to delete it.

Hiding the Currencies box

If you only operate with one currency, the US Dollar for example, you may wish to delete all other currencies and set the exchange value to 1.

With only one currency in use, you will most likely want to stop the currency selection box from being displayed.

To do this:

1. Click on **Tools | Layout Boxes Controller**.

2. Find **sideboxes/currencies.php** in the list. It may appear at the bottom.

3. Click on it, and then click on **edit** and set both **Left/Right Column Status** and **Single Column Status** to **OFF**.

4. Finally, click **Update**.

sideboxes/specials.php	ON	RIGHT	45	0	OFF	
sideboxes/product_notifications.php	ON	RIGHT	55	85	ON	
sideboxes/tell_a_friend.php	OFF	RIGHT	65	0	OFF	
sideboxes/languages.php	ON	RIGHT	70	50	ON	
sideboxes/currencies.php	OFF	RIGHT	80	60	OFF	
sideboxes/whos_online.php	OFF	RIGHT	200	200	OFF	

Reset All Box Sort Order to match DEFAULT Sort Order for Template: **packt**
This does not remove any of the boxes. It will only reset the current sort order

reset

Languages

Zen Cart has a multi-lingual feature which you can use to provide multiple languages for your online shop. This feature allows us to add and translate the Zen Cart interface into new languages. By default, the store will be shown in the English language. You can add another language and translate the strings into that language. When you activate this new language, Zen Cart shop will be displayed in that language. The following sections describe how to convert a Zen Cart shop into a multi-lingual shop.

Using Character Sets

You can set locales for the site from the language file. For each language, there is a file named after that language. For example, for the English language, you will find the `includes/languages/english.php` file. For viewing a locale, open this file in your favorite text editor, and find the following line:

```
@setlocale(LC_TIME, 'en_US.ISO_8859-1');
```

For the English language, the locale is set to `en_US.ISO_8859-1`. For other languages, it may be different. For example, for the Bangla language it is `bn_BD`.

For each language, you can set the character set encoding. The character set encoding needs to be set correctly, otherwise, the language characters shown may be wrong. To change the character set, find the following line:

```
define('CHARSET', 'iso-8859-1');
```

For the English language, the character set `ISO-8859-1` may work fine, but for languages that use Unicode or some other encoding, you must set the appropriate character set. For example, to use the Bangla language, the character set must be set to `UTF-8`.

Creating a New Language

You can add a new language from the **Localization | Languages** screen. Click on the **new language** button on this screen, and a form will appear. Now, enter the following information in the form:

- **Name**: This is the name of the language, probably best expressed in itself, for example, Francais for French, Español for Spanish, Deutsch for German, and so on.
- **Code**: This is ISO 639 two-letter language code; for example, en for English, fr for Francais, es for Español, bn for Bangla, and so on.

- **Image**: This would be a small icon used to identify the language. This would most likely be a `.gif` image of the national flag for a country commonly associated with that language.

- **Directory**: This is the directory where the translated `.php` source files for this language are located. For example, if `www.example.com` is running Zen Cart, and its files are located in the zencart directory, then the directory for English is located at `http://www.example.com/zencart/includes/languages/english`. The value for other languages needs to be changed to the appropriate values.

- **Sort order**: This is the order in which the languages should appear in. Lower numbers are shown higher in the front-end.

- **Set as default**: Check this box if this is the default language for your shop.

Once you have provided this information, click on the **insert** button to add the new language. Alternatively, click on the **cancel** button if you change your mind.

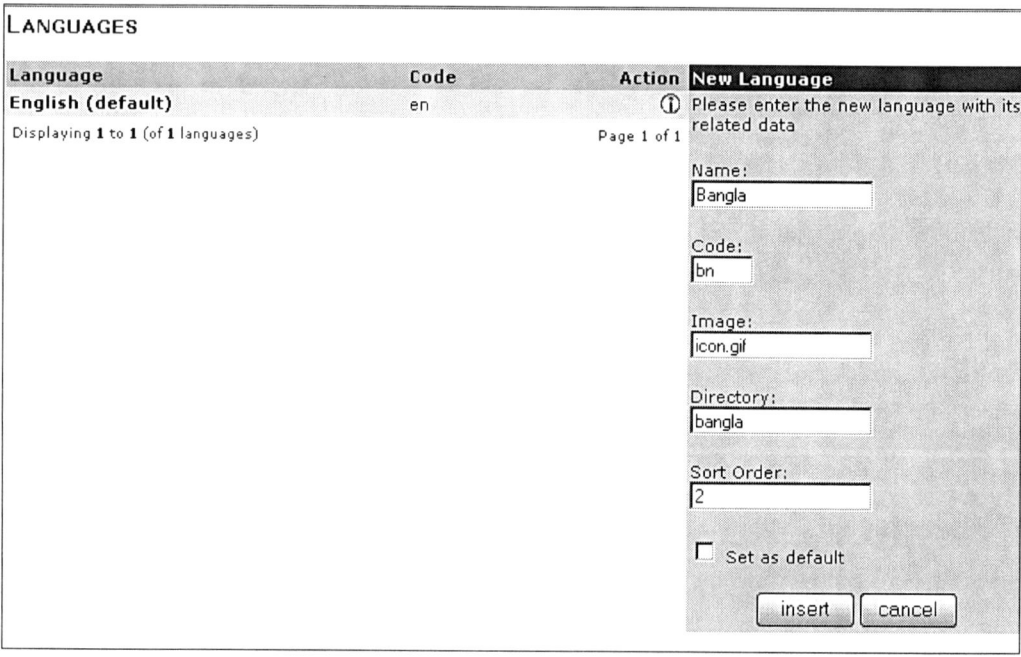

Although you can create a language without uploading the language files to the appropriate directories, the language will not work until you do so. Therefore, before creating a new language in the **Localization | Languages** screen, you need to download a language pack from Zen Cart's website and copy those files to the `includes/languages/` folder with the language name.

Before creating a new language, make sure that the following files and directories are uploaded to the appropriate places:

- `includes/languages/<language_name>.php`
- `includes/languages/<language_name>/*`
- `admin/includes/languages/<language_name>.php`
- `admin/includes/languages/<language_name>/*`
- `includes/templates/template_default/buttons/<language_name>/`

Replace `<language_name>` with the name of your language. Also remember that although most of the files go in the `includes/languages` directory, language-specific buttons need to be placed in the `includes/templates/template_default/buttons/<language_name>` folder.

Editing a Language

To change information about an existing language, do the following:

1. Click on the named language so that the right-arrow appears in the Action column.
2. Click on the **edit** button.
3. Now edit the settings. The fields on the screen are the same for adding a language.
4. After you have finished editing, click on the **update** button to save the changes, or click on **cancel** to discard them.

 Remember that editing a language and translating a language is not the same. You can translate a language by editing the individual language files, that you have uploaded to the language directories.

Deleting a Language

To remove a language, click on the named language so that the right-arrow appears in the Action column, and then click on the **delete** button. If this is not the default language, you will be asked for confirmation. Click on the **delete** button again to delete the language, or click on **cancel** if you do not wish to delete this language. If this is the default language, only the **cancel** button will appear, as you cannot delete the default language.

Remember that deleting a language from the list does not delete the language files automatically. If you want to delete the language files too, you need to delete those manually.

Translating Language Files

At present, more than 25 language packs are available for download from the Zen Cart website. Packs for most of the major languages are available, including Arabic, French, Spanish, Portuguese, Norwegian, Japanese, Simplified Chinese, and so on. If you do not find your language pack there, don't be upset. You can always create your own language pack.

Zen Cart gives you the flexibility to translate any language. In fact, translating language strings in Zen Cart becomes very easy if you understand the basics of its language structure. In Zen Cart, all of the language strings are defined as constants in the language files.

The best way to start translating the language files is to copy the English language files into a new directory. Then, open each file and translate the strings.

For each language, there is a file in the `includes/languages/` directory named after the language name. For example, you will find `english.php`. Rename this file to your language name, for instance, `bangla.php`.

First change the locale in `@setlocale(LC_TIME, 'en_US.ISO_8859-1');` line. For Bangla, change `en_US.ISO_8859-1` to `bn_BD`. Remember that you have to change the string inside the quotation mark keeping the constants in UPPERCASE unchanged.

You can also change the date format via the `DATE_FORMAT_SHORT` and `DATE_FORMAT` settings. For some languages, dates are expressed as `m/d/y` and for some, it is `d/m/Y`. Set the appropriate format for your language.

The language strings for each front-end file are located in similarly-named `.php` files. For example, language strings used in `create_account.php` page are located in the `includes/languages/english/create_account.php` file. You will find lines such as:

```
define('NAVBAR_TITLE', 'Create an Account');
```

You have to translate only the second part, that is, Create an Account. Make sure that the quotation marks are intact after translating the strings. You will need to change all of the strings in all of the files, one by one.

```
bangla - Notepad                                          _ |□| x|
File  Edit  Format  View  Help
// text for gender
  define('MALE', 'জনাব');
  define('FEMALE', 'জনাবা');
  define('MALE_ADDRESS', 'জনাব');
  define('FEMALE_ADDRESS', 'জনাবা');

// text for date of birth example
  define('DOB_FORMAT_STRING', 'dd/mm/yyyy');

//text for sidebox heading links
  define('BOX_HEADING_LINKS', '  আরো');

// categories box text in sideboxes/categories.php
  define('BOX_HEADING_CATEGORIES', 'শ্রেণীবিভাগ');

// manufacturers box text in sideboxes/manufacturers.php
  define('BOX_HEADING_MANUFACTURERS', 'প্রকাশক');
```

Remember to select UTF-8 or Unicode encoding when saving the modified language file, if that file contains Unicode characters. Saving these .php files in ANSI format will degenerate the Unicode strings.

Order Status

Every order has a status. For example, when an order is placed by a customer, it is assigned either a **pending** status, or a **processing** status. This may be expressed in different ways for different languages. Therefore, Zen Cart allows us to add new order status entries, edit existing order status name entries, or delete an order status name entry, in the **Localization | Order Status** screen.

By default, there are four order status defined:

- **Pending(default)**
- **Processing**
- **Delivered**
- **Update**

When an order is placed, **Pending** is the default status of that order. Of course, you can set the default order status for each type of payments while configuring the payment modules. **Processing** means that the order is currently being processed, and will be shipped soon. Once the order has been shipped and delivered to the customer, you may set the status to **Delivered**. Similarly, a status of **Update** can be assigned to any order when you are updating it for some reason. You may like to inform the customer of any order status change. This is done from the order editing screen.

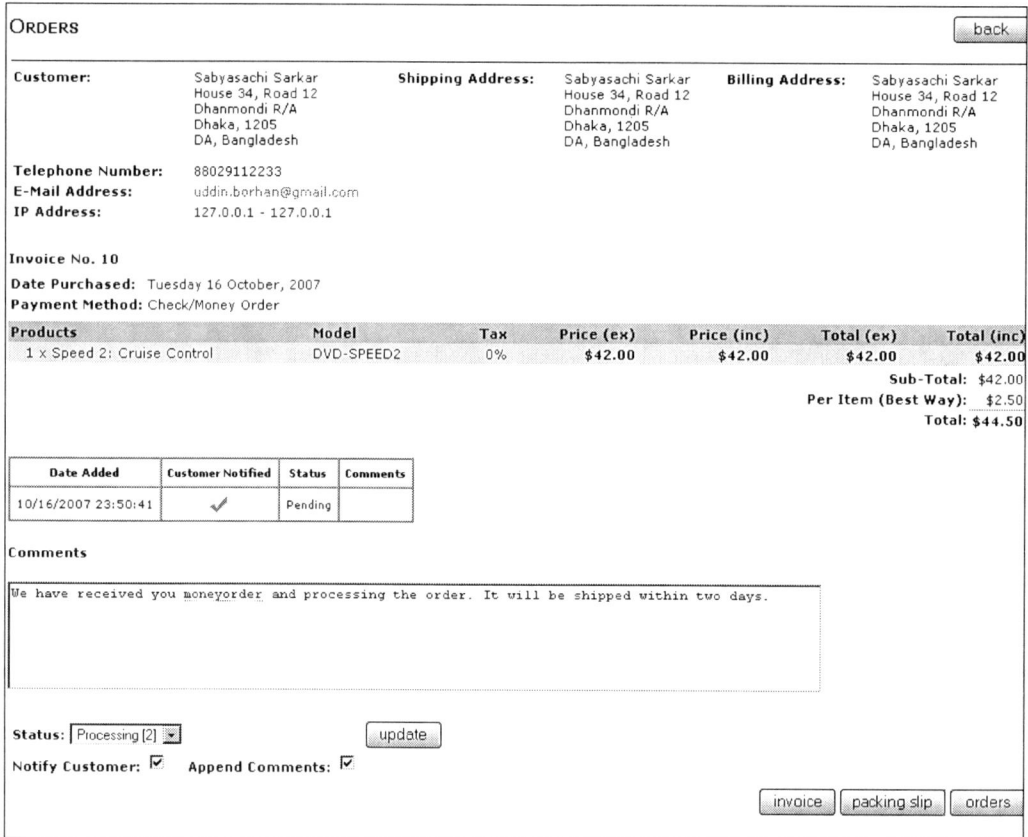

Adding a New Order Status

You may need to add a new order status. For example, you may want to add a **Shipped** status, so that you can inform the customer when their order has been shipped. Adding this order status is simple. You can add a new order status from the **Localization | Order Status** screen.

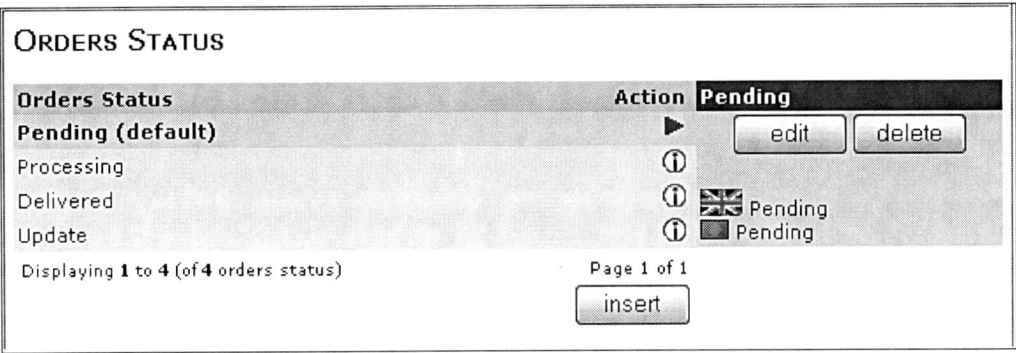

To add a new order status, click on the **insert** button. A box allowing you to enter
the name of the status will appear. You will find one or more text boxes to type the
name of that status in all installed languages. Give a meaningful name to the order
status. If this is the default status (applied to all new orders), check the **set as default**
checkbox. Click on the **insert** button to save this new status, or click on the **cancel**
button if you want to discard the changes.

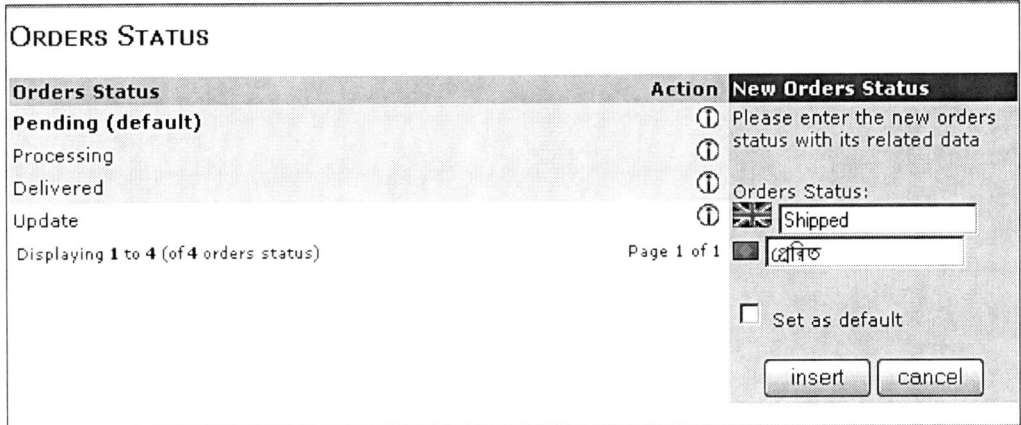

Editing an Existing Status

You may need to edit an existing order status to reflect the actual meaning of that
status. For example, you may want to change **Pending** to **Waiting for Payment**, to
explain why the order is pending. For other installed and supported languages, you
also need to edit the order status.

To edit an existing order status, select the status and click on the **edit** button. The **Edit Orders Status** box will be shown. Again here, you will see one or more text boxes, each showing a language icon alongside it. You can change the name of that order status for any or all of the languages in these text boxes. If you want to set that status as the default status for upcoming orders, check the **Set as default** checkbox. Once you have finished editing the status names, click the **update** button to save your changes, or click **cancel** to discard the changes.

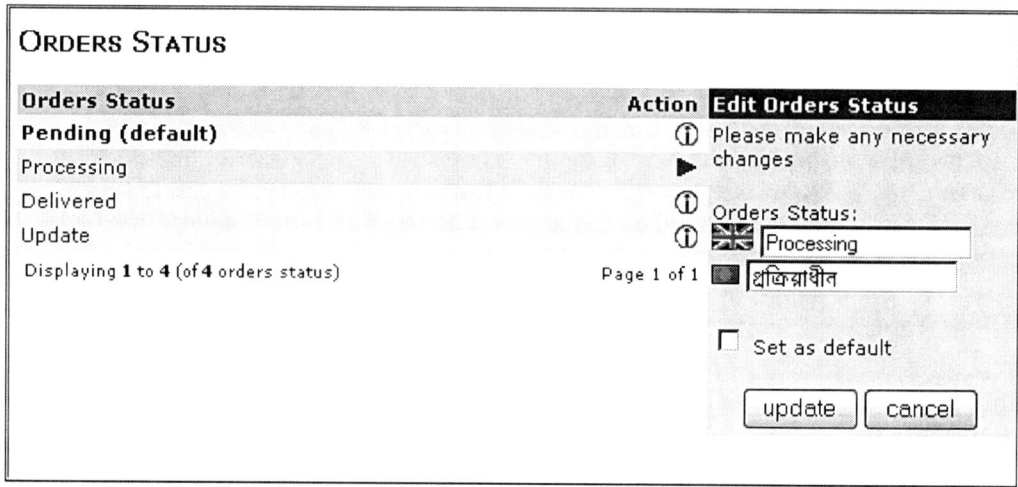

 Order statuses can be very useful for your online business. First, plan the status of the orders according to your selling process. Then add appropriate order status in **Localization | Order Status**. For example, you may add **Returned** and **Refunded** statuses to indicate that the product has been returned for a refund, and has subsequently been refunded.

Summary

In this chapter, we have discussed important configuration options for localizing Zen Cart. First, we discussed how to define countries and zones. Then you learned about defining zones for taxes, tax classes, tax rates, and assigning tax rates to specific zones. We also discussed adding, editing and updating currencies in a Zen Cart shop that uses multiple currencies. You also learned about creating and editing languages for the Zen Cart shop and translating language files into another language.

With this knowledge in localizing the Zen Cart shop, you will be able to make the shop online after localizing it. In the next chapter, we will discuss how to promote your products and maintain public relationships through Zen Cart tools.

6
Promotions and Public Relations

Every online store's success depends on promotion and public relations. As a marketer, the more you promote your products to the target market, the greater the chance of getting more customers. Good online stores have built-in promotional activities and public relations tools. Zen Cart has a set of tools for promotion and public relations. In this chapter, you are going to be introduced to these tools.

On completion of this chapter, you will be able to:

- Use Zen Cart's promotional tools such as banner ads, discounts, salemaker, cross-sell and up-sell, specials, and featured products.
- Use gift certificates and coupons to attract more customers.
- Use newsletters and product notifications to keep in constant communication with your customers and reward their loyalty.
- Optimize your site for search engines.

By now, you should have learned how to add products to your catalogue and how to manage customers.

Promotions

For any business, promotion is a must and Zen Cart has built-in tools for promotional activities. Features such as banner ads, promotional discounts, salemaker, products on special list, cross selling, and up selling can be used effectively for promotions. In this section, we are going to discuss how these features can help to promote your products.

Banner Ads

If you have been operating a shop or have started building a shop using Zen Cart, you will know what a banner ad is. A banner ad is a form of advertising on the Web used frequently to display product advertisement into a web page. Clicking on a banner ad takes you to a site or a webpage.

Banner ad tool in Zen Cart can be used for advertising both external and internal products. You can display any banner ad through this tool. In Zen Cart, there are three places where you can display banner ads.

You can control banner ads in your Zen Cart shop from **Tools | Banner Manager**. From here, you can add, delete, and edit the banners:

- To add a new banner, click the **new banner** button.
- To edit an existing one and change its link, its picture, and so on, click on the banner you want to change, and click the **edit** button.
- You can enable and disable any particular banner by clicking on the red/ green status button.

Types of Banners

Two types of banners can be used in Zen Cart: sidebox and wide banners. Sidebox banners are just like a sidebox suitable to be shown in the left or right column. Wide banners span the width of your page.

Each banner is assigned to a group, and you can give it any name. A group contains multiple banners and one from the group will be randomly shown at a time . For each group, you also need to indicate the position where it is to be displayed. This is done from **Configuration | Layout Settings**.

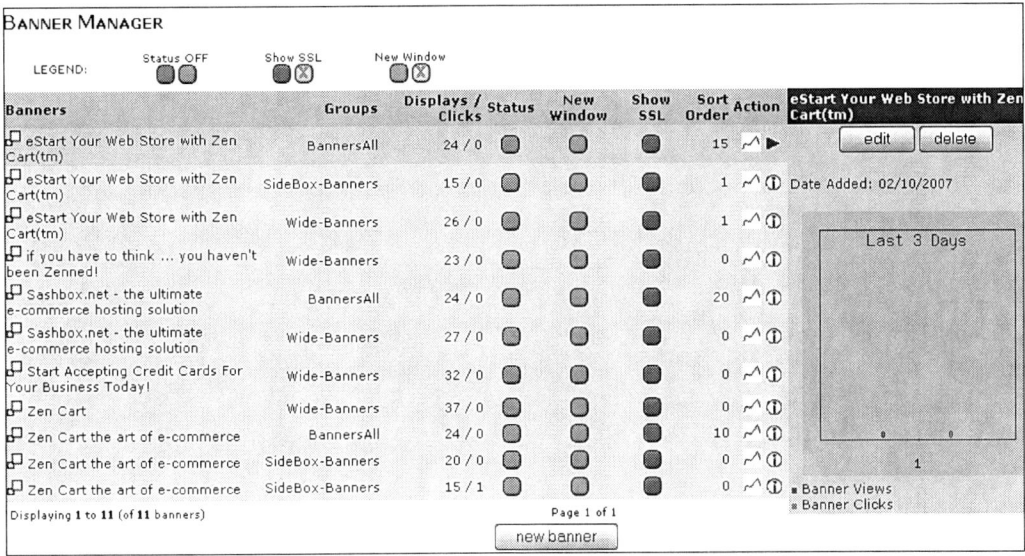

By default, Zen Cart has three predefined banner groups: **BannersAll**, **SideBox-Banners**, and **Wide-Banners**.

Banner statistics are also tracked on a day-to-day basis. You will see the banner views and clicks statistics for the last three days on this window.

Displaying Banner Groups

Each group is assigned to be displayed in a position on the shop front-end. You define this position by editing the **Banner Display Groups** position group names under **Configuration | Layout Settings**.

For sidebox banners, only one banner group on a particular sidebox can be displayed at a time. For others, you can have multiple banner groups.

By default, the BannersAll group is assigned to be displayed in SideBox — BannersAll position. This means that banners from the BannersAll group will be shown in this sidebox, one at a time. SideBox-Banners group is assigned to two sidebox locations — SideBox-Banner Box and SideBox — Banner Box 2. Wide-Banners group is assigned to be shown in footer position 3.

Remember that, wide banners are only suitable for showing at the header and footer positions. Assigning such a banner to a sidebox will create a layout problem, and is hence should be avoided. Similarly, assigning sidebox banners to the header or footer positions will result in too much blank space at both sides of the banners.

Designing Banners

Banner sizes are of your choice. However, there are standard sizes of banners to be used on websites. You should use these standard sizes for consistency. But you can make them any size that you want as long as those sizes match your template layout.

Standard sizes for banners and their suitable display position are shown in the following table:

Size (pixel)	Style	Zen Cart Position
468 x 60	Full Banner	Header, footer
728 x 90	Leaderboard	Header, footer
336 x 280	Square	Sidebox, if layout permits
336 x 280	Square	Sidebox, if layout permits
300 x 250	Square	Sidebox, if layout permits
250 x 250	Square	Sidebox, if layout permits
180 x 150	Square	Sidebox, if layout permits
160 x 600	Skyscraper	Sidebox
120 x 600	Skyscraper	Sidebox
120 x 240	Small Skyscraper	Sidebox
240 x 400	Fat skyscraper	Sidebox, if layout permits
234 x 60	Half banner	Sidebox, header, footer – depending on layout
125 x 125	Square button	Sidebox
120 x 90	Button	Sidebox
120 x 60	Button	Sidebox
88 x 31	Button	Sidebox

 There are several tools for designing banner ads. Some of them are wizard driven and only take a few minutes. If you are not a graphic designer, try these tools to create attractive banner ads quickly.

Adding/Editing a Banner

You can add/edit banners from **Tools | Banner Manager** from the administration panel. To edit the properties of a banner, select the banner and click on the **edit** button. For adding a new banner, click on the **new banner** button. This will open the following screen:

```
BANNER MANAGER

Banner Status:          ⊙ Active  ○ Not Active
                        NOTE: Banner status will be updated based on Scheduled Date and Impressions

Banner New Window       ⊙ Yes  ○ No
                        NOTE: Banner will open in a new window

Banner on SSL           ⊙ Yes  ○ No
                        NOTE: Banner can be displayed on Secure Pages without errors

Banner Title:           Zen Cart the art of e-commerce          * Required

Banner URL:             http://www.zen-cart.com

Banner Group:           BannersAll       , or enter a new banner group below

Image:                  [                ] Browse , or enter local file below
                        e:/www/zencart/images/ banners/bw_zen_88wide.gif

Image Target (Save To):  e:/www/zencart/images/
Suggested Target location for the image on the server: e:/www/zencart/images/banners/

HTML Text:              NOTE: HTML banners do not record the clicks on the banner

                        NOTE: The banners_box_all sidebox will display the banners in their defined sort order
Sort Order - banner_box_all  10

Scheduled At:           [          ] ▽
(dd/mm/yyyy)

Expires On:             [          ] ▽ , or at
(dd/mm/yyyy)            0       impressions/views.        [ update ] [ cancel ]

Banner Notes:
   • Use an image or HTML text for the banner - not both.
   • HTML Text has priority over an image
   • HTML Text will not register the click thru, but will register displays
```

You have to fill or edit the following information in the banner editing/adding screen:

- **Banner Status:** Select **Active** or **Not Active** to indicate the banner status. If **Not Active** is selected, then the banner will not be shown.

- **Banner New Window:** Indicates whether the banner will open in a new window when clicked, or open in the same window. Selecting **Yes** will open the banner in a new window.

- **Banner on SSL:** To display a banner in secure pages without any errors, select **Yes** in this field.

- **Banner Title:** Type the title of the banner. Each banner must have a title.

- **Banner URL:** Type the URL to which the browser will be redirected when the banner ad is clicked.

- **Banner Group:** Select the group for this banner. If you do not see appropriate groups in the drop-down list, type a new group name in the text field next to this.

- **Image:** Indicate the image to be used in the banner ad. This file needs to be uploaded or the path of the image should be indicated in the textbox below this field. For uploading the banner ad image, click on the **browse** button and select the appropriate banner ad image which you want to upload.

- **Image target (Save To):** Indicates the folder where images will be uploaded to. Type the name of the folder relative to your images folder under the Zen cart installation directory. The directory name should end with a slash, as in banners/ .This directory must exist at the server and should be writable.

- **HTML Text:** If you want to show a HTML banner instead of an image banner, type HTML text in this box. Remember that the HTML text will take precedence over the image banner. This means that if you type HTML text and provide the image banner link, only the HTML banner will be displayed. The clicks for the HTML text banners will not be counted.

- **Sort Order-banner_box_all:** As there are multiple banners under the **banner _box_all** category, a sort order or each banner needs to be specified here. The banners will be displayed in that sort order – a lower order banner will be displayed first. For other categories, this field does not carry any importance.

- **Scheduled at:** You can schedule a banner for a specified date. Select the date from which you want to start showing the banner. Keeping it blank will immediately activate that banner.

- **Expires on:** Select the date on which you want to stop showing the banner. If you want to show the banner for a number of impressions, type the number of impressions in the **impressions/views** field. You have to fill either the expiry date or the number of impressions/views. If you don't want to stop showing the banner, keep the expiry field blank.

Promotional Discounts

Promotional discounts are often used in online shops. You can offer special discounts to customers on different occasions such as the New Year, Christmas, and so on. Zen Cart has built-in tools to configure promotional discounts on products in specific categories or on selected products. You can also configure the promotion start and end dates.

Special prices can be configured from **Catalog | Products Price Manager**. First, select a category to show the products under it. Once the product list is shown, select the product for which you want to assign a special price. Then click on the **install** button to the right of the **Special Price Info** field.

A special screen will display a list of products in the **Product** list box. Select a product from the **Product** list box. Then assign the special price in the **Special Price** field. You can assign a new price for the product, or assign a percentage discount (say 20%) in this field. Then select the start date at the **Available Date** field and the end date at the **Expiry Date** field. If you want to start the discount immediately, keep the **Available Date** field blank. Similarly, if you want to keep the discount continuing for an indefinite period, keep the **Expiry Date** field blank.

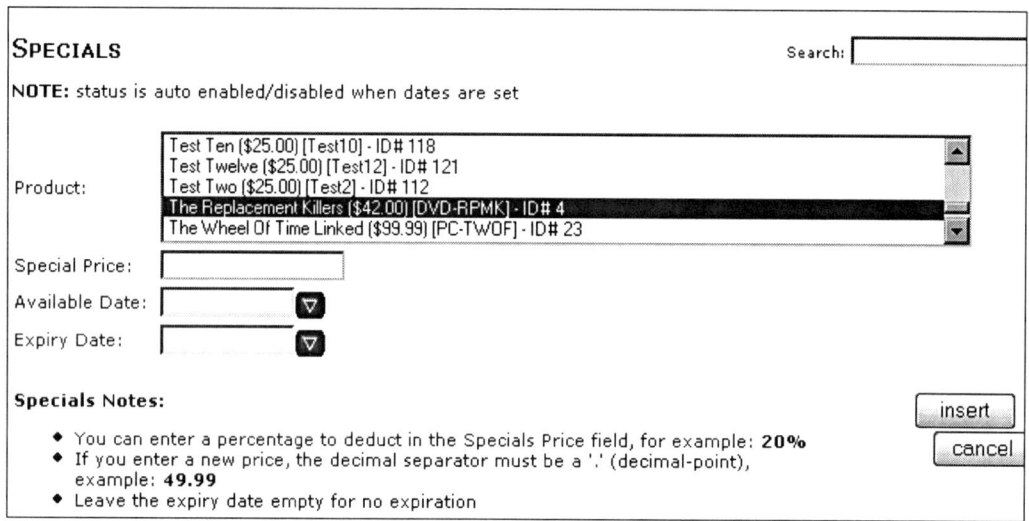

 Although you can keep a discount for an unlimited period, it is not a good idea to keep it open-ended, as it actually attracts fewer customers. Always assign an **Expiry Date** so that customers feel an urge to buy it immediately.

Cross-Selling and Up-Selling

Cross-selling, up-selling and better-together are some of the sales techniques used widely in online shops. Although Zen Cart has no built-in capability of doing these, you can implement these features by adding contributed modules. In this section, you are going to learn how to implement cross-sell, up-sell and better-together features.

Cross-Selling

The idea of cross-selling is to sell additional products or services to a customer. Cross-selling may be of different forms. For example, while you are selling a novel, you may try to sell other novels by the same author; while selling a computer, you may try to sell other accessories; or when you are selling a product which requires maintenance, you may sell servicing and extended warranty along with that product. The idea of cross-selling is to sell relevant products—not substitutes for that product.

Zen Cart has no built-in capability for cross-selling. However, several modules for cross-selling are available at the Zen Cart website. You can use one of those and start cross-selling. We are going to discuss one such module—Cross Sell by Tony Corbett. This module allows you to add up to 6 products as relevant in your product information page.

The installation process of the module is described in the `Install.txt` file in this package. Follow the instructions for installation. First, you have to apply a patch (in `products_xsell.sql`) from **Tools | Install SQL Patch**. Then, upload the files in to the appropriate directories. Replace `YOUR_TEMPLATE` with your template's name, for example, `packt`. Then you have to edit two files:

- Add `define('TEXT_XSELL_PRODUCTS', 'We Also Recommend :');` just above the final `?>` in `includes/languages/english/product_info.php` and save it into `includes/languages/english/packt/product_info.php`.

- Edit the product-info template file `/includes/templates/template_default/ tpl_product_info_display.php` and insert the following code at the point where you wish the Cross-Sell box to appear. Usually, best at the end of the file:

```php
<?php
require($template->get_template_dir ('tpl_modules_xsell_products.
php', DIR_WS_TEMPLATE, $current_page_base,'templates'). '/' .
'tpl_modules_xsell_products.php');
?>
```

Save the file as `/includes/templates/packt/ tpl_product_info_display.php`. Add the above codes for any other product type for which you wish to enable cross-sell display (for example, files such as `tpl_product_music_info_display.php`).

After successful installation, you can configure the options for this module from:

- **Configuration | Minimum Values | Display Cross-Sell Products** - This is the minimum number of configured Cross-Sell products required in order to cause the Cross-Sell information to be displayed.

- **Configuration | Maximum Values | Display Cross-Sell Products**:This is the maximum number of configured Cross-Sell products to be displayed.
- **Configuration | Product Info | Cross-Sell Products Columns per Row**: This refers to the Cross-Sell Products Columns to be displayed per Row. A value of 0 means off. You can set a sort order.
- **Configuration | Product Info | Cross-Sell - Display Prices?**: Select whether to display prices in the list of cross-sell products.

Once you have configured these options, you can start using the Cross-Sell module from **Catalog | Cross Sell Products**. The screen will list all the available products. Select a product for which you want to assign cross-sells. Another screen will appear, where the selected product will be shown at the top, and you will have the option to check the products that you want to sell with the selected product. Select all the related products and click the **update** button.

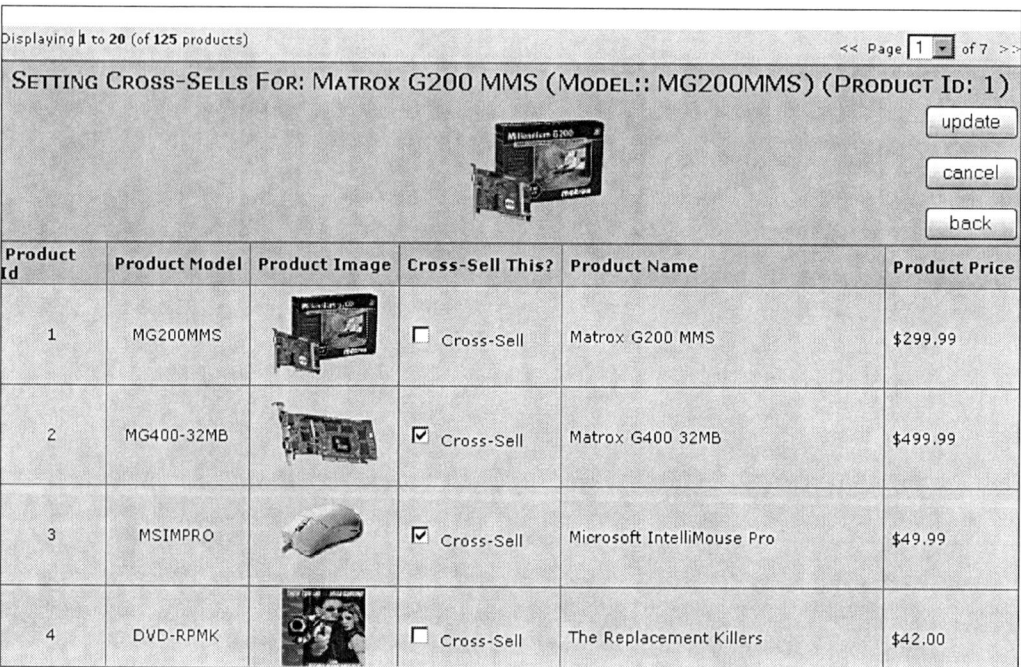

Once you have configured the cross-sells, you can work on the product details page. Click on the product for which you have configured Cross-Sell, for example, Matrox G200 MMS. Another centerbox, which looks like the following, will be displayed at the bottom of product description page:

One of the limitations of the Cross-Sell module is that the cross selling is configured one way. If you configure product A to sell with product B and product C, you will get cross-sell listing only for product A. When a customer clicks on product C, she will not see product A as a recommendation. This can be solved by using **Cross Sell - Just Another Cross Sell Mod**, available for download from the Zen Cart website.

The `Read_me.txt` file with this package describes the installation of this Cross-Sell module. Before installing this module, you must have installed Cross-Sell module first. Upload all the files to the `admin` and `js` folders. Then, apply `sql_patch.sql` through **Tools | Install SQL Patches**. With the patching of SQL, the installation would be complete, and you will see one option in **Configuration | Cross Sell** and a set of options under **Catalog | Advanced Cross Sell**.

In **Configuration | Cross sell**, you will find the field **Input type to be used in form**. If you set this to **id**, you have to use the product ID when you insert new cross-sell in the cross-sell form at **Catalog | Advanced Cross-Sell**. If you set this to **model**, you have to use the product model when you insert a new Cross-Sell. You can insert all Cross-Sells from **Catalog | Advanced Cross-Sell**. The screen looks like this:

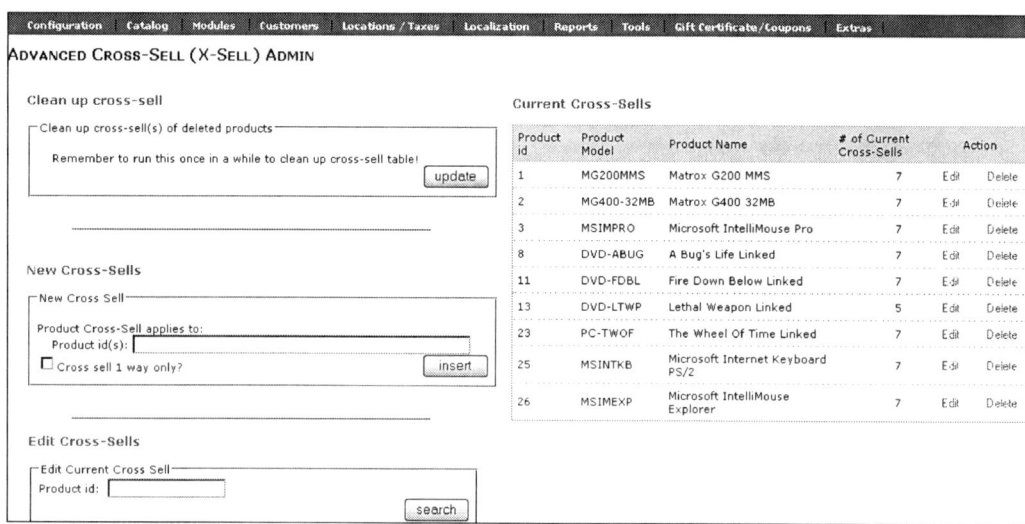

Up-Selling

Now, let's talk about up-selling. You may have seen up-selling several times in your life. When you go to buy a dress, the salesperson may recommend you buy a dress that is of a better quality and higher price. So, up-selling is a sales technique where a salesperson attempts to have the consumer purchase more expensive items, upgrades, or other add-ons in an attempt to make a more profitable sale.

Upselling in Zen Cart can be implemented by the **Cart Upsell/Cross sell** module available from the Zen Cart website's download section. The installation process for this module is described in the `install.txt` file. First, you have to upload all the files as per the directory structure. Then, edit the `tpl_shopping_cart_default.php` file and add the following code before the last `</div>` tag:

```php
<?php
require(DIR_WS_MODULES . zen_get_module_directory(FILENAME_CART_
UPSELL));
?>
```

The last thing you have to do is edit the `includes/modules/YOUR_TEMPLATE/cart_upsell.php` file, and replace YOUR_TEMPLATE with the name of your template, for example, `packt`. You will find the following set of variables defined in this file:

```
// number of upsells/xsells to display
define('NUMBER_UPSELLS_DISPLAY', '9');
define('NUMBER_XSELLS_DISPLAY', '9');

// number of upsells/xsells columns to display
define('UPSELLS_COLUMNS_DISPLAY', '3');
define('XSELLS_COLUMNS_DISPLAY', '3');

// upsells/xsells box title to display
define('UPSELLS_TITLE_DISPLAY', 'Customers who selected the items in
your cart also chose...');
define('TEXT_XSELL_PRODUCTS', 'To go with the items in your cart we
also recommend...');
```

Among these some are for displaying the number of up-sells, and some are for defining texts for the up-sell headings. Change these to suit your needs.

If you have installed the Cross-Sell module, edit the `includes/languages/english/packt/product_info.php` file, and add the following line (if it is already not there):

```
define('TEXT_XSELL_PRODUCTS', 'We Also Recommend For: ');
```

By doing this, your installation is complete. Now, you can see the up-sell feature in the product info page. Just below the product description, you will find the 'Customers who purchased this item also purchased...' box as shown here:

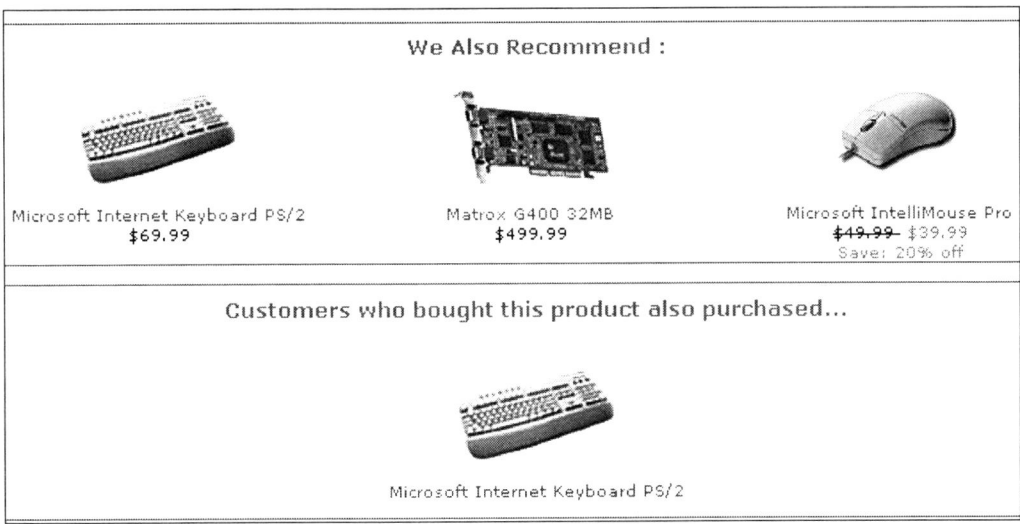

Don't panic if you do not see the box for up-sell after installing this module. If you have no successful record of a completed order, then the 'also purchased' box will not be displayed. As there is no buying history based on which "customers who purchased this item also purchased..." can be displayed. Add some orders first, and then you will see this box.

The single configuration of this module is setting the number of columns per row to display in the up-sell box which is done under **Configuration | Product Info.** Set the appropriate number in the **Also Purchased Products Columns per Row** field. You can also change this value by editing the `includes/modules/YOUR_TEMPLATE/cart_upsell.php` file.

Better-together

If you have ever visited `Amazon.com`, you will know what 'Better Together' is. Whenever you view a product description, the 'Better Together' title will suggest more products to be bundled with your chosen product. Packt online shop (`www.packtpub.com/books`) also suggests better-together products. You can implement this feature in Zen Cart by using the **Better Together** module written by Scott Wilson and available from the Zen Cart website's download section.

For installing this module, upload all the files as per their directory structures. Then, login to the administration panel. In **Modules | Order Total**, you will see **Better Together** listed along with all the other modules available. Click on **Better Together** to highlight the module, and click on **Install**. Then, you have to assign a sort order. You may also decide whether to show taxes with the Better Together offer, or whether taxes will be calculated based on the better together price offer.

One of the pitfalls of this module is that you cannot configure the discounts from the Administration panel. For this, you need to edit the `includes/modules/order_total/ot_better_together.php` file. You have to provide links for the products and mention discounts. Find `function setup()` at line 497 in this file. You will see some commented examples. First, uncomment the examples and provide your product ids and discounts. You may add the discounts as follows:

```
// Buy product 10, get product 11 at 50% off
$this->add_prod_to_prod(10, 11, "%", 50);

// Buy product 21, get one free
$this->add_prod_to_prod(21, 21, "%", 100);
```

```
// Buy product 1, get an item from category 3 free
$this->add_prod_to_cat(1, 3, "%", 100);

// Buy an item from category 1, get an item from category 2 free
$this->add_cat_to_cat(1, 2, "%", 100);

// Buy item 14, get a second one free.
$this->add_twoforone_prod(14);

// Buy any item from category 3, get a second identical one free
$this->add_twoforone_cat(19);

// buy two and get one free
$this->add_prod_to_prod(11, 12, "%", 100);

//buy 14 & 15, get 50% discount on 15
$this->add_prod_to_prod(14, 15, "%", 50);

// buy item 16 & 17, get 25% discount on item 17
$this->add_prod_to_prod(16, 17, "%", 25);

//buy two items from category 2 & 3, and get another item from these
categories free
$this->add_cat_to_cat(2, 3, "%", 100);

//buy two and get another item at 50% discount
$this->add_prod_to_prod(22, 25, "%", 50);
```

After adding the discounts, save the file. Now, you need to edit tpl_product_info_display.php to advertise your discounts. Add the following code in this file below the product description block:

```
<?php
require($template->get_template_dir('/tpl_better_together_marketing.
php',DIR_WS_TEMPLATE, $current_page_base,'templates'). '/tpl_better_
together_marketing.php');
?>
```

Save the file in the `includes/templates/<Your Template>/templates` directory. Replace `<Your Template>` with your custom template directory, for example, `packt`. Be sure that you have installed `tpl_better_together_marketing.php` in this same directory. Now, the **better together** module is ready for use. Browse to a product and you will see the following:

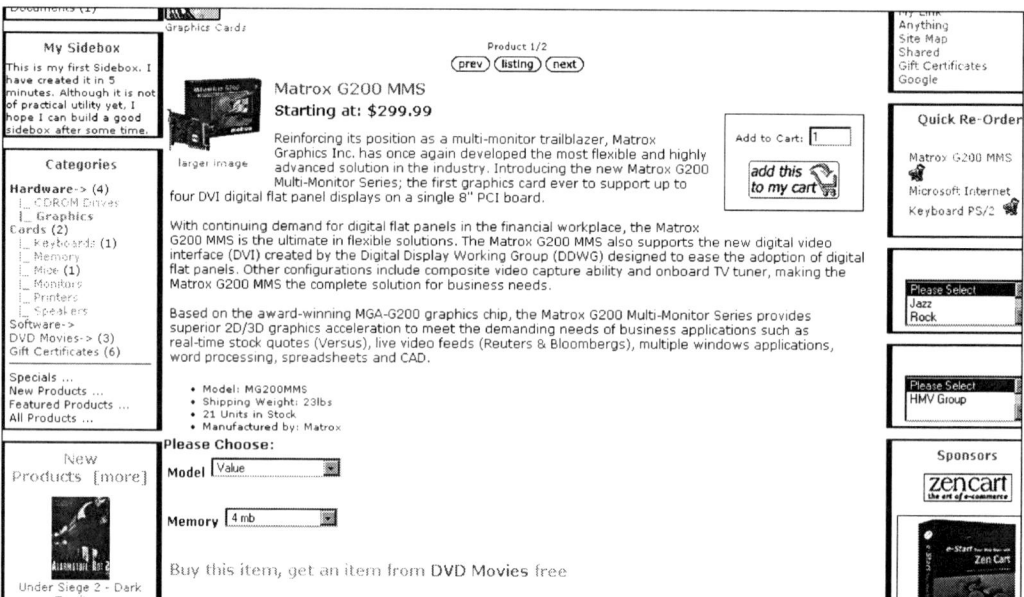

Remember that you have configured to give DVD free with a Matrox G200 MMS. You can make it vivid by adding the following declaration in the `stylesheet.css` file:

```
#betterTogetherDiscountPolicy {
font-weight: bold;
font-size: 1.5em;
color: red;
}
```

Now, the **better together discounts** screen will look like this:

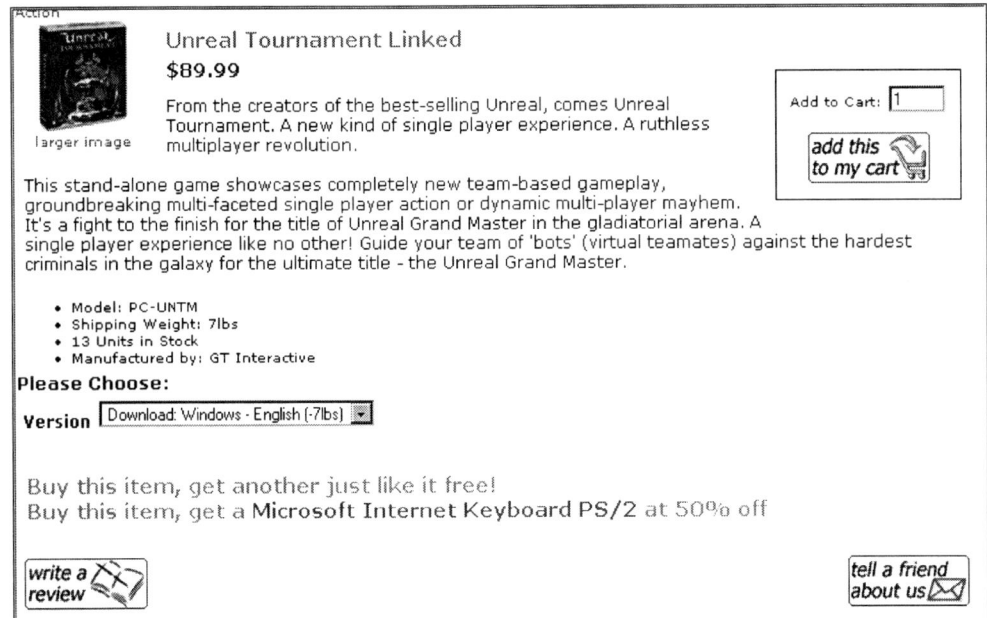

When you order both Unreal Tournament and Microsoft Internet Keyboard PS/2 together, you get a 50% discount on Microsoft Internet Keyboard PS/2. This discount will be shown in the Order Total Section in the **Payment Information** Step (Step 2) during checkout:

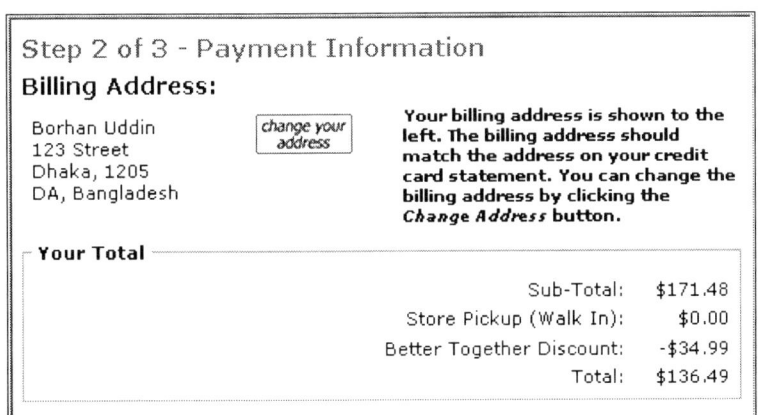

SaleMaker

Online shops often introduce a sale for special events, or a season, to attract more customers, or to clear stock quickly. For example, a book shop may offer a 35% discount on all books for the New Year. Zen Cart has an excellent tool called **SaleMaker** to manage such sales. You can access SaleMaker from **Catalog | SaleMaker**.

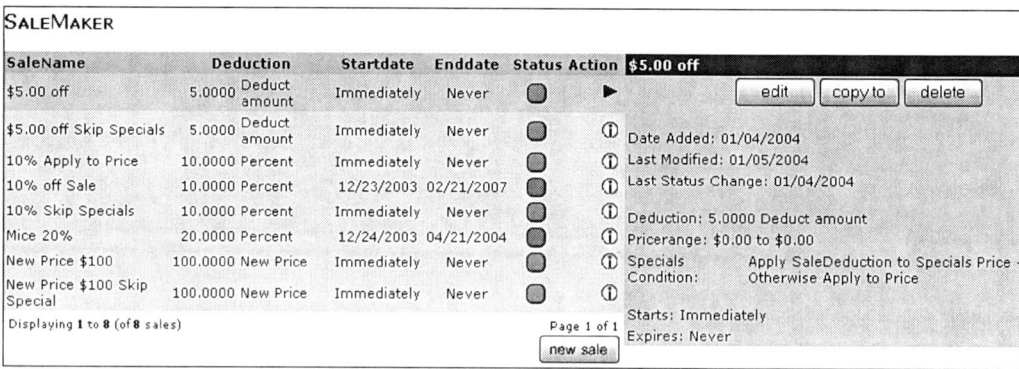

In the **SaleMaker** screen you will see the list of sales including the deduction amount, the **Start Date** and the **End Da**te, and the status of those sales. Selecting one Sale will give you the option to edit, copy to or delete that sale. You will also get information about that sale by selecting it.

You can add a new sale by clicking on the **new sale** button. It opens a screen that looks like this:

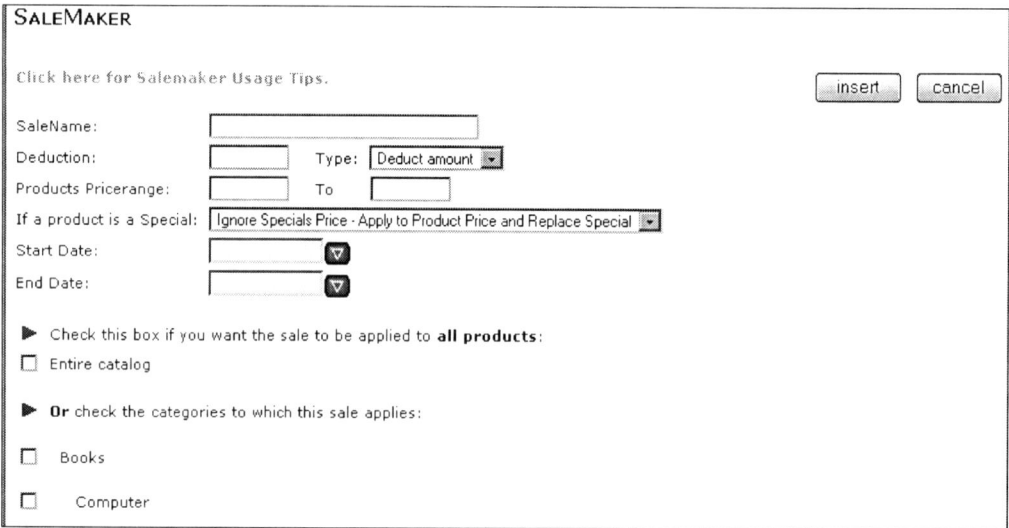

Suppose that you want to offer special discounts on all books during Christmas for two weeks. Type the sale name, Christmas Book Discount, in the **SaleName** field. Then, type the discount. You can specify the discount as a percentage of the price, or as an absolute amount. For example, if you want to offer a 35% discount, type 35 in the **Deduction** field, and select Percent from the **Type** drop-down list. You will get three options here: **Deduct Amount, Percent**, and **New Price**. This means that you can specify a new price for the product. In the product price range field, you may specify the product price range for which the discount is applicable. For example, you may want to apply a 35% discount on books whose price ranges from $ 30 to $ 150.

Some products may already be having specials. In that case, the sale discount to be applied can be configured from the **If product is a special** drop-down list. You have three options: **Ignore Specials Price – apply to product price and replace special, Ignore Sale condition – No Sale applied when Special exists**, and **Apply SaleDeduction to Specials Price – Otherwise Apply to Price**. Choose one option from these.

Then select the **Start Date** and the **End Date** of that sale. If your sale is open-ended, keep the **End Date** blank. Keeping the **Start Date** field blank will activate that sale immediately.

You may apply the sale to a whole product catalog or some specific categories. If the sale is only for books, then check the **Books** category. Remember that applying the sale to a parent category automatically applies it to its child categories. Therefore, if you apply a sale to the **Books** category, that will also be effective for other sub-categories under **Books**. While selecting categories, you can also see the categories that are already on sale. A **more** link will be shown beside such categories to display the details of the products on sale.

Special, Featured, and New Products

By this time, you may have already noticed on the homepage a center box that shows New Products for that month. It also shows a center box called Monthly Specials for that month. New products are displayed according to the date when they were added to the product catalog. But for Specials, you have to specify the products that fall under that category. Specials often have discounted prices. This is another way of attracting customers.

You can decide whether New Products, Special Products, Featured Products, and Upcoming Products center boxes should be displayed in the main page or not. To do this, select **Configuration | Index Listing** from the Administration panel and find the following options:

- **Show New Products on Main Page**
- **Show Featured Products on Main Page**
- **Show Special Products on Main Page**
- **Show Upcoming Products on Main Page**

A value of **0** means that the center box will not be displayed. If you want to show the box, just type the sort order. A lower sort order will display that center box in a higher position.

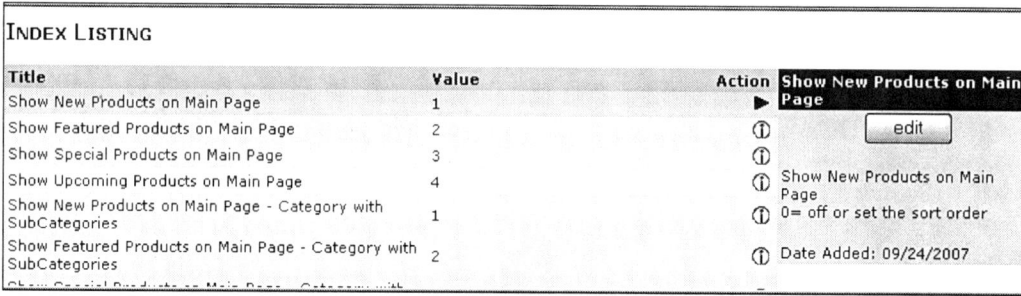

As said earlier, new products are chosen based on the date they were added to the catalog. However, you can define what the New Products, Featured Products, and Specials Products mean. Select **Configuration | Maximum Values** and find the following options:

- **Products on Special**: From here, you can configure the number of products that will be displayed on the Specials box. The default is **9**, and you can change it to another value.

- **New Products Module**: From here, you can define the number of new products which will be displayed in the New Products Module.

- **Upcoming Products**: Assign the number of upcoming products to be displayed. The default is **10**.

- **New Products Listing- Number Per Page**: Assign the number of products to be listed per page. The default is **10**.

- **Maximum Display of Featured Products - Main Page**: Assign the number of products to be displayed in the Featured Products box. The default **is 9**.

- **New Product Listing Limited to**: This option defines the products **that** will be considered new for displaying in the center box. A value of **0 indicates All Products**, **1** means **Current Month**, **7** means **7 Days**, **14** means **14 days**, **30** means **30 days**, and a value of **60** means **60 days**, **90** means **90 days**, and **120** means **120 days**. Therefore, if you want to show new products for that month assign a value, **30**.

Special Products

You can manage Special products from **Catalog | Specials**. The screen will list the products on **Specials** and display their special prices. You can add, edit, or delete a product from **Specials**, or manage special prices from this screen.

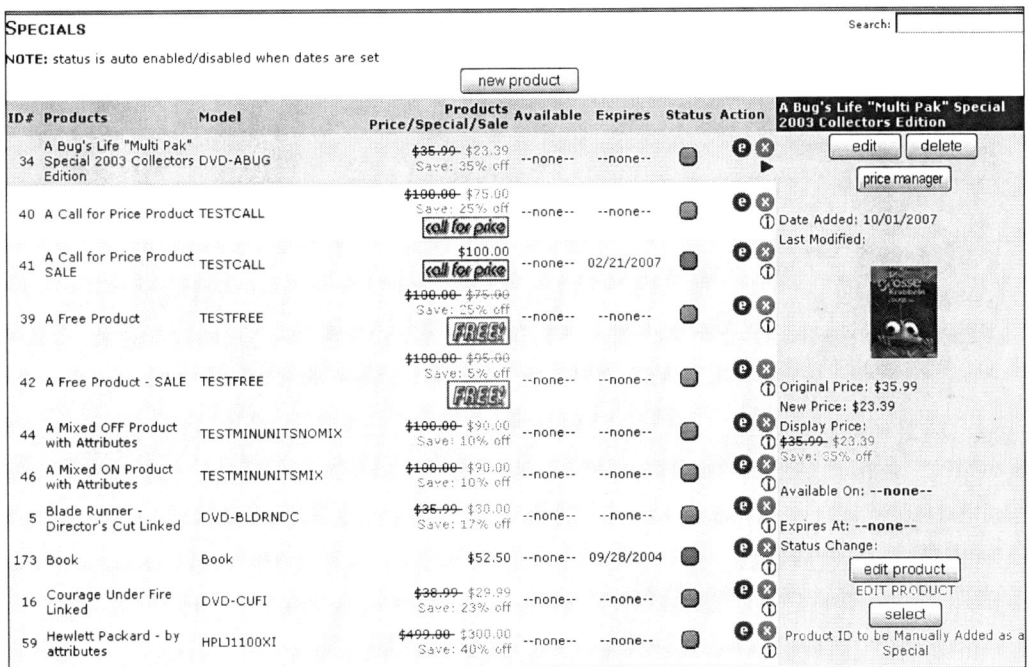

To create a new special product, click on the **new product** button. Then, select a product from the list of available products, assign special prices, available date and expiry date. Special Price can be set as a new price or as a percent deduction (for example, 14.70 or 25%). Once the values are set, click on the **insert** button.

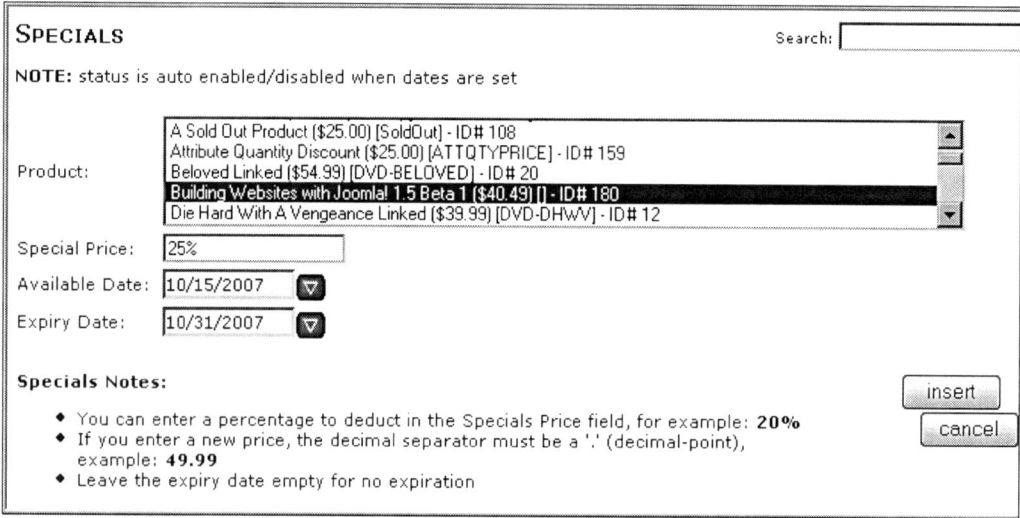

Featured Products

Featured products are like special products but they have no discount price. You can add some products to the Featured Products to draw the customers' attention to them. Featured Products are managed from **Catalog | Featured Products**. The screen is similar to the **Specials** screen. You can add a new product to the featured list by clicking on the **new product** button. Then, you have to select the product, assign an **availability date** and an **expiry date**.

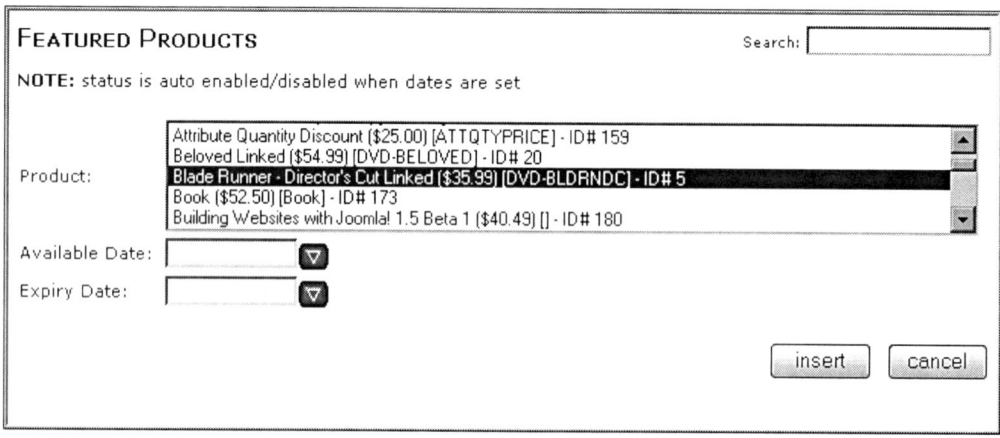

For a large product catalog, it's difficult to select a product from a list. For such product catalogs, you can add a product to the featured and specials list by clicking on the **select** button on **Catalog | Specials** or **Catalog | Featured Products** screen, and then typing the product id.

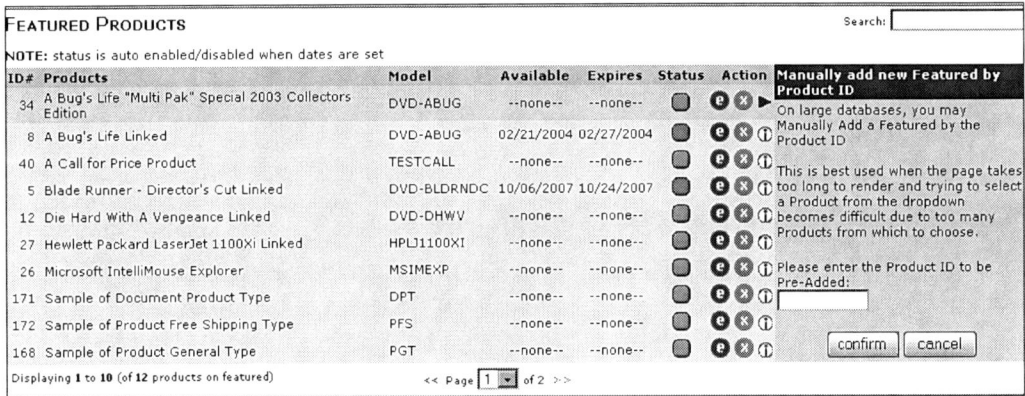

New and Upcoming Products

New Products and Upcoming Products lists are built dynamically based on the product availability. When you add a product to the catalog, you assign **Product Availability Date**. If the product is already available, it will be shown in the New Products list. If it is expected to be made available in the future, then that product will be added in the Upcoming Products list. You can see a list of Upcoming Products from **Catalog | Products Expected**.

Gift Certificates & Discount Coupons

Gift certificates and coupons are excellent ways to attract customers to your shop and to make them buy your products. Zen Cart has built-in features for Gift Certificates and Discount Coupons.

Gift certificates are sent by the shop owner to a group of customers. Customers can use that certificate while buying from that shop. Gift certificates can also be sold as a product, where customers can use them later for purchasing products from that shop.

Discount coupons are slightly different from gift certificates. Shop owners can give discount coupons to both individuals and a group of customers. Customers can use the coupons to get a discount while purchasing products from that shop. Unlike gift certificates, a customer cannot buy a product using only the discount coupons.

You can configure the discount coupon options from **Configuration | GV Coupons**. Here, you can configure the default Order Status when a gift voucher has a zero balance. By default, it is set to **Processing[2]**. You may change it to **Pending[1]**. Also configure **Length of the Redeem Code**. Remember that the longer the redeem code, the more secure it is. The default value is **10**, You can change it to 20 or more. You may also like to offer a discount coupon to new customers who sign up. If you want to do so, select the gift voucher in **New Signup Discount Coupon ID#**, and assign the amount you want to give through this voucher in **New Signup Gift Voucher Amount**.

Sending a Gift Certificate

As a shop owner, you can send Gift Certificates to any customer, whenever you want. To send a Gift certificate, go to **Gift Certificates/Coupons | Mail Gift Certificate**. The **Send Gift Certificate to Customers** screen will be displayed.

SEND GIFT CERTIFICATE TO CUSTOMERS	Text Editor Plain Text
Customer:	Please Select
Email To:	Use this for sending single emails, otherwise use dropdown above
From:	suhreedsarkar@gmail.com
Subject:	
Amount	
Rich Text Message: Text-Only Message:	We're pleased to offer you a Gift Certificate
	send mail

Fill in the following fields:

- **Customer**: Select the individual customer or the appropriate group to whom you want to send this Gift Voucher. Options in this drop-down list are – **All Customers, All Newsletter Subscribers, Dormant Customers (>3 months) (Subscribers), Active Customers in Past 3 Months (Subscribers), Active Customers in Past 3 Months (Regardless of Subscription Status)**, and then individual customer names. Select the appropriate option for sending the Gift Voucher.

- **Email To**: If you want to send the Gift Certificate to a non-customer, then type his/her email address in this field. This will go to a single person. For sending to multiple customers, select the drop-down in **Customer** field.

- **From**: By default, the shop owner's or administrator's email address is shown in this field. You may type a separate address in this field.

- **Subject**: Give a subject to your Gift Voucher email. For example, Special Gift from Packt Publishing.

- **Amount**: Specify the amount you are giving to the customer by this gift voucher. The amount you type in this field will be in the default currency of the shop. Remember that your total gift amount will be the amount typed in this field multiplied by the number of customers you are sending it to.

- **Rich Text Message:** If you are using Rich Text Editor, such as HTMLArea or FCKEditor, then type the formatted text in this field. This field may contain graphics, links, and so on.

- **Text Only Message**: As all email clients may not render the rich text message, it is always advisable to type the message in a text-only format. The message typed in this field will be shown to the text-only email clients.

Once all these fields are filled up, click on **send mail** to send the gift voucher to the customer.

Creating Gift Certificate Products

You can sell Gift Certificates through your shop, just like your other products. Customers who buy Gift Certificates can redeem it and pay for their purchases. They can also send that Gift Certificate to others. Therefore, it is a convenient way to send gifts to friends and family members—you send the Gift Certificate—and your friends and family members can buy the product of their choice.

Gift Certificates can be added from **Catalog | Categories/Products**. First, create a category named Gift Certificates. Then add a product named Gift Certificate and configure it as follows:

- **Products Status**: Set to **In Stock**.

- **Date Available**: Leave it blank.

- **Products Manufacturer**: Leave it blank.

- **Products Name**: **Gift Certificate**

- **Product is Free**: **No**

- **Product is Call for Price**: **No**

- **Product Priced by Attributes**: If you want to display products priced by attributes, then select **Yes**. You may opt for this because, pricing by attributes only needs one gift certificate product. Then by attribute you may change the price only.

- **Tax Class**: Choose the appropriate tax class in this field.

- **Products Price (Net)**: Set the price here. If you choose **Yes** in the **Product Priced by Attributes**, set zero in this field.

- **Products Price (Gross)**: It is figured automatically based on the value in the Products Price (Net) field.

- **Product is Virtual**: As virtual products like gift certificates do not need shipping address and shipping charge, select **Yes, Skip Shipping**.

- **Always Free Shipping**: Select **No**, Normal Shipping Rules.

- **Products Quantity Box Shows**: Select **Yes, Show**.

- **Product Qty Minimum**: Leave it blank.

- **Product Qty Maximum**: Set **0** (Unlimited) so that customers can buy as much as they want.

- **Product Qty Units**: Leave it blank.

- **Product Qty Min/Unit Mix**: Select **No**.

- **Products Description**: Give a description of the product. Try to explain the benefits that the customer will get by purchasing this gift certificate.

- **Products Quantity**: Type a large number so that you can track the number of gift certificates sold. When customers cannot add a Gift Certificate to their cart, check the stock and try adding a quantity here.

- **Products Model**: Type GIFT-0001 or something similar.
- **Products Image**: Upload an image for this Gift Certificate. Although the Gift Certificate is virtual, it is good to have a nicely designed image for it.
- **Upload to directory**: Choose the directory to which the image will be uploaded.
- **Products URL**: Leave it blank.
- **Products Weight**: Leave it blank.
- Click **Preview** and then **Save** the Gift Certificate.

Now, go to **Modules | Order Total** and click **install** to install or the **edit** button to configure the **Gift Certificate (ot_gv)** module. Define whether tax is to be included and how to recalculate tax.

Selling and Using Gift Certificates

Once the Gift Certificate product is added to the catalog, and the Gift Certificate module is enabled in **Modules | Order Total**, that will be displayed in the catalog. Customers can see it through the Gift Certificates category in the main page. However, you may draw attention to gift certificates on your store by creating a homepage graphic with a link to your Gift Certificate category. A new sidebox for displaying such graphics can also be used.

Customers can buy a gift certificate just like the other products. They can add it to the cart and pay for it through the checkout process. When Gift Certificates are purchased, as an Administrator, you have to log into your administration area and release them. Once a Gift Certificate is released by an Administrator, funds will be made available to the customer.

Upon the release/approval of Gift Certificates, emails with a redemption code are sent to the customers. Then customers can redeem that code either by clicking on the link, or by keying in the code on the checkout-payment page (or the **Gift Voucher Redemption** screen). Once a gift voucher is redeemed, funds for that gift voucher will become available to the customers, and they can use them in future transactions. Customers will see their gift voucher balance in their **My Account** page.

Customers can use those funds for themselves, or send it to their friends and family members. They can email as much as they want, to various people, for the amount they have purchased. Whoever they email it to will receive a new redemption code and must follow the same redemption process. They can in turn email the code whoever they wish to.

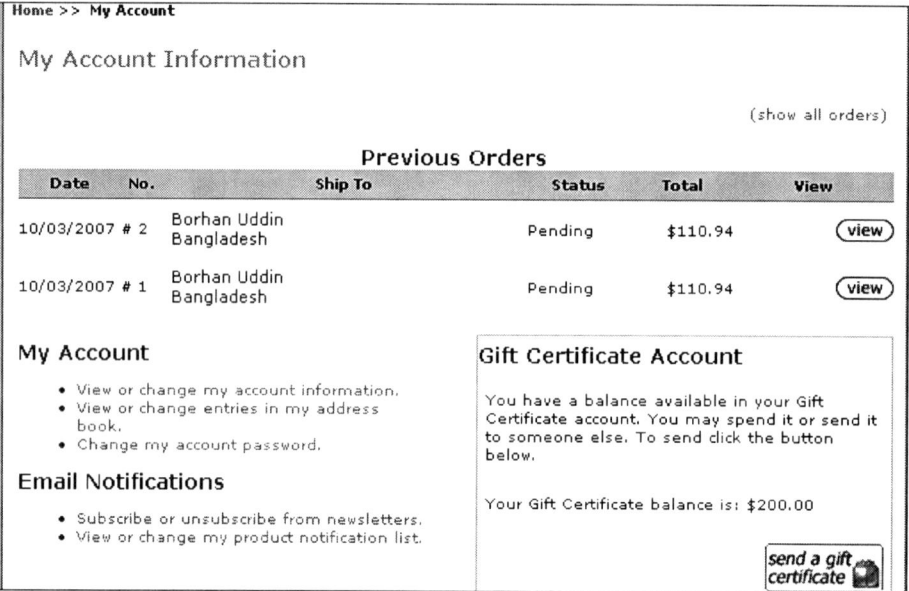

Coupon Administration

In Zen Cart, discount coupons are managed from **Gift Certificates/Coupons | Coupon Admin**. The coupon list is displayed in this screen. You can insert a new coupon, delete old one, send a coupon already configured, and view **Report** of coupon usage.

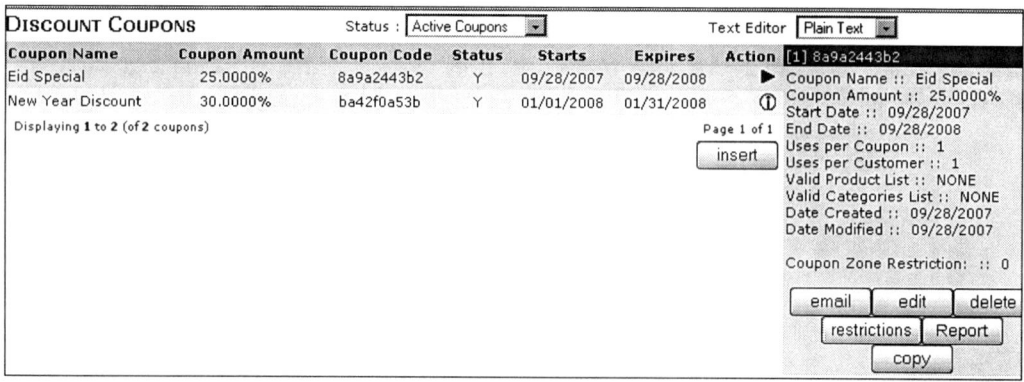

You can edit, copy or delete a coupon by clicking on the **edit**, **delete** or **copy** button respectively. Click on the **email** button to mail a coupon to the customers. You can also assign restrictions on the usage of this coupon.

To create a new coupon, click on the **insert** button. The **Discount Coupons** screen will be displayed as follows:

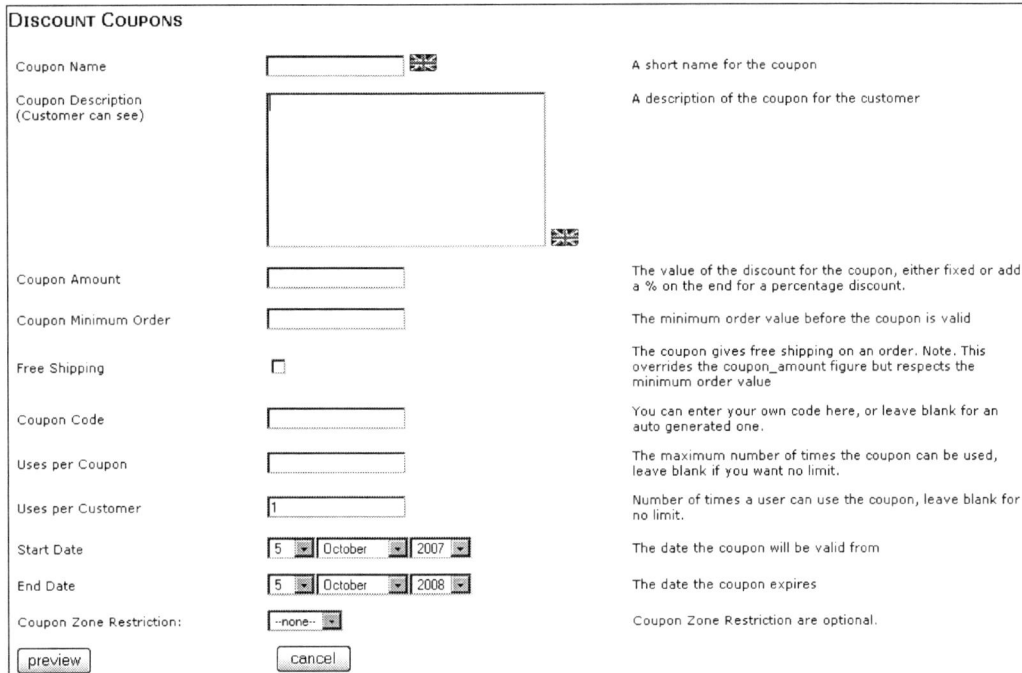

The following fields have to be filled up for a new coupon:

- **Coupon Name**: Give a short name for the coupon, for example, Happy New Year Discount.

- **Coupon Description**: Type a description of the coupon. This is your message to the customers. Explain why you are giving this coupon, and how they can use it for shopping.

- **Coupon Amount**: Type the value of the discount for the coupon. This can be a fixed amount or a percentage discount. Use a % sign to denote the percentage discount.

- **Coupon Minimum Order**: Specify the minimum order value for which the coupon will be considered valid. For example, if you want to give a 35% discount to customers who buy books for US$ 100 or more, the discount coupon cannot be used for a sale value lower than US$ 100. .

- **Free Shipping**: You may use this coupon to give customers free shipping on the purchase of some products. If you want to do so, check this checkbox. While using the coupon for free shipping, the discount amount will be overridden, that is, the customers will get only free shipping, not discounts on purchases.

- **Coupon Code**: Every discount coupon needs a unique code. You may type your own code, or keep it blank to auto generate the code. It's better to auto generate the coupon code than write your own. Auto generation ensures uniqueness.

- **Uses per Coupon**: Specify the number of times a coupon can be used. Leaving it blank implies that it can be used without limit.

- **Uses per Customer**: Specify the number of customers can use the same coupon. Generally, a single coupon is for a single customer. It is better to keep the default value **1** in this field.

- **Start Date**: Specify the date from which the coupon will be valid.

- **End Date:** Specify the date the coupon will expire on. The coupon will never expire if you keep this field blank.

- **Coupon Zone Restriction**: The coupon can be restricted for a specific zone. Select a Zone from the drop-down list. Keeping this field blank will allow the coupon to be used for all zones.

Once the above fields are configured, click on **preview** to see the discount coupon, and click on the **confirm** button to save it.

Creating a coupon does not send it to customers instantly. To send a coupon to customers, select that coupon, and click on the **email** button in **Gift Certificates/ Coupons | Coupon Admin** screen. The **Discount Coupons** screen will be displayed. Select an individual or a group of customers, just as in Gift Vouchers, type, subject line, and a message. Then click on the **send mail** button to send it to the customers.

Another way of creating similar discount coupon is to copy that coupon and change some properties as needed. You can copy a coupon by selecting that and then clicking on the **copy** button.

As a shop owner, you may want to see which of your discount coupons are used. You can see uses of discount coupons by clicking on the **report** button. You will be able to know which customer has redeemed the coupons, and on which date, and from which IP address.

You can apply restrictions on using this coupon by clicking on the **restrictions** button. In the **Discount Coupons Products/Category Restrictions** screen, you can assign the products and categories for which the coupon can be used. For example, if you want New Year 2008 Discount Coupon to be used only for the purchase of books, limit the use of this coupon to the Books category—allow for this category and deny for all other categories.

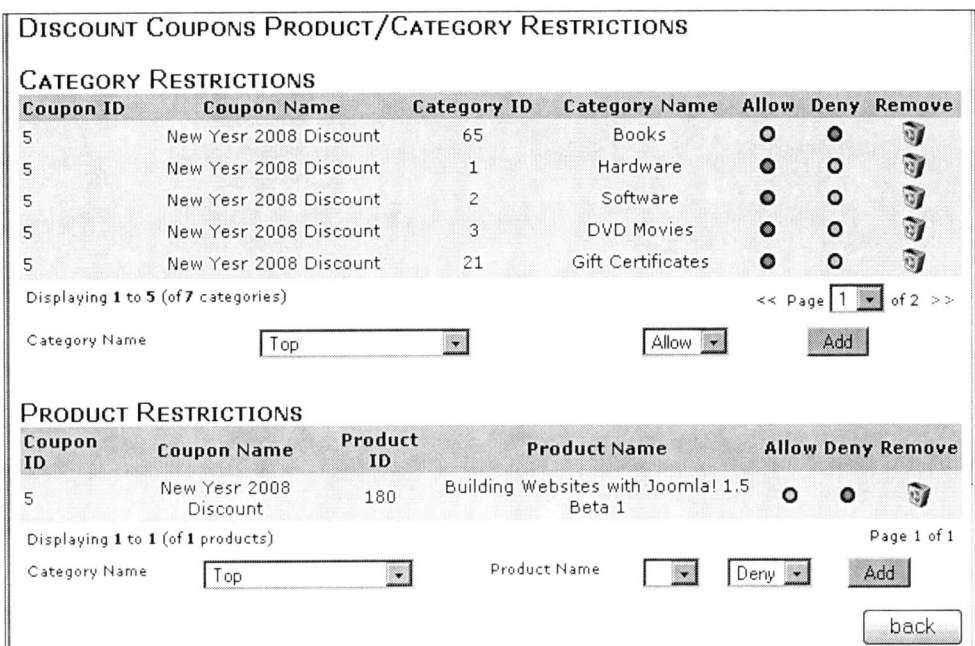

Newsletters/Product Notification

Newsletters/Product notification is an excellent feature of Zen Cart for keeping the customers informed about new products and products of interest to them. Zen Cart's built-in newsletters/product notification management system allows you to send newsletters and product notifications to your customers as and when required. Effective use of this tool may boost your sales. You are going to learn about the newsletters/product notifications feature of Zen Cart in this section.

Product Notification Subscription

Product notifications can be sent to customers who have opted to receive them. While browsing products, customers can sign up for product notifications via the notifications sidebox. This sidebox is visible only on actual product pages (if it is enabled by administrator).

You can also subscribe to product notifications by clicking the checkboxes shown upon checkout success. Checking the boxes and clicking the **submit** button will allow the customers to view the notifications for a product. For this, the customers should have an account with the online shop. The customers can also manage the products for which they want to receive notifications.

As an administrator, you can also enable/disable the Product Notification System for the customers. To enable/disable the Product Notification System, go to **Configuration | Customer Details**. Change the setting for **Customer Product Notification Status** to on or off. If Customer Product Notification Status is on, the customer will be asked about product notifications after checkout success and in account preferences.

Customers themselves can modify their product notification subscriptions from their **My Account** area. Click on **View or change my product notification list** link to edit the subscription to product notifications. If you have subscribed to any product notification, it will be shown here. You may subscribe to **Global Product Notifications** by checking the **Receive notifications on all available products** checkbox.

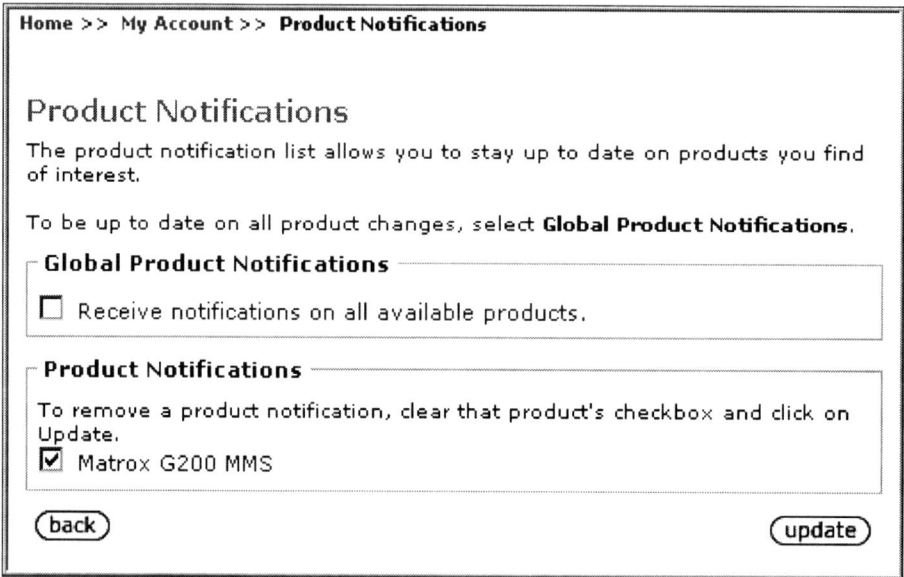

Creating Newsletters/Product Notifications

Newsletters/Product notification system is not automatic. You have to send newsletters/notices to the people who have subscribed to newsletters and product notifications.

To send notifications to those who have signed up, go to **Tools | Newsletter & Product Notifications Manager**. Then, create a newsletter/notice by clicking **new newsletter** button, choose product notification as the module. While sending the notifications, it will ask you for the products which the notice applies to. Select products to which the notification applies and click on the **send** button. You may click on the **Global** button to indicate that the notification is for the whole product catalog.

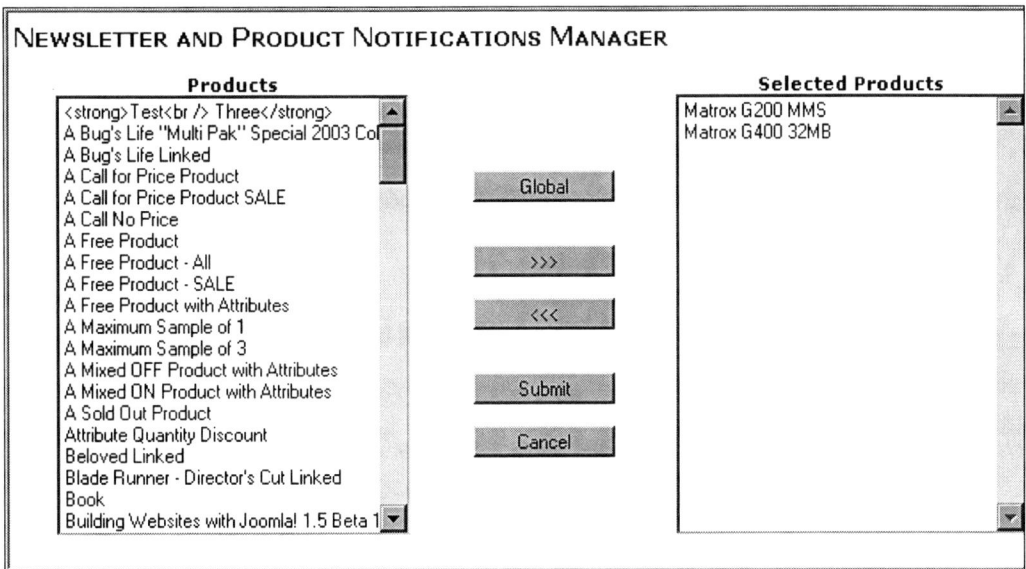

Sending Newsletters

Newsletters also need to be created and saved first. The process of creating a newsletter is the same as creating a product notification, except that you have to select **newsletter** in the **Module** field. Then, you will see the newsletter on the **Tools | Newsletter and Product Notification Manager** screen. Select the newsletter you want to send, and click on the **send** button. Then, you have to select an audience to whom the newsletter will be sent. The options in this drop-down list are: **All Newsletter Subscribers, Dormant Customers (>3 months)(Subscribers), Active Customers in the past 3 months (Subscribers), Active customers in the past 3 months (Regardless of subscription status)**. Once a customer group is selected, click on the **select** button. A preview of the newsletter will be displayed in the next screen. Click on the **send mail** button to mail it to the customers.

Product Reviews

The Product Review system in Zen Cart can be used as a promotional tool. Customers registered with the shop can write reviews for a product. It also has a rating system. The reviews by customers help attract other customers to the product. You may encourage customers to write product reviews and award gift vouchers to top reviewers.

Customers can write a product review while they are in the Product Details page. Clicking on the **Write a review on this product** link in the **Reviews** sidebox will open up a **Reviews** screen.

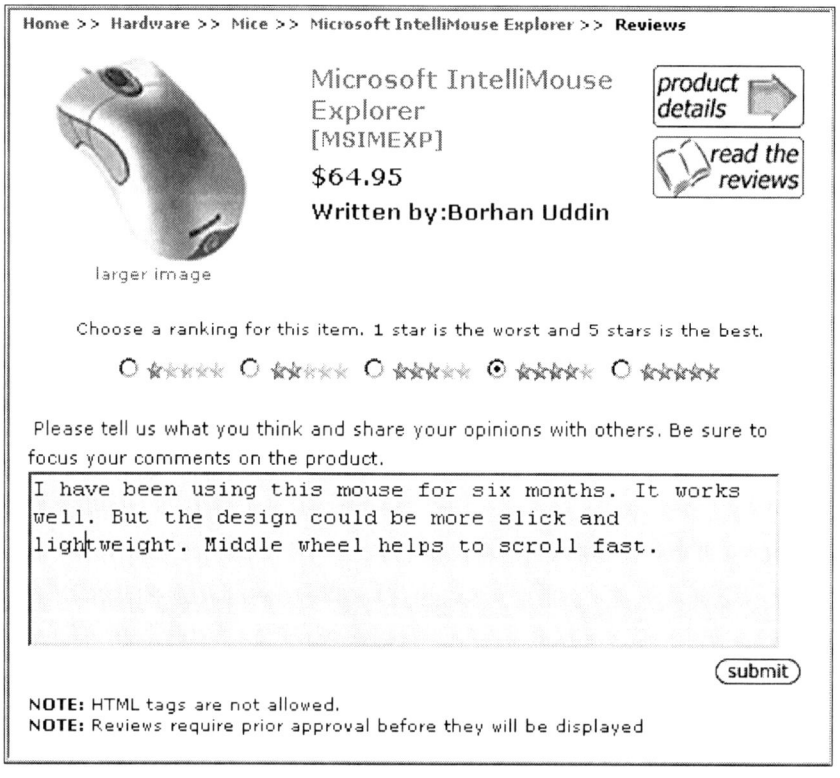

Select a ranking (1 to 5 stars) and write your review in the text box. Then, click on the **submit** button. Remember that customers cannot use HTML tags in writen product reviews. This is disabled to strengthen the security of the shop. Review needs to be a minimum 50 characters. Once a review is submitted, the review will be available to other customers only after approval by the administrator.

As an administrator, you can approve the reviews from **Catalog | Reviews**. All product reviews are listed in this screen indicating their status. A red box indicates **disabled**. You need to read the review first to approve it. Select the review from the list and click on the **edit** button. The **Reviews** screen will show the product review. Here, you can edit the review and ranking, and change its status. To publish the review, select **Approved** in the **Status** drop-down list.

Once the product review is approved, it will be displayed in the **Reviews** sidebox while the customer is in the Product Detail page of that product.

Once written and submitted by the customers, Product Reviews can be published instantly. To do this, you have to change the option in the **Configuration | Product Info** screen. Click on the **Product Reviews Require Approval** option, click the **edit** button and set its value to **0 =Off**. If you want to approve the reviews before publishing, set its value to **1 =On**.

Search Engine Optimization

People come to know about your online shop mostly through search engines. Therefore, it is imperative to have a good ranking in the search engines, or at least ensure that your site can be found through a search engine. Some techniques are used to optimize your site so that it gets listed in a search engine and appears first in the search results. Using meta-tags for products and categories is one way of optimization. Another way is to use search engine friendly URLs. We are going to learn about these in this section.

Using Meta-tags

The first step in search engine optimization is to use meta-tags properly. Zen Cart has a built-in feature for adding meta-tags for categories and products. You can add meta-tags to each product and category so that a search engine can index them appropriately.

Site-Wide meta-tags

You can define site-wide meta-tags such as charset, keywords and description from the `includes/languages/english/meta_tags.php` file. Edit the file for keywords, site title, site tagline and site description and save them to your override template directory, for example, `packt`.

Some of the meta-tags you want to add may not be present in the above file. To adding your custom meta-tags, copy the `includes/templates/template_default/common/html_header.php` file to your `includes/templates/packt/common/` folder. Open it and add your own meta-tags to those already there by default.

Meta-tags for Categories

You can define meta-tags for each category from **Catalog | Categories/Products**. Here, you will find a list of all defined categories. Now, click on the meta tag icon, which is the last one to the right. A new screen will be displayed where you have to provide the following information:

- **Title**: The title of the page will be defined in this field.
- **Keywords:** Add the keywords that will be used for searching products in that category. These are the keywords that are going to be used during a search. Appropriate keywords result in better search results.
- **Description**: Give a description of the category. Try to accommodate as many keywords as you can. The description should be brief, but comprehensive, so that customers know exactly what is in a category.

A meta-tag must contain keywords and a description, or it will not be considered complete, and will eventually be ignored. Do some research about the keywords for each category beforehand. You may use some online tools for such keywords and get synonym keywords. One such tool can be found at: http://www.webmaster-toolkit.com/keyword-research-tool.shtml.

Meta-tags for Products

You can also define meta-tags for each product. Go to **Catalog | Categories/Products** and browse to the individual product lists. Then, click on the meta-tag icon to define it. Here also, you have to define the title, keywords and description. Your descriptions need to be content-rich and keyword-rich. There are custom settings in Product Types that can include the Product Name, Title, Model, Price and Title tagline in the meta-tag title. You have to select Yes/No for these fields.

 Generally, search engines will index all your pages in the shop. Therefore, build your pages with proper text to increase their content value for search engines. Although meta-tags are helpful, they are not the be all and end all. Content is more significant than meta-tags. The content should also be relevant to the meta-tags. If there is a difference between the keywords used in meta-tags and the actual content, a search engine may consider it keyword spamming. Remember that the lack of content is the major issue if your site is not getting good search engine rankings.

Using Search Engine Friendly URLs

If you are a long time user of the internet and have some interest in search engine optimization, you will find that one of the drawbacks of using shopping carts such as Zen Cart is its URLs. If you look into your browser's address bar, at the first sight, you may be perplexed. The URL reads something like: http://www.yourdomain. com/ /index.php?main_page=product_info&products_id=12. In fact it is a link to a DVD titled Die Hard. As a human, you cannot remember the URL. On the other side, robots from Google and other search engines also dislike these types of URLs. URLs with '?' are usually not indexed by search engines. This means your shop may be out of the search engine, or in the worst case, Google may index only your store's homepage, and not all the products. This is awful!

Several attempts have been made to use Search Engine Friendly (SEF) URLs in such shopping carts. Although other CMSs like Joomla! have built-in SEF feature, Zen Cart is yet to develop such SEF URLs on its own. However, third-party contributions are available for implementing SEF URLs in a Zen Cart shop. We will know how to use the **Ultimate SEO URLs** module in Zen Cart.

The **Ultimate SEO URLs** module can be downloaded from Zen Cart's download section. It is located in the **Other Modules** category. Its installation is simple, and works perfectly in most of the cases.

After downloading this from the web, extract it on to your computer. Then, upload the files from `_zen_cart_folder` to your Zen Cart installation directory. Now see the files in the `v137-specific-files` folder. Backup these files in your Zen Cart installation. Then, upload these files to your Zen Cart installation. A sample `.htaccess` file is included with the package. Rename it to `.htaccess`, and edit the word `/shop` to reflect your site's installation directory. Once done, you can configure this module from **Configuration | SEO URLs.**

SEO URLs

Title	Value	Action	Enable SEO URLs?
Enable SEO URLs?	true	▶	edit
Add cPath to product URLs?	false	ⓘ	
Add category parent to begining of URLs?	true	ⓘ	Enable the SEO URLs? This is a
Filter Short Words	0	ⓘ	global setting and will turn them off completely.
Output W3C valid URLs (parameter string)?	true	ⓘ	
Enable SEO cache to save queries?	true	ⓘ	Date Added: 10/06/2007
Enable product cache?	true	ⓘ	Last Modified: 10/06/2007
Enable categories cache?	true	ⓘ	
Enable manufacturers cache?	true	ⓘ	
Enable articles cache?	true	ⓘ	
Enable information cache?	true	ⓘ	
Enable automatic redirects?	true	ⓘ	
Choose URL Rewrite Type	Rewrite	ⓘ	
Enter special character conversions		ⓘ	
Remove all non-alphanumeric characters?	false	ⓘ	
Reset SEO URLs Cache	false	ⓘ	
Enter pages to allow rewrite	index, product_info, products_new, products_all, featured_products, specials, contact_us, conditions, privacy, reviews, shippinginfo, faqs_all, site_map, gv_faq, discount_coupon, page, page_2, page_3, page_4	ⓘ	

You have to configure the following options for Ultimate SEO URLs:

- **Enable SEO URLs?:** You can enable or disable search engine friendly URLs from this option. Select **true** to enable, and **false** to disable SEO URLs.

- **Add cPath to product URLs?:** Selecting **true** in this option will append the category path to the product URL. In such cases, the URL will look like `http://yourdomain.com/matrox-g400-32mb-p-2.html?cPath=xxx`. Keep this setting to **false**.

- **Add category parent to beginning of URLs?:** This setting will add the category parent name to the beginning of the category URLs (that is—parent-category-c-1.html).

- **Filter Short Words:** This setting will filter words less than or equal to the value from the URL. For example, you want to keep the filenames 20 characters long. Then type a value of 20 in this field. Longer product names will be shortened to that having 20 characters.

- **Output W3C valid URLs (parameter string)?:** Enabling this setting will output W3C valid URLs.

- **Enable SEO cache to save queries?:** This is a global setting and will turn on/off caching completely.

- **Enable *** cache?:** There are five options for enabling cache for. These settings will enable/disable cache for products, categories, manufacturers, articles and information pages.

- **Enable automatic redirects?:** Enabling this will activate the automatic redirect code and send 301 headers from old to new URLs.

- **Choose URL Rewrite Type:** Choose which SEO URL format to use. At present you will get only one option, Rewrite. In future, there may be more options.

- **Enter special character conversions:** This setting will convert special characters in URL into normal characters. The format must be mentioned in the form char=>conv,char2=>conv2, etc.

- **Remove all non-alphanumeric characters?:** This will remove all non-letters and non-numbers from rewritten URLs. This should come in handy while removing all special characters with one setting.

- **Reset SEO URLs Cache:** This will reset the cache data for SEO. From time to time, you may need to refresh the SEO URLs to get updated SEF URLs.

- **Enter pages to allow rewrite:** This setting will allow the rewrite only in the specified pages. If it is empty, all the pages will be rewritten. The pages must be mentioned in the following for at: page1,page2,page3. The pages mentioned by default will be alright in most cases.

Once you have configured the SEF URLs, you can browse products in your store and see their rewritten URLs. These will look like: `yourdomain.com/matrox-g200-mms-p-1.html`, `yourdomain.com/hewlett-packard-laserjet-1100xi-linked-p-27.html`, and so on.

 There are some other modules for SEF URL in Zen Cart. For example, SEFU is one of the modules which modifies Zen Cart core files and database tables. While using any third-party module, always keep track of the files which are being modified. Module which do not modify any core files or database tables are safer to use. For Ultimate SEF URLs module, it only replaces three files for v.1.3.7: `admin/categories.php`, `admin/product.php`, and `includes/functions/html_output.php`. Before uploading these files to the server, rename the original files with a suffix `.SEO`. When you want to remove SEF URLs, you can get back to the original files by changing their names to their original ones.

Summary

In this chapter, you have learned about several promotion and public relations tools available for a Zen Cart shop. Use of these tools effectively, and in a planned manner can enhance your sales dramatically. Amongst the tools, Featured Products, Special Products, SaleMaker, Cross-sell, Up-Sell, Gift Certificates, and Gift Vouchers can be used for the promotion of your products. On the other hand, tools such as Newsletters/Product Notifications manager can be used to communicate with your customers and inform them about new offers. The Review system can also contribute in promoting your products and acting as testimonials. Finally, you have learned how to get the attention of the search engines by using meta-tags for the site, category, products, and using search engine friendly URLs in your online shop.

After knowing all these attractive features of Zen Cart you may be tempted to move your existing shop to Zen Cart. In the next chapter, you are going to learn how to migrate from osCommerce to Zen Cart.

7
Migrating from osCommerce to Zen Cart

For several reasons, you may think of migrating from osCommerce to Zen Cart. In fact, people often install osCommerce when start their business. After some time, they discover Zen Cart and find that it has more features to offer than osCommerce. This chapter will show you how to migrate from osCommerce to Zen Cart.

On completion of this chapter, you will learn:

- Why you need to migrate from osCommerce to Zen Cart.
- What points you need to consider before migrating to Zen Cart.
- How to migrate the database, the product catalogue, the product images, and other files in addition to the look and feel of the site.
- How to minimize interruption to service during migration.
- How to convert an osCommerce module to a Zen Cart module.
- What the common problems during migration are, and how to overcome them.

This chapter will show you a step-by-step migration process from osCommerce to Zen Cart.

The Need for Migrating to Zen Cart

Most of the time, the first-time online entrepreneur starts their shops using osCommerce. They choose it because osCommerce has been around for a long time, and is widely used. But after some time, administrators of osCommerce find that it is difficult to customize and lacks so many essential features. They often need to install contributed modules for osCommerce.

osCommerce administrators face the greatest difficulties in customizing its look and feel. As discussed in Chapter 1, osCommerce does not follow an easy to understand template system. Conversely, Zen Cart has improved on its templating system. In Zen Cart, you can apply a new template without modifying the original core files.

osCommerce templates also use extensive HTML which is difficult to edit. The tables are buried in PHP codes. The CSS also needs refining. Zen Cart's HTML is more up-to-date, and easier to edit. Considering this, many developers prefer Zen Cart to osCommerce.

One may migrate to Zen Cart after observing the differences between osCommerce and Zen Cart. The features of Zen Cart and osCommerce are discussed in Chapter 1, *Introduction to Zen Cart*. You may revisit those and find out why many online shop owners want to migrate to Zen Cart.

 Migrating data from one database to another needs some experience in database systems. In the case of migrating osCommerce to Zen Cart, we assume that you are familiar with MySQL and phpMyAdmin. You know how to connect to a database, create/modify tables, and insert data into the tables. Knowledge of relational database management system concepts is a must before attempting the procedures explained in this chapter.

Points to Consider Before Migration

Every migration is complicated. Before migrating data to a new shopping cart, you have to consider the following points:

- Ensure that your product data is migrated in its original form (as it was in the osCommerce shop).
- Ensure that critical data, for example, customers, orders, products, product options, prices, and so on are retained as in the original.
- Ensure that no data is lost during the migration.

 Always backup your database before you attempt to modify any tables. As this exercise will deal with two of them, we recommend backing up both databases before proceeding to migration.

Depending on the types of shops you are using, you may fall into one of the following cases:

1. **Migrating from a live osCommerce shop to new Zen Cart shop**: You have an osCommerce shop online. You have been using it for years or months, and now you want to migrate to Zen Cart (maybe after reading this book and knowing about Zen Cart's advantages). In this case, migration will be simple. Once you extract data from an osCommerce shop, you can insert it to a new Zen Cart shop database. There will be no issues of conflicting data for the two databases, as the Zen Cart database will have no existing data.

2. **Migrating from a live osCommerce shop to a live Zen Cart shop**: Suppose you have two shops running: one on osCommerce, and another on Zen Cart. Now you want to merge these two shops and want to continue with the Zen Cart shop only. In this case, you have to migrate osCommerce data to Zen Cart and at the same time ensure that the Zen Cart shop has minimum interruption. You also have to consider existing data items in Zen Cart. Conflicts may arise during exporting data from osCommerce to Zen Cart as there are some data items already. Problems of duplicate IDs are prominent in this case. You have to resolve these conflicts in order to migrate successfully.

You have to consider some other aspects of migration, depending on what you are migrating – only products and categories, or other data as well. The more data you are trying to migrate, the more complex the process will be. The following sections discuss some other aspects which need to be considered before migration.

Product Catalogue

Zen Cart product catalogue includes product categories and product information including descriptions for the products. osCommerce also follow the same database structure, but product tables in osCommerce have fewer fields than in Zen Cart. This structural difference should be taken into consideration while migrating from osCommerce.

While migrating the product catalogue from osCommerce to Zen Cart, you should also be aware that besides migrating the database we also need to migrate the product images to appropriate folders from osCommerce to Zen Cart.

osCommerce does not support product types. So the default value for the products type field will be used for products imported to Zen Cart. This means that all products will belong to the **Product – General** type.

If you are migrating other data, such as customers, orders, and so on, besides product catalogues, you have to consider interrelations among these tables. Remember that products are related to orders and orders are also related to customers. Thus, customers are related to some products. These interrelations must be understood beforehand and planned accordingly to decide which tables need to be migrated.

Database Structure

You have to remember that Zen Cart and osCommerce databases are not identical. Some of the tables in Zen Cart database have more fields. However, the fields available in osCommerce tables are mostly available in Zen Cart tables with similar names. For some fields, the data type or length is different. However, this will not create a problem while migrating data from osCommerce to Zen Cart, as new field types and their length in Zen Cart tables can accommodate the original data types and the length of the osCommerce table fields.

Considering the differences in both the databases, you have to understand that all fields in Zen Cart tables will not have values except the default values for those fields. For example, osCommerce categories have no descriptions, but Zen Cart categories have. While exporting osCommerce categories data to Zen Cart, the description field will remain blank. You have to add the descriptions to these fields manually.

Look and Feel

The general look and feel will not be exported to the Zen Cart shop. Usually, Zen Cart shops have their own look and feel, and you can adapt their look and feel to the old osCommerce shop by modifying the Zen Cart template. Customizing the Zen Cart template has been discussed in detail in Chapter 4 , *Customizing Look and Feel*.

Some other elements of look and feel are the display of product categories, display of product images, and so on. osCommerce cannot have images for categories. Therefore, in Zen Cart, you need to assign icons for categories manually after migration. You also need to transfer the product images to the `images` directory of Zen Cart installation.

Uninterrupted Service

While migrating your osCommerce products to Zen Cart, you have to ensure that service on both shops remains uninterrupted. If you are migrating from a live shop, ensure that the interruption to the shop is minimal. And also for migrating to a live shop, you have to pay special attention to ensure minimum interruption to services.

It is best to do all preparatory work beforehand and then make the shop offline for some time to complete the migration. Before the actual migration, do some testing on your local server.

As taking the shop offline will not be possible all of the time, you can run the shop in its original location and make a copy in another folder. Then, try to migrate to the new instance of Zen Cart. This will allow you more time to migrate data from osCommerce. Once the instance works fine after migration, make this instance the main shop.

osCommerce versus Zen Cart Database Structure

By now, you will have understood that migration from osCommerce to Zen Cart mainly involves migration of osCommerce categories and products data to the Zen Cart database. Generally, exporting osCommerce data and importing that to Zen Cart database will work if the structures of both the databases are similar, or compatible to each other. In this section, we are going to explore the similarities and differences of the data structure of Zen Cart and osCommerce tables for categories and products.

You can explore the database structure by exporting the structure of both the databases into a `.sql` file. For this, you can use phpMyAdmin. To export the Zen Cart data structure, login to cPanel (if applicable) and open phpMyAdmin. Then, select the Zen Cart database. Click on the **Export** tab. Now, select all the tables beginning with:

- categories_*
- products_*

In Zen Cart, you have to select the following tables:

- categories
- categories_description
- products
- products_attributes
- products_attributes_download
- products_description
- products_discount_quantity
- products_notifications
- products_options

- products_options_types
- products_options_values
- products_options_values_to_products_options
- products_to_categories

In the **Options** section to the right-hand side, check only the **Structure**. Uncheck all the other options. At the bottom of the page, check **Save as File**. Now, click on the **Go** button and save the file with a name such as `zendb_structure.sql`.

Exporting the osCommerce data structure is similar to exporting the osCommerce data structure. Similarly, you can do it from phpMyAdmin. Select the existing osCommerce database that you want to extract the information from. Click on the **Export** tab. Under the **Export** section, highlight all the tables that begin with:

- Categories_*
- Products_*

Under the **Options** section, select the **Structure** options. At the bottom of the page, check **Save as File**. Uncheck all other options. Click on **Go**, save the file with some name, say `osc_structure.sql`.

Now, open the files in a text editor and compare the tables. An analysis of the tables will show the differences as discussed in the following sections.

> You can also use a file comparison utility such as WinMerge or Kompare. Another commercial file comparison tool is Beyond Compare. Use any of these tools, or just open it in text editor and compare manually.
>
> I have used WinMerge to compare Zen Cart v.1.3.8 and the osCommerce MS2.2 database structures. The following sections are based on these findings. Please remember that you may get different results when comparing different versions (different from those I have used).

Tables for Categories

First, compare the categories tables for osCommerce and Zen Cart. The tables are almost similar, except for one field. Zen Cart's `categories` table has an extra field named `categories_status`. So, while migrating data from the `osc_categories` table, you will not get data for this `categories_status` field. However, this will not create a problem as it takes a default value of 1 (meaning active).

The `categories_descriptions` table contains descriptions of each category. Both `zc_categories_descriptions` and `osc_categories_descriptions` tables are identical. So, migrating data from `osc_categories_descriptions` table to `zc_categories_descriptions` will be straightforward.

Tables for Products and Attributes

There are many differences between the `zc_products` and the `osc_products` tables. There are at least 22 extra fields in the `zc_products` table. Fields available in the `osc_products` table are also available in the `zc_products` table, although, there are differences amongst common fields. For example, the `products_model` field in `zc_products` table is `varchar(32)` whereas same field in `osc_products` table is `varchar(12)`. This means that exporting data from `osc_products` to `zc_products` is not a problem for this field, but exporting from `zc_products` to `osc_products` may create a problem as the `zc_products.products_model` field is larger than the `osc_products.products_model` field. On the otherhand, `zc_products.product_weight` is of `float` type which is `decimal` in `osc_products`. As a `float` type can accommodate a `decimal` type, it will not be a problem. Analyzing the structure of both the tables, you can see that exporting data from `osc_products` to `zc_products` will be not a problem, but the reverse may be.

Similarly, `zc_products_attributes` table has 27 fields, whereas the `osc_products_attributes` table has only 6 fields. These 6 fields are also available in the `zc_products_attributes` table in an identical form. So, there will be no problem exporting data from `osc_products_attributes` to the `zc_products_attributes` table.

Product options are stored in the `product_options` table. `Zc_product_options` table has 11 fields while the `osc_product_options` table has only 3 fields, which are identical to the 3 fields available in the `zc_product_options` table.

Regarding product options, Zen Cart has an extra table – **products_options_types**. This table contains three fields: **products_options_values_id**, **language_id**, and **products_options_values_name**. osCommerce has no such table and you will not get these fields.

The `Zc_products_options_values` table has one extra field - `products_options_values_sort_order`. The other two fields are identical to `osc_products_options_values`.

The following tables in both Zen Cart and osCommerce are identical:

- products_attributes_download
- products_description
- products_notifications
- products_options_values_to_products_options
- products_to_categories tables are identical

Product types are not supported in osCommerce. So, you will not find the `product_music_extra`, `product_types`, `product_types_to_category`, and `product_type_layout` tables in osCommerce.

Migrating Databases

First, you have to migrate categories and product data from osCommerce to Zen Cart. We assume that you have installed both osCommerce and Zen Cart, and both are in operation. Now, you want to migrate the product data to Zen Cart. The following is a step-by-step guide for migrating categories and product data from osCommerce to Zen Cart.

Step 1: Backup Existing Data

Back up both the osCommerce and Zen Cart databases. It is always recommended that whenever you make any change manually to the database, you back it up first. Once the data is lost you cannot get it back unless you have a recent backup. For both the databases, backup at least the categories and the products tables. You can do it easily from phpMyAdmin tool by exporting the whole database.

Step 2: Export osCommerce Data

Login to cPanel (if applicable), and open phpMyAdmin. Select the existing osCommerce database that you want to extract information from. Now, click on the **Export** tab.

Under the Export section, highlight all tables that start with `categories_` and `products_`. You have to select at least the following tables:

- categories
- categories_description
- products

- products_attributes
- products_attributes_download
- products_description
- products_notifications
- products_options
- products_options_values
- products_options_values_to_products_options
- products_to_categories

Under the SQL options on the right hand side of the page, check **Data** and **Complete Insert** options.

Now, at the bottom of the page, check **Save as File**. Click on **Go**, save the file on your hard disk and name it something like `osc_data.sql`.

Step 3: Import osCommerce Data to Zen Cart

You have already extracted information from the osCommerce database, which needs to be imported to the Zen Cart database. Now, importing to Zen Cart can be simple or complex depending upon your situation:

1. You may want to migrate osCommerce product data to a new Zen Cart shop. In that case, the Zen Cart shop has no product data. This makes the import from osCommerce simple, as there will be no conflict between the existing and imported `categories_id` and `products_id`.

2. You may want to migrate from an osCommerce store to another Zen Cart shop which already has some categories and products. In that case, importing osCommerce data adds some complexities as you have to consider unique id issues for `categories_id` and `products_id`. As there are categories and products already in the Zen Cart shop, some of the ids used by osCommerce categories and products may already be used by the Zen Cart categories and products. You have to ensure that all categories and products have unique ids and the ids are appropriately changed in all related tables.

We will discuss importing data for both cases, but start with the simple migration process.

Migrating to a Zen Cart Shop that does Not have Products

First, let us suppose that we are migrating our osCommerce categories and products to a new Zen Cart shop which has been installed and configured, but no categories or products have yet been added to it. In that case, the `categories_*` and `products_*` tables are empty. It may also happen that you have installed sample data, and these tables are populated with the data. In that case, just delete the records from these tables and make them empty.

Once you find the tables empty, you are ready to import the osCommerce data. Start phpMyAdmin, and go to the **Import** tab. In the **File to Import** section, click on the **browse** button and select the `osc_data.sql` file on your hard disk (which you have saved in Step 2). Then, click on the **Go** button. Your data will be imported if everything is alright. Otherwise, some error messages will be thrown up, and from those messages, you will get clues to look into the problems.

On the successful completion of the import of the osCommerce product data into the Zen Cart database, you need to import product images from osCommerce. Generally, product images in osCommerce are stored in the `/images` directory under osCommerce installation root. Copy the images and sub-directories (e.g. dvd, matrox, sierra, and so on) to the `/images` directory under the Zen Cart installation root. Both the images for categories and for products need to be imported.

You can download two contributions from the Zen Cart website. The first one is osCommerce Data importer contribution by Albert Savage, available for download from `http://www.zen-cart.com/index.php?main_page=product_contrib_info& cPath=40_41& products_id=918`. This package includes three separate scripts which import customers, products, product description, categories, category descriptions, category structure, specials and reviews. You have to extract the zip file and upload these three scripts to the Zen Cart installation directory. For all the three scripts, you have to configure the following variables:

```
//Source Database with OSC records
$source_db_host = 'localhost';
$source_db = 'database';
$source_db_username = 'user';
$source_db_password = 'password';
$source_db_table_prefix = '';
```

The above variables are for the source database, that is, the osCommerce database from which data will be imported. Then, you have to configure variables for the destination database, that is the Zen Cart database to which you want to import the data.

```
//Target Database with ZEN records
$target_db_host = 'localhost';
$target_db = 'database';
$target_db_username = 'user';
$target_db_password = 'password';
$target_db_table_prefix = '';
```

After changing the configurations and saving the file, point your browser to one of the above files, for example, `http://yourdomain.com/import_osc_customers.php` to run the script.

The script will display the progress of exporting and importing data, and finally notify you of its success. You have to run the other two scripts: `import_osc_products.php`, and `import_osc_orders.php` as well.

> **Warning**
>
> Remember that running these scripts will erase all product data in the target database. Therefore, use these scripts in a new store only when no product or category data is available.

The second contribution that can be used for importing data from osCommerce to Zen Cart is osCommerce to Zen Cart Conversion Script by Michael Morris, available from `http://www.zen-cart.com/index.php?main_page=product_contrib_info& cPath=40_41&products_id=946`. This package contains a single script named `oscommerceimport.php`. Once downloaded, extract the zip package and upload the `oscommerceimport.php` file in your admin directory. Now, point your browser to the file, that is, `http://yourdomain.com/admin/oscommerceimport.php`. The page will ask you for the osCommerce database name and the table prefix. Enter this information and click on the **Go** button. The data from osCommerce will be imported to the Zen Cart database. Like the other script, it will destroy all the product, category, and order data in Zen Cart. As you need to use this script only once, delete the file once the data import is complete.

Migrating to a Zen Cart Shop that has Products

We have already mentioned that when your Zen Cart shop has existing categories and products, importing categories and products from osCommerce database becomes more complex. This is because the Zen Cart categories and products use the same category and product IDs, which results in conflicts of uniqueness of these primary keys. Before importing osCommerce data, we have to modify them in osCommerce to avoid conflict with the Zen Cart table IDs.

First, check the highest ID assigned to categories and products. For example, your existing Zen Cart shop has 66 categories, and the highest value of the `categories_id` field is 66. You can determine this by running the following query in the Zen Cart database:

```
SELECT MAX( categories_id )
FROM categories;
```

This will return the highest value for the `categories_id` field. Similarly you can get highest value for `products_id` field:

```
SELECT MAX(products_id )
FROM products;
```

It may return something like 181. Now, we have got the values which we cannot have in osCommerce data. In our osCommerce data file, we must not have any category whose `categories_id` is less than 67, and any product whose `products_id` is less than 182.

 Backup your osCommerce database tables before trying any of the following methods. As the following instructions are going to change the primary keys of some tables, it is crucial that you back up your entire database so that you can get the original data if something goes wrong.

Changing the values of the `categories_id` and `products_id` fields is tricky, as these are also used to link to the other tables. The following tables we have selected from the osCommerce database use the `categories_id` field (as the primary or foreign key):

- categories (Primary key)
- categories_description (foreign key)
- products_to_categories (foreign key)

So, if we change the value of the `categories_id` for one category, we have to change that value in all these three tables simultaneously. We can use the UPDATE statement for this. As a rule, we may increase the value of all category ids by 100. So we will add 100 to the value of the `categories_id` field. We can do this by running the following query in the osCommerce database:

```
UPDATE categories SET categories_id = categories_id + 100;
UPDATE categories_description SET categories_id = categories_id + 100;
UPDATE products_to_categories SET categories_id = categories_id + 100;
```

These three UPDATE statements will add 100 to the value of the `categories_id` field.

Warning
Run the above queries only once. Running any of the queries above more than once will give unexpected results, and the relationship between tables will be lost or misleading.

Now, we will update the values of the `products_id` field. The following tables use the `products_id` as the primary/foreign key:

- orders_products (Foreign Key)
- products (Primary Key)
- products_attributes (Foreign Key)
- products_description (Foreign Key)
- products_notifications (Foreign Key)

Similar to the `categories_id`, we will change the `products_id` in these tables by executing the following queries:

```
UPDATE orders_products SET products_id = products_id + 200;
UPDATE products SET products_id = products_id + 200;
UPDATE products_attributes SET products_id = products_id + 200;
UPDATE products_description SET products_id = products_id + 200;
UPDATE products_notifications SET products_id = products_id + 200;
UPDATE products_to_categories SET products_id = products_id + 200;
```

These queries will update the `products_id` values in related tables.

Warning
Run the above queries only once. Running any of the queries more than once will produce unexpected results, and the relationship between tables will be lost or misleading.

There is another thing that we have to update in the categories table. The `parent_id` field in the categories table indicates the parent category ids. If the value of `parent_id` is 0, it is the root category, and if it has a value, it is under some category. As we are changing the category's id, we must also change the value of the `parent_id` to reflect the exact category id. But for root categories, we will not change the `parent_id`. So, we have to run the following UPDATE statement:

```
UPDATE categories SET parent_id = parent_id + 100 WHERE parent_id > 0;
```

We also need to update the `products_options_*` tables. As the `product_options_id` field may have duplicate values with Zen Cart the `products_options_*` tables, we need to increment the values in osCommerce first. Similar to categories and products, determine the highest value of `products_options_id` in Zen Cart, say 90. Then increment the value of `products_options_id` in osCommerce tables as follows:

```
UPDATE products_options SET products_options_id = products_options_id
+ 100;
UPDATE products_options_values_to_products_options SET products_
options_id = products_options_id + 100;
```

And for updating `products_options_values_id`, run the following queries (assuming that existing highest value of this field is 95):

```
UPDATE products_options_values SET products_options_values_id =
products_options_values_id + 100;
UPDATE products_options_values_to_products_options SET products_
options_values_id = products_options_values_id + 100;
```

After these updates, you are ready to export data from the osCommerce database. Follow the procedures described in Step 2 to export data from osCommerce. Save the exported data file as `osc_data2.sql`.

Now, it is time to import `osc_data2.sql` into the Zen Cart database. Start phpMyAdmin and go to the **Import** section. In the **File to Import** section, click on **Browse** and select the `osc_data2.sql` file. Then click on the **Go** button. All data will be imported to the Zen Cart database.

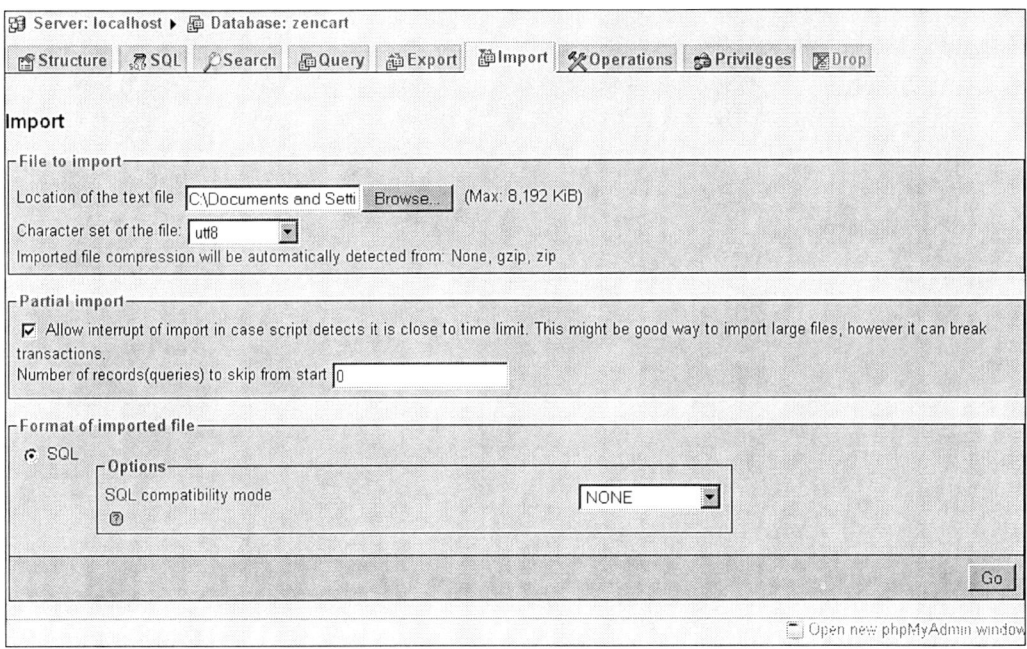

Adjusting the Look and Feel

During migration from osCommerce to Zen Cart, you are actually migrating the product, category, order and customer data only, not any `.php` files from osCommerce. The Zen Cart shop will use its own templates for look and feel. However, you may customize the Zen Cart template to have the same look and feel of the osCommerce store. Customizing of Zen Cart templates has been discussed in Chapter 4, *Customizing Look and Feel*.

Another thing about look and feel is that osCommerce categories do not use images, but in Zen Cart, you can use images for categories. Assign these icon images for categories.

When you import categories from osCommerce, they do not have images assigned. For a consistent look with other Zen Cart categories, you need to add the category images manually. The following picture shows that only the Fisher Price category shows an image, which has been added manually. But other categories shown have no images, as they have not been imported from osCommerce.

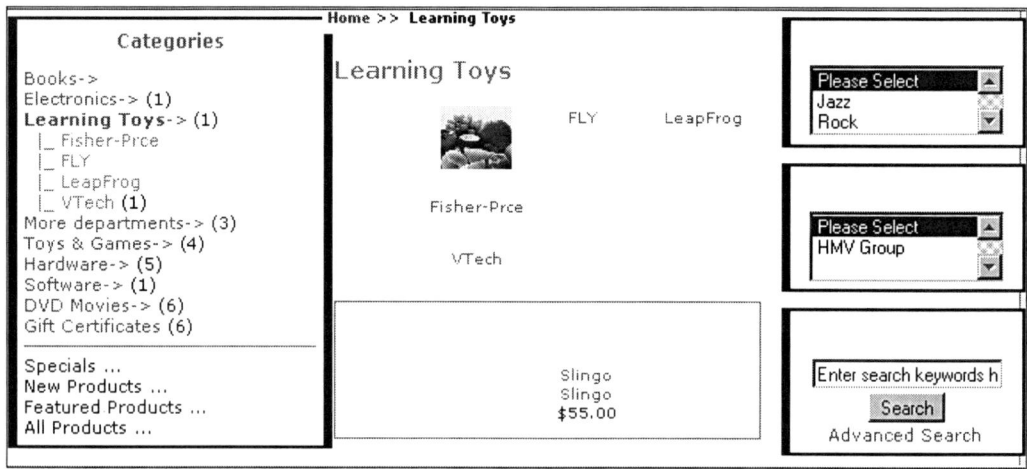

Also, you have to move the product images to the appropriate directories. In Zen Cart, product images can be stored in separate sub-directories. But in osCommerce, no subdirectory can be used. You have to put all osCommerce product images into your Zen Cart product image folder's root that is, in the `images` directory. So, move the images from the osCommerce's `images` directory to Zen Cart's `images` directory. Then the products will display pictures as shown in the following screenshot:

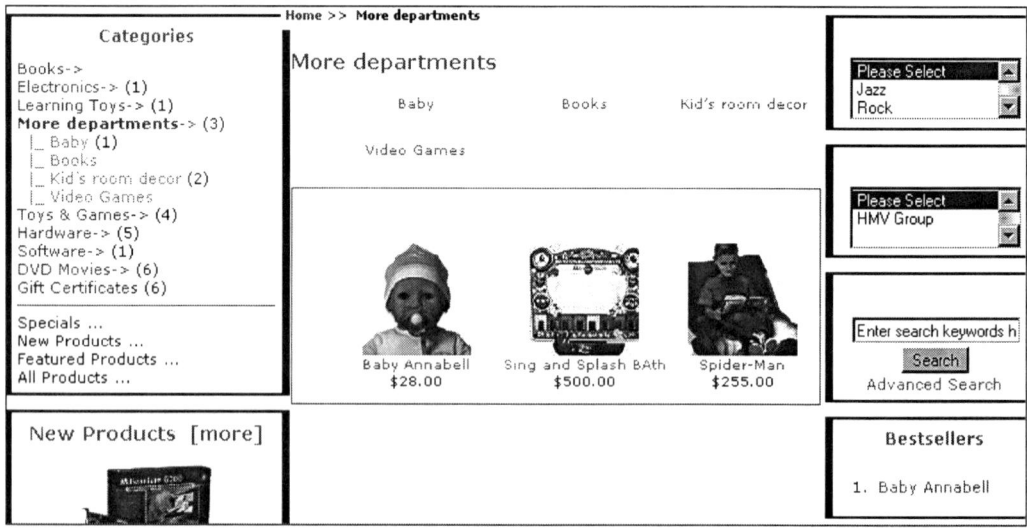

Converting osCommerce Modules

In Chapter 1, *Introduction to Zen Cart*, we discussed some programmatic differences between osCommerce and Zen Cart. These programmatic differences prevent osCommerce modules from working with Zen Cart. If you want to use a osCommerce module in Zen Cart, you need to modify that module first. There are a few general rules for converting osCommerce code to Zen Cart code. You must follow the rules of conversion.

Most of the essential modules are available on the Zen Cart website for your download. Before trying to convert any osCommerce module, first check the Zen Cart website and search for equivalent or alternative modules. Converting an osCommerce module may be your last resort. However, you are always encouraged to do so if you really want to learn how Zen Cart modules work, and if you have enough time to invest in it.

First, osCommerce uses the `tep_db_query()` and `tep_db_fetch_array()` functions to run queries on a database and assign the query results to some variable or array. You will find some codes like this:

```
$my_var_query = tep_db_query("query stuff");
$my_var = tep_db_fetch_array($my_var_query);
```

In the first line, the query result has been assigned to the `$my_var_query` variable. It seems that the query result will be a scalar variable. But for the second line, the result is expected to be an array and will be assigned to `$my_var`. For running queries in Zen Cart, the `$db->Execute()` function is used. So, whenever you see lines like the above code, replace them with something like the following:

```
$my_var = $db->Execute("query stuff");
```

Remember that in Zen Cart, one statement is enough for both scalar and array variables. You do not need to use different functions such as `tep_db_fetch_array()` just for the arrays.

In osCommerce, both the `tep_db_query()` and `tep_db_fetch_array()` functions are used with `if` and `while` statements to loop through the results. You will often find the following codes in osCommerce:

```
$my_var_query = tep_db_query("query stuff");
if ($my_var = tep_db_fetch_array($my_var_query))  {
    do_stuff;
}
```

and

```
$my_var_query = tep_db_query("query stuff");
while ($my_var = tep_db_fetch_array($my_var_query)) {
    do_stuff;
}
```

As Zen Cart does not use those functions, you have to rewrite the above codes as follows:

```
$my_var = $db->Execute("query stuff");
if (!$my_var->EOF)  {
 do_stuff;
}
```

and

```
$my_var = $db->Execute("query stuff");
while (!$my_var->EOF) {
    do_stuff;
    $my_var->MoveNext();
}
```

Note that, in both cases, you have used `!$my_var->EOF`, which means that until you reach the end of the variable, you have to execute the following instructions.

There is also a difference in referencing query fields. In osCommerce, query fields are referenced as follows:

```
$my_var_query = tep_db_query("query stuff");
$my_var = tep_db_fetch_array($my_var_query);
$i = $my_var['db_key'];
```

In Zen Cart, you have to reference the query field as follows:

```
$i = $my_var->fields['db_key'];
```

In osCommerce, the number of rows is returned by the `tep_db_num_rows($my_var)` function. In Zen Cart, you simply use `$my_var->RecordCount()`. For a new insert id, osCommerce uses the `tep_db_insert_id()` function, whereas Zen Cart uses a simple `$db->Insert_ID()` function. Another difference is in declaring `$db`. In Zen Cart, for every function you have to declare `global $db`, as all functions refer to `$db`.

In osCommerce, the session id is referenced by `$osCid`, which must be changed to `$zen_session_id()` in Zen Cart. Also, change all the `tep_` prefixes in the remaining functions to the `zen_` prefixes in Zen Cart.

osCommerce uses registered globals which Zen Cart does not. Instead, Zen Cart uses $_SESSION superglobal. For every registered globals $var, replace it with $_SESSION['var']. Also replace all $HTTP_x_VARS with $_x in Zen Cart. For example, $HTTP_POST_VARS will be $_POST, and $HTTP_GET_VARS will be $_GET. You also need to remove any global $HTTP_x_VARS declaration inside the functions, because new superglobals do not need a global declaration.

These are the changes you need to make to an osCommerce module port into Zen Cart. However, simply importing products from osCommerce to Zen Cart will not need conversion of modules, as Zen Cart has most of the essential modules needed for the online store.

Common Problems during Migration

You may face some problems during migration, most of which are related to the export/import of data. These problems occur when there is a mismatch in your data fields, or there is some existing data with the same primary keys.

As we have discussed earlier, it is more difficult to import data from osCommerce to a Zen Cart shop when it has some categories and products. In this case, you have to ensure that the primary keys for the categories and products tables are unique. Otherwise, conflicts will arise during import. Possible ways to avoid these unique id conflicts are discussed earlier in this chapter.

There may be a problem in displaying products in the appropriate categories. Products in categories may be misplaced if products_id are not appropriately updated in the products_to_categories table. Entries in this table maintain relationships with the products and categories table. So be careful about maintaining these relationships while migrating from osCommerce to Zen Cart.

Summary

In this chapter, you have learned about migrating from osCommerce to Zen Cart. First, you learned about the various scenarios in which you may need to migrate, and points to be considered before migration. Then, you learned the differences between the osCommerce and Zen Cart database structures. Finally, we discussed the actual data migration from osCommerce to Zen Cart, converting osCommerce modules for Zen Cart, and common problems during migration. This chapter discussed only the migration of categories and products data, but other data on customers and orders can also be migrated similarly.

8

Integrating Zen Cart with Other CMS

There are various types of **Content Management Systems (CMS)** which are widely used for building and managing a website. Although Zen Cart is very good for running an online shop, it cannot be used for building a company website. Your organization may have a website running a CMS, and as you are going to open an online shop, you may need to integrate Zen Cart with that existing CMS.

In this chapter, you will learn:

- In which cases you can integrate Zen Cart with a CMS
- What you need to consider before integration
- What the basic principles of integration are
- How to integrate Zen Cart with popular CMSs

This chapter will give you the conceptual and practical know-how required to integrate Zen Cart with other CMS.

Why should you Integrate Zen Cart with CMS?

Every CMS has its own merits. If you consider the features of other CMSs, you will find a particular one that you like the most. After having tested so many CMSs you may be interested in getting all the best features of your favorite one. In spite of this, you may also need to add shop functionality to your existing website, or you may need more than a shop. You may be tempted to use the best CMS in order to have a better website and may want to start an online shop later. In these cases, you need to use both Zen Cart and a CMS.

The general principles of integrating web-applications are as follows:

- **Seamless integration**: The Integration of any two CMSs should be such that users see it as a single application. Both applications' look and feel and workings should be integrated to give this impression to the users.

- **Data integrity**: Data of both applications should be synchronized instantly. For example, when a user registers at a Zen Cart shop, the same user should be created or replicated to the other CMS. Attempts to synchronize databases by running periodic updates such as cron or scheduler applications should be avoided.

- **Integration codes should be as simple as possible**: For all integration attempts, code should be minimized. This will help maintain the code as well as develop the integration quickly.

- **No forking**: All the applications should maintain their own code and should support their own upgrade path. The core files for the applications should not be modified. Instead, attempts should be made to develop some plug-ins for which code will be maintained separately.

The following sections illustrate some scenarios where you may need to integrate Zen Cart with a CMS.

A Well Established Site Starts a Shop

You may have been running a website for a long time and now you may want to sell products from this site. As you want to sell products directly from your site, you may think of adding Zen Cart.

In real life, it is most likely that your organization will establish a website first, to prove its online presence. When the website becomes popular and your organization observes the benefits of the website, it may be tempted to start an online shop. If the website has been established for a long time, it becomes branded for your company. Switching over from that site may become harder due to various other reasons. Now, you may want to start the online shop and integrate that shop with the existing site with a similar look and feel.

Increase the Scope of Your Shop

Zen Cart or osCommerce is well suited for running an online shop. But in some cases, you may want to establish a site which is more than a shop. Suppose that you are producing e-books and selling those in a Zen Cart shop. Now you think that adding a blog will be appropriate as authors will be able to write articles on their favorite topics, and these articles will add value to the e-books you publish.

In that case, keeping the online shop intact, you have to establish a blog. From your experience, you know that WordPress is feature-rich and will meet your expectations. Now the challenge is to integrate Zen Cart with WordPress. You have to integrate these two so that customers think that the blog and the shop are the same site—it is crucial for your web branding.

Single Sign-in Benefits

One of the benefits of integrating one or more CMS or shopping carts is a single sign-in facility. A single sign-in provides users with the benefit of having logged into one CMS and use the other CMS without logging in again. If we integrate Zen Cart with some other CMS, it may happen that logging in into either Zen Cart or the CMS will allow you to use both Zen Cart and that CMS. You may want to integrate both Zen Cart and the existing CMS to give a single sign-in facility to your visitors.

How to Integrate with CMS?

While attempting integration of one CMS with another, some simple principles should be remembered. For all integration attempts, you have to consider the following aspects:

- **Master–slave relationship**: While integrating one CMS with the other, one of the applications act as the master and the other as the slave. If you integrate application A to application B, then application B will be considered as master. Master applications maintain authentication and sessions for both applications. While integrating Zen Cart with some other CMS, first consider whether Zen Cart will be the master or the slave. If you are integrating Zen Cart with an existing website, Zen Cart is going to be the slave. On the other hand, when you are adding blogging functionality to the Zen Cart shop by integrating WordPress with Zen Cart, Zen Cart is going to be the master.

- **User and Group Management**: One purpose of integrating two CMSs is to have a common user and group management system. Zen Cart integration may be tight, where both Zen Cart and an other CMS will use the same database for user and group management. On the other hand, loose integration will allow periodic or event-based synchronization of user or group databases. Tight integration becomes easier when both CMSs use the same type of user database. If the user databases are very different from each other, then tight integration may not be possible and some sort of fallback solution such as synchronizing the databases may be used.

- **Visual integration**: Users see the integration only through the visual integration. In fact, visual integration should be such that users will be unaware of integration attempt. While integrating the two CMSs, the visual template of the master should preferably be used for both CMSs. However, using a master's template system is difficult and a central template system should be developed which can be used for both applications.

Now, we will see how to integrate Zen Cart with other CMSs. You will notice that at least one of the above-mentioned aspects is present in such integrations.

Joomla!/Mambo

If you are using Joomla!/Mambo and want e-commerce functionality, you have a number of choices. Among these, the best one is using the **VirtueMart** component. The VirtueMart component for Joomla!/Mambo is quite similar to Zen Cart or osCommerce. Only a few features of Zen Cart or osCommerce are missing in VirtueMart. However, if you still want to integrate Zen Cart into the existing Joomla!/Mambo website, you have two options—and neither is easier than the other: Use Zen Cart as a wrapper or, develop a component based on Zen Cart.

Using Zen Cart as a wrapper is in its true sense not an integration. It runs separately and Joomla! provides a menu link. Clicking on this link will show Zen Cart in a wrapper window. If you are experienced with Joomla! or Mambo, you can figure out how a menu item can be added to show the application in a wrapper. However, adding a wrapper may appear to be an integration if you modify the Zen Cart template accordingly. As the Zen Cart shop appears in the wrapper, it would be wise not to use headers and sidebars in the Zen Cart template. Links to the categories and other menus can be provided in the headers. A separate login mechanism should also be provided in the Zen Cart template.

Developing a bridge for Zen Cart and Joomla! is a hot topic in the Zen Cart forum. Users of both Joomla! and Zen Cart agree that integration or bridging of these two will be of great value. However, due to the framework of these two systems, developing such a bridge has some complexities and takes some time. Recently, a discussion on this topic has led to the development of such a bridge by the open-source enthusiasts. Please watch the following thread: http://tinyurl.com/65ypyu.

Another possibility is JFusion plug-in for Joomla! (available at www.jfusion.org) which is a framework for integrating several forums to Joomla!. The developer of JFusion has proposed developing such a plug-in for Zen Cart as well. It is hoped that JFusion will be able to integrate Zen Cart to Joomla! soon.

Drupal

Drupal is a powerful CMS and is widely used. There are a wide range of modules available for Drupal and it is used for different types of websites. There are a great number of Drupal users who want to integrate Drupal and Zen Cart—as both are considered useful in their category. Until recently, there was no easy way to integrate Drupal and Zen Cart. Very recently, Zen Cart Integration module has been released as a development version. For now, it works on Drupal 5.x and Zen Cart 1.3.7. Once this module is installed and configured, you can create Zen Cart categories and products from Drupal. As other nodes, these products and categories will be displayed as nodes in Drupal. When visitors click on these products they see product details as a Drupal node, but when the product is added to cart, it redirects to the Zen Cart shop. This module also provides a single sign-on facility.

For integrating Zen Cart into Drupal, download the module from `http://drupal. org/project/zencart`. Before we proceed with the integration of Drupal and Zen Cart, assume that you have installed Drupal and Zen Cart on the same server. Let us suppose, Drupal is installed in `e:\www\drupal57` directory and Zen Cart 1.3.7 is in `e:\www\zc` directory, and these two uses separate database on the same MySQL server.

Follow these steps:

1. **Download and unzip Zen Cart integration module**: For integrating Zen Cart into Drupal, download the module from `http://drupal.org/project/ zencart`. On your computer, unzip the `zencart-5.x-1.x-dev.tar.gz` package. You will get a folder named `zencart`, under which there are some files and a subfolder named `zencart`.

2. **Copy files for Zen Cart**: Inside the `zencart` subfolder you will find the `includes` folder. Copy this subfolder, that is `/zencart/includes`, to your Zen Cart installation directory, that is `e:\www\zc`. This will overwrite the `e:\www\zc\includes` directory, but will not overwrite any files. Once you have copied all the files in this folder, you are finished with Zen Cart.

3. **Install Zen Cart installation module in Drupal**: Copy the `zencart` directory with all the files inside it, except the `zencart` subfolder, to Drupal's installation directory, that is `e:\www\drupal57`. As an administrator in Drupal, you can install this module from Drupal's **Administer | Site Building | Modules** section. In the module list you will see the **Zen Cart Integration** module group. You will find the following modules in this group:

   - **Zencart**—This is the main module for integrating Zen Cart shopping cart to Drupal. This is required by other modules in this group.

- **Zencart Catalog** — This module allows creation of Drupal nodes for Zen Cart products and categories.
- **Zencart Category Node Hierarchy** — This module depends on the Node Hierarchy module and organizes Zen Cart products and categories. Download the Node Hirarchy module from `http://drupal.org/ project/nodehierarchy` and install it before enabling this module.

To enable these modules, select checkboxes in **Enabled** column and click **Save configuration** button at the bottom of the list.

Zencart Integration

Enabled	Throttle	Name	Version	Description
☑	☐	**Zencart**	5.x-1.x-dev	Module to integrate Zencart shopping cart with Drupal. You must have version 1.3 of Zencart installed - http://zencart.org Required by: Zencart Catalog (enabled), Zencart Catalog Node Hierarchy (enabled), Zencart Users (enabled)
☑	☐	**Zencart Catalog**	5.x-1.x-dev	Module to allow creation of Drupal nodes which are Zen Cart products and categories. Depends on: Zencart (enabled) Required by: Zencart Catalog Node Hierarchy (enabled)
☑	☐	**Zencart Catalog Node Hierarchy**	5.x-1.x-dev	Module to use yhe Node Hierarchy module to organize the Zen Cart Catalog. Depends on: Zencart (enabled), Zencart Catalog (enabled), Node Hierarchy (enabled)
☑	☐	**Zencart Users**	5.x-1.x-dev	Module to integrate Zencart and Drupal users. Allows login accross tools. Depends on: Zencart (enabled)

4. **Configure Zencart Integration module in Drupal:** After enabling the modules, you can configure those from **Administer | Site Configuration | Zencart Integration** screen.

Zencart Integration

▷ Zencart status

▽ Zencart settings

Path to Zencart:

e:\www\zc

Enter the full directory path where the Zencart installation.

▷ Zencart Page Redirects

▽ Zen Cart Catalog

☐ Update product info on cron

If this is checked, price, weight and stock info for products will be copied from the Zencart DB to the Drupal DB whenever cron is run. Leave this checked if you plan to edit product info through the Zencart admin tool (using the Zencart Salemaker, for example). You can also Click here to sync manually whenever you make a change with the Zencart admin tool.

☑ Redirect Product Info Pages

Automatically redirect Zencart product info pages to their Drupal equivalents.

The **Zencart Integration** screen has the following sections:

- The **Zen Cart Status** section will provide you information about your Zen Cart installation. The module will search and find the Zen Cart installation and show its version, path to Drupal installation and other information.

- The **Zen Cart Settings** section will give you the opportunity to mention the Zen Cart installation directory path. Type it into the **Path to Zencart** field.

- The **Zen Cart Page Redirects** section allows you to configure page redirects from the Zen Cart page to Drupal node.

- **Zen Cart Catalog** section allows you to configure redirect from the Zen Cart catalog items to Drupal. While using this integration module, you create Zen Cart catalog and products from Drupal. If you want to create these categories and products from inside Zen Cart and synchronize those with Drupal, then check **Update product info on cron**. This will synchronize product information both on Drupal and Zen Cart by running **cron** command on linux/unix. Checking **Redirect Product Info Pages** will automatically redirect visitors from the Zen Cart product info pages to equivalent Drupal nodes. Similarly, checking **Redirect Category Listing Pages** will automatically redirect visitors from the Zen Cart category pages to equivalent Drupal nodes.

- The **Zen Cart Users** section allows you to configure single sign-on options for Drupal and Zen Cart. If you want to allow Zen Cart existing customers to login to Drupal, then check the **Allow Zen Cart Customers to login to Drupal** checkbox. On the other hand, if you want to allow Drupal users to login to Zen Cart as customers, check **Allow Drupal Users Customers to login to Zen Cart as Customers**. Checking **Allow Single Sign-On** will allow users to login once and access both Drupal and Zen Cart.

Once you have configured these options, click the **Save configuration** button, or revert to defaults by clicking the **Reset to defaults** button.

5. **Create Content Type in Drupal for Zen Cart categories and products**: If you have ever used Drupal, you know how to create content types in Drupal. You can add new content type from **Administer | Content Management | Content types | Add content type**. Now you will get a Zen Cart Catalog group. From this section you can define whether this type will be used as a Zen Cart product or category. You can also configure node hierarchy— ability to be parent or child (default is parent). In the **Identification** section, type a human readable name, for example Zen Cart Product, in the Name field. Then type a machine readable name of this content type, for example zc_product, in the Type field. Provide a description of this content type in the **Description** field.

   In the **Submission Form** section, provide a label for the title and body field, minimum number of words, and explanation or submission guidelines. Configure default options in the Workflow section. Finally, click the **Save** content type button.

   Create two content types—one for the Zen Cart category and another for the Zen Cart product.

6. **Add Category and Product in Drupal:** You can create categories and products from **Create Content** section. In the list, click on **Zen Cart Category**. This will open **Submit Zen Cart Category** form. In this form, type the category name in **Title** field, type a description of this category in **Body** field. In the **Node Hierarchy** section, you can select a parent category. Check **Category is Active** to make this category visible. Configure other options like **Menu settings**, **URL path settings**, **Publishing options**, and so on and click the **Submit** button to create the category.

Similarly, you can create Zen Cart products by clicking on the **Zen Cart Product** content type. This will display the **Submit Zen Cart Product** form.

Home > Create content

Submit Zen Cart Product

Title: *

Zencart Product Information

Product Model #:

Quantity In Stock:

Tax Class:
Taxable Goods ▼

Base Price:

☐ Product is Free

☐ Product is "Call for Quote"

☐ Product is Priced by Attributes

☑ Show Quantity Box

Minimum Order Quantity:
0

Maximum Order Quantity:
0

Fill in the **Submit Zen Cart Product** form with appropriate information, such as product name, model, quantity in stock, tax class, base price, and so on. You can select its parent category in the **Node Hierarchy** section. Check the **Create Menu** option to make a menu item for this product. Configure other options like **Menu settings**, **URL path settings**, **Publishing options**, and so on and click the **Submit** button to create the product.

7. **Test Zen Cart Integration to and from Drupal:** Now it is time to test whether the Drupal-Zen Cart integration is working or not. First, go to your Zen Cart shop, for example, `http://localhost/zc`. There you will find the categories and products you have added. Click on any of these, and you will be redirected to the respective Drupal node. Again, in the Drupal, click on a product link, type a quantity and click the **Add to Cart** button. That will redirect you to the Zen Cart shop's **Your Shopping Cart Contents** page.

Similarly you can test single sign-on features by signing in to either Drupal or Zen Cart and trying to purchase items from these two shops.

Gallery 2

Gallery2 is a web-based software product that lets you manage photos on your own website. It creates a catalog of photos which visitors can view as thumbnails as well as in its original size. It has an intuitive interface to create and maintain albums. It can create thumbnails automatically and can be used for image resizing, rotation, ordering, captioning, searching, and some other functions.

You can use Gallery2 to build a community site for sharing photos. You can create the community using Gallery2 and registered users can share their photographs by uploading their own photos.

You need to integrate Gallery2 with Zen Cart if you want to sell photos from your photo gallery. Gallery2 has a great mechanism to integrate with Zen Cart. The Gallery2/Zen Cart integration module is available at the Gallery2 download site `http://dakanji.com/g2stuff/zcg2-3_2_1a-full.zip`. Using it, users can organize their photos and other multimedia files into Gallery2, and offer them for sale through Zen Cart.

In integrating Gallery2 with Zen Cart, you have to configure Zen Cart first. Follow these steps for Zen Cart:

1. Download the **Gallery2/Zen Cart Integration** module and extract it.

2. Copy the `zencart/includes` folder into your Zen Cart installation directory. This directory contains some templates for Zen Cart. Copying these files will not overwrite any existing file.

3. Login to your Zen Cart administration panel and create a new product category, such as **Photographs**. Photo items from Gallery2 will go to this category.

4. Select **Tools | Template Selection** and choose one of the Gallery2 Integration templates provided. You can take a copy of the template folder (`../includes/templates/pgxxx`) and modify `stylesheet.css`. You can modify these templates as described in Chapter 4, *Customizing Look and Feel*.

5. Edit `../includes/languages/pgxxx/english.php` if you want to change language strings or date formats.

6. Replace `../includes/templates/pgxxx/images/logo.gif` with your site's logo.

Remember that for Gallery2/Zen Cart integration, both Zen Cart and Gallery2 data tables need to be in one database.

In Gallery2, you need to make the following changes:

1. Upload the module files in the `gallery2/` directory to your Gallery2 installation's modules directory.

2. In Gallery2 Site Administration, click on **Plugins** and find **Zen Cart** under the **Commerce** heading. Then click **Install**.

3. After Installation, click **Configure**.

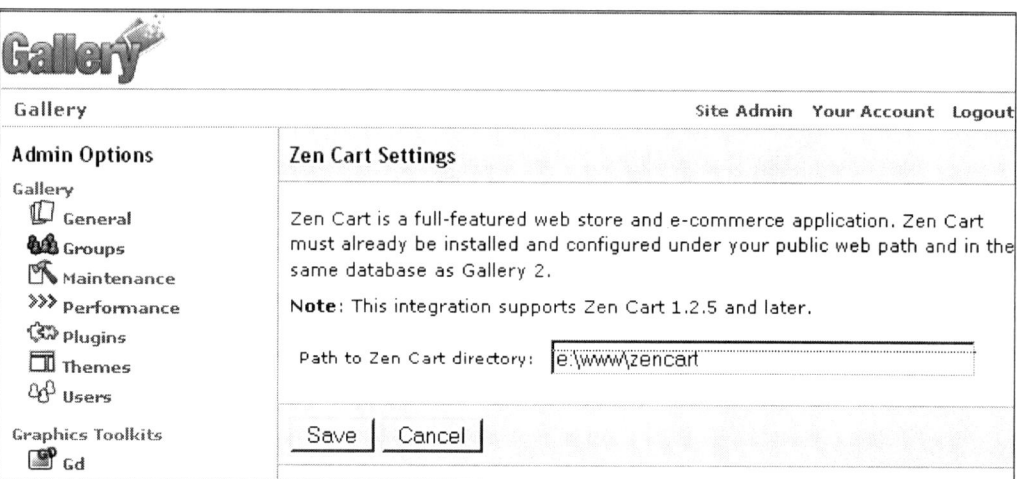

3. Enter the entire server path to your Zen Cart installation, for example, `/home/your_name/public_html/zencart/`.

4. Select the category you created in Zen Cart earlier (for example **Photographs**) from the drop-down menu.

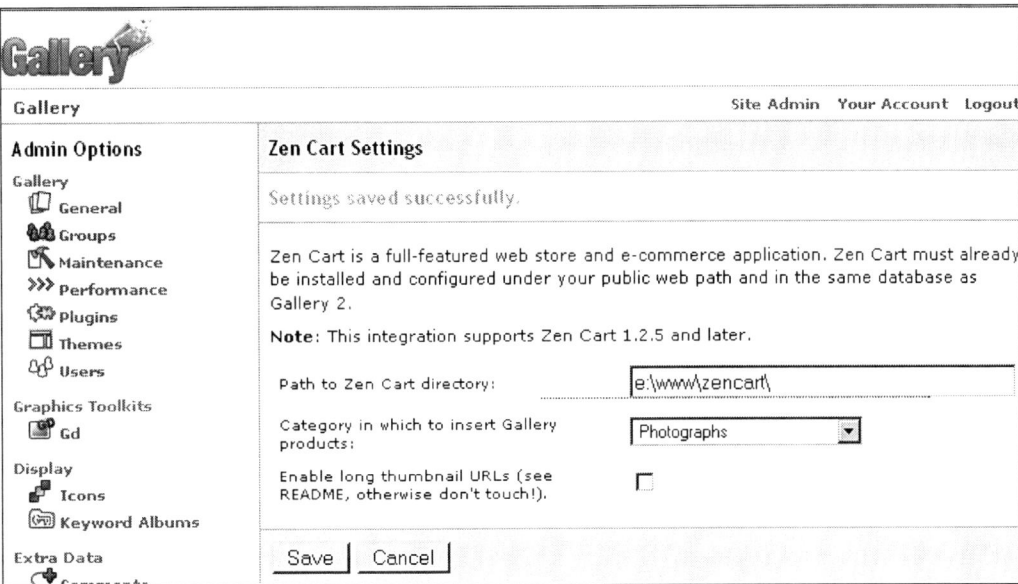

5. Click **activate** next to the Zen Cart listing on the module page.

6. Refresh the page and click on the Zen Cart link under **Admin Options** to edit product details.

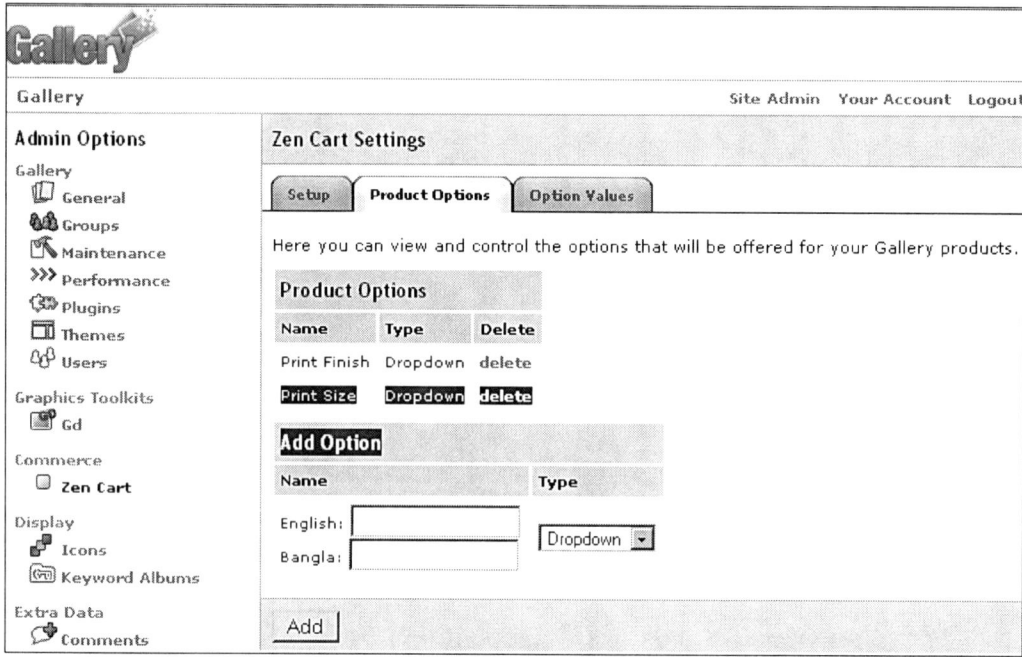

6. Edit permissions for the individual items as you wish. The module will have assigned permissions to non-album items on activation.

If you do not want to sell an item, you will need to disable that item in Zen Cart as the module adds all data items in your gallery to Zen Cart.

You can add photograph items from Gallery2. Adding any item to the Gallery2 album will simply show that item in Zen Cart. You can add product options from Gallery2 by clicking on the Zen Cart link in your Gallery2 site administration menu.

When you have installed the Gallery2/Zen Cart bridge, you will find a product type in Zen cart named **Product-Gallery**. All the items from Gallery2 need to be of this type. If you edit any item from Zen Cart and change the product type of any Gallery2 item, the link with the Gallery2 will be broken. Also, note that the Gallery2 bridge will co-exist with Zen Cart image handler and lightbox add-on for Zen Cart. These will handle product images for Zen Cart, whereas Gallery2 add-on only handles images added in Gallery2.

You cannot assign the **Main** category in Zen Cart as the root product category for Gallery2. The category you are selecting in the Gallery2 bridge configuration must be a sub-category product.

Once the configurations are done, you can see the photographs from Zen Cart. Visitors can also order photographs from Zen Cart. While you are in Gallery2, you can also place an order by clicking the **add to cart** link, which is redirected to Zen Cart.

WordPress

WordPress is an extremely powerful and widely used open-source blogging platform. It has a wide community of developers and users, and almost all kinds of plugins are available for it. Although there are some shopping cart plugins for WordPress, they are not full-blown shopping carts like Zen Cart or osCommerce. E-commerce plug-ins available for WordPress have limited features.

Those who are running blogs using WordPress may want to integrate it with Zen Cart to provide e-commerce functionality to their blogs. In fact, there is a Zen Cart module for integrating these two. You can download that module from www.zen-cart.com.

After downloading the plug-in **WordPress on Zen Cart**, you have to install it on the webserver. You can install the plug-in in two ways: first, in an environment where you have a working WordPress installation, and second, when you have not installed WordPress.

WordPress and Zen Cart Installed in Separate Directories

When you have an existing installation of WordPress, generally it will be in a separate directory from that of the Zen Cart installation. If your web document root directory is public_html, then the installation directories may be: /public_html/blog and /public_html/shop. Follow these procedures to install WordPress on Zen Cart plug-in:

Step1: Install WordPress

If you have not installed WordPress yet, then download the WordPress files from `www.wordpress.org` and unzip the files. Then, upload the files to your webserver's `/public_html/blog` directory. Now, change the permission of this directory to 777 and point your browser to `http://yourdomain.com/blog/wp-admin/setup-config.php`. The installation wizard for WordPress will be displayed. Follow the instructions on the wizard and give the necessary information. Once all of the information is given, WordPress will be installed.

Step 2: Configure WordPress

During installation, an administrative account will be created. Note the username and password for this account. Then, point your browser to `http://yourdomain.com/blog/wp-admin/`. The login page will be displayed. Type the username and password for the administrative account and click on the **Login** button.

You will see the dashboard for administering WordPress. Go to **Options | General**. Now, change the Blog Address (URL) to Zen Cart's URL `http://yourdomain.com/shop/`. From the administration dashboard, go to **Presentation | Themes** and select **WordPress Default 1.6**.

Step 3: Upload WordPress on Zen Cart

When you unzip the WordPress on Zen Cart plug-in zip file, you will find that there is a directory called `ZC_ROOT` and `WP_ROOT`. Now, upload the contents of `ZC_ROOT` directory to Zen Cart's installation path on the server, that is, `/public_html/shop/`. Similarly, upload the contents of the `WP_ROOT` directory to WordPress' installation path, that is, `/public_html/blog`. Before uploading the contents of the `ZC_ROOT` directory, please change the name of the `/ZC_ROOT/includes/templates/MY_TEMP/` directory to that of the template directory you are using for your Zen Cart shop.

Step 4: Edit WordPress File

For older versions of WordPress, you may need to edit the `/wp-include/template-loader.php` file. Open the file in a text editor and replace all `exit;` with `return;`. However, you may not need this for the newer versions of WordPress. WordPress 2.3.1 can work without this modification. First, try without this modification.

Step 5: Edit Zen Cart File

You also need to edit another file in the Zen Cart installation. Open the `/includes/extra_configures/wordpress-config.php` file under the Zen Cart installation folder and find the following line:

```
define ('ABSPATH','/var/www/vhost/example.com/public_html/blog/');
```

Type the appropriate WordPress path, that is, `/home/username/public_html/blog/`. The above line will look like this:

```
define ('ABSPATH','/home/suhreed/public_html/blog/');
```

If you are trying it on Windows, you may need to put the absolute path, as in, `e:/www/blog`.

Step 6: Configure Sideboxes from Layout Boxes Controller

Once the file modifications have been done, login to the Zen Cart administration panel. Go to **Tools | Layout Boxes Controller**. The screen will notify you that some new sideboxes—`wp_cats.php`, `wp_archives.php`, `wp_pages.php`, `wp_links.php`, and `wp_sidebar.php`—have been found. To use these sidebars, click on the **reset** button at the bottom. To show these sideboxes on your Zen Cart shop, click on the sidebar and change its left/right column status.

Step 7: Test your Integration

Now, it's your time to see how the Zen Cart and WordPress integration works. Point your browser to your Zen Cart shop, that is, `http://yourdomain.com/shop/`. If everything is ok, you will find the screen as shown in the following screenshot:

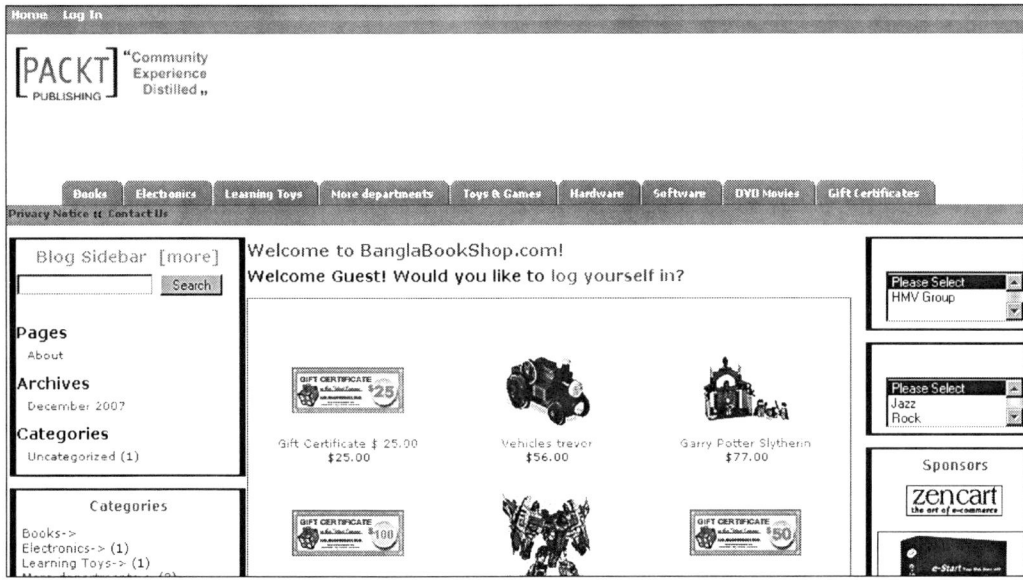

If the **ABSPATH** value in `wordpress-config.php` file is not entered appropriately, you will get a message saying that `wp-config.php` file in a particular path is not found. In that case, edit the `wordpress-config.php` file and enter the correct path to the WordPress installation.

Note that a left sidebox named **Blog Sidebar** is shown in your Zen Cart shop. You will find links to pages in the blog, links to archives, and links to categories. Click on a link and that category, archive or page will be displayed.

You may be disappointed when you look at the result because the whole WordPress page with headers, footers, and sidebars is displayed. If you have some knowledge of customizing WordPress themes, you can work out a nice solution by removing the header, the footer, and the sidebar from the theme layout.

> For learning WordPress theming, check the excellent tutorials at
> www.wordpress.org. You can also read *WordPress Themes*,
> published by Packt.

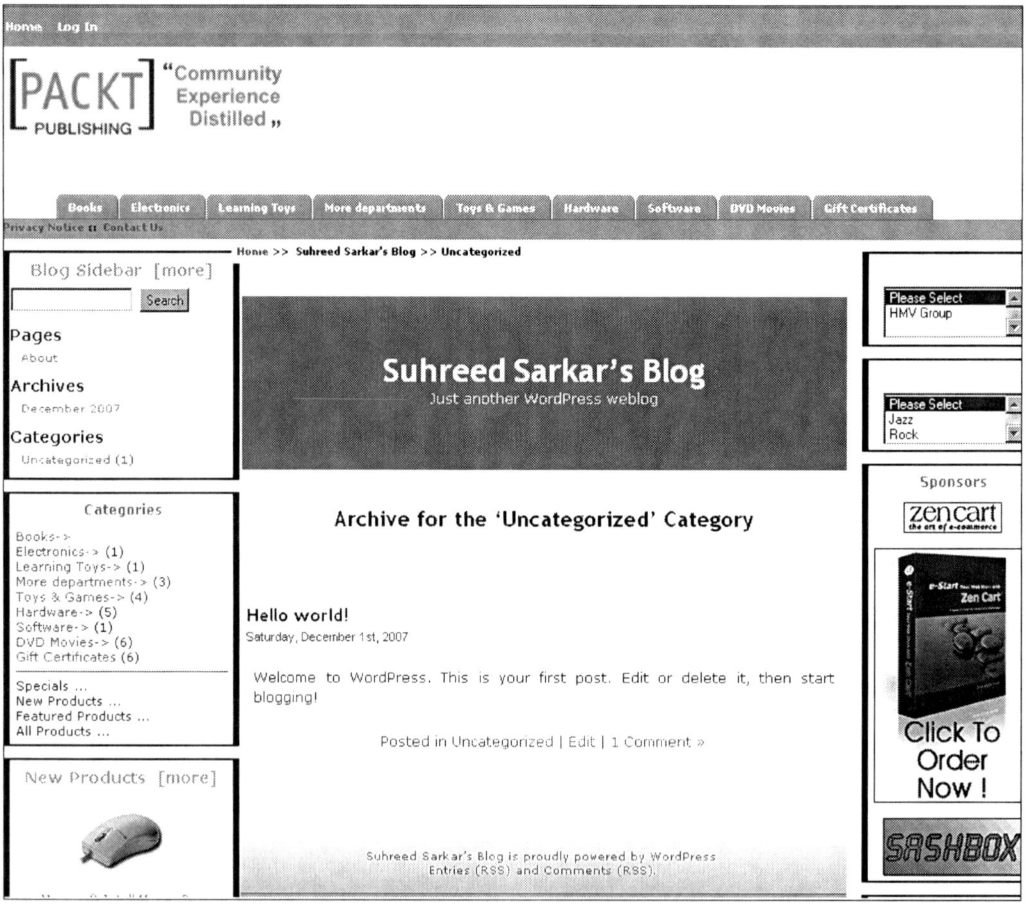

WordPress and Zen Cart Installed in the Same Directory

You can also install WordPress and Zen Cart in the same directory. In such a case, install Zen Cart first. Configure it for normal use, and then proceed with the installation of WordPress. For example, if your Zen Cart installation is in `/public_html/shop/`, then WordPress will also be installed at `/public_html/shop/`. First, download the WordPress installation package, unzip it, and upload all files, except `index.php`.

After uploading the files to the Zen Cart directory, i.e. `/public_html/blog/`, change the access permission of these to 777. Now, point your browser to `http://yourdomain.com/shop/wp-admin/setup-config.php`. The installation wizard for WordPress will be displayed. Follow the instructions of the wizard and provide the necessary information. Once all information is made available, WordPress will be installed.

Now, follow Steps 2 to 7 as described in the previous section. In this case, the paths to Zen Cart and WordPress will be same.

[ When you use other themes, it is necessary to revise the header of the WordPress theme, a footer, a sidebar, and a style sheet.]

XOOPS

XOOPS is a CMS written in PHP. It uses a modular architecture allowing users to customize, update, and theme their websites. XOOPS is an acronym of **eXtensible Object Oriented Portal System**. It aims to serve as a web framework for use by small, medium, and large sites through the installation of modules. For example, a small XOOPS installation can be used as a personal weblog or journal, but this can be expanded upon and customized. For example, users might add the appropriate modules (freeware and commercial) to store content in news, forums, downloads, and more.

If you have a XOOPS-based website and want to add e-commerce functionality to that website, you can use Zen Cart with XOOPS. There is a Zen Cart XOOPS Integration module which can be used to integrate Zen Cart with XOOPS.

After downloading the module, upload the files to your XOOPS installation directory. Then, install it as a normal module for XOOPS. Ensure that the **Use custom session** value in **Preferences | System | General Settings** is on.

You need to change the permissions of some files and folders. CHMOD the following folders to 777:

- `shop/images`
- `shop/images/banners`
- `shop/images/categories/`
- `shop/images/uploads`
- `shop/blocks/cache/english`
- `shop/blocks/cache/additional_language`

The default admin URL for the Zen Cart shop will be `shop/admin` with username and password admin.

XOOPS Zen Cart has a built-in Zen Cart installation. Zen Cart files are included with this module and are installed as a module of XOOPS. This module has the following features:

- It integrates the languages of both XOOPS and Zen Cart. When selecting a language at the XOOPS site, Zen Cart's language is also changed. However, the same language needs to be installed in both XOOPS and Zen Cart. Extra language packs for Zen Cart can be downloaded from `www.zen-cart.com`.

- It also integrates the XOOPS theme with Zen Cart. The template applied to XOOPS site also applies to the Zen Cart shop. You can use the template variable `$isshop` to determine if the module is currently open through your theme.

- It also integrates blocks. You can select all the static sideboxes of Zen Cart which can be seen through the Zen Cart blocks. Once the blocks are assigned to show in Zen Cart blocks, these must be rebuilt in the Zen Cart XOOPS administration panel through **Tools | Layout Boxes Controller**.

- This module is based on Zen Cart v.1.2.7d and supports the feature of Zen Cart v.1.2.7d.

e107

e017 is a comparatively new CMS with lots of features, and ease of use. It has hundreds of plug-ins through which you can extend its capability. You will find a plug-in to bridge with Zen Cart too. Bridging through this plug-in is easier for the layperson.

This plug-in is available at: `http://plugins.e107.org/e107_plugins/psilo/ psilo.php?artifact.178`. Download it, unzip it and copy the `zencart_bridge` folder in your e107 installations `e107_plugins` folder. Then, install the plug-in from the administration panel's **Plugins | Plugin Manager**. You will see the list of installed and available plug-ins. Click on the **Install** button beside the **ZenCart Bridge** plug-in. It will be installed without any prompt.

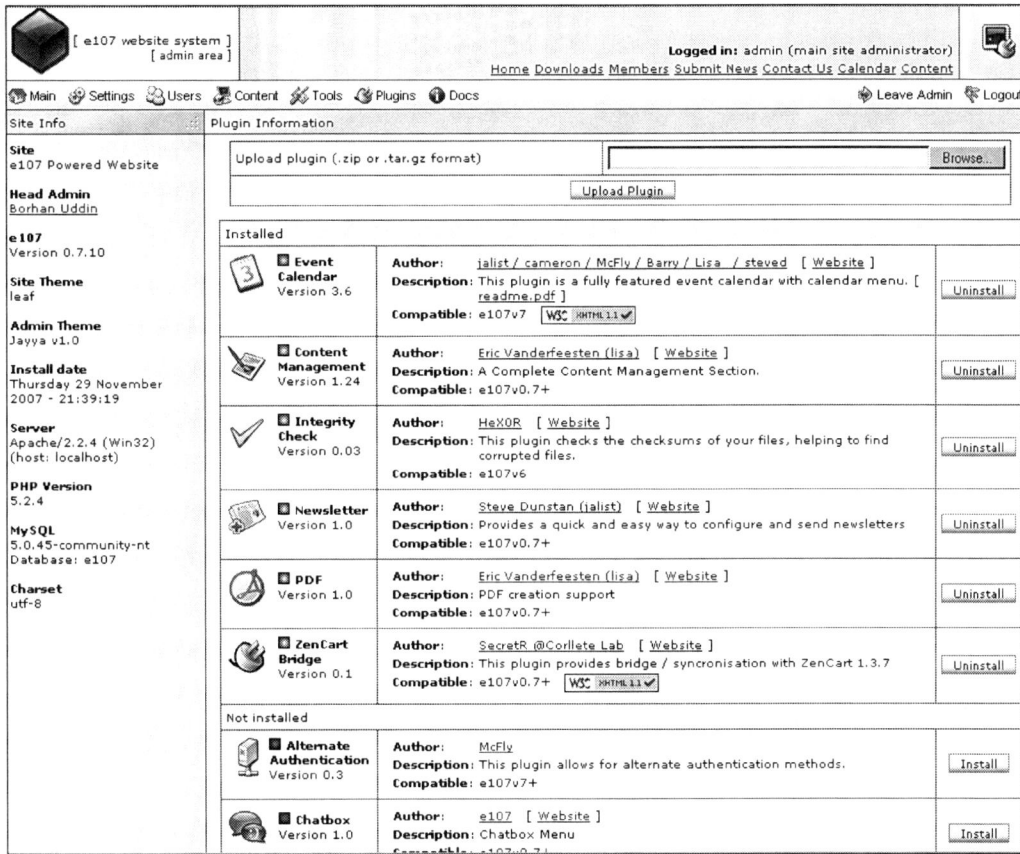

Once the Zen Cart bridge is installed, you will see the list of installed plug-ins in the main administration panel. You can also access configuration options by selecting **Plugins | ZenCart Bridge**. You have to configure the following options:

- **Try to create ZenCart user account on e107 signup event:** Selecting **Yes** will create a Zen Cart user account when a user registers on e107 CMS.

- **Try to update existent ZenCart user account when found on e107 signup event:** Select **Yes** if you want to update the existing user account in Zen Cart when a user registers with the same name in e107. For example, suppose that a user registers with the name 'borhan' in e107, and Zen Cart has an account named 'borhan'. Zen Cart bridge will update user 'borhan' in Zen Cart. If the password chosen for e107 user is different from that of the Zen Cart user password, the password in Zen Cart will be changed for that user.

- **Try to update existing ZenCart user account on e107 profile update event** (Zen Cart password will be synchronized only if the user changes his or her e107 password): Select **Yes** if you want to update the Zen Cart user profile from e107. Whenever a user in e107 changes profile information, including password, the user profile at Zen Cart will also be changed.

- **Go online—Try to synchronize e107 and ZenCart user sessions on e107 login/logout events:** Select **Yes** if you want to keep e107 and Zen Cart user databases synchronized always. Selecting **Yes** in this field will automatically synchronize user accounts when the user logs in or logs out from e107.

- **Synchronize e107 site admins as well:** Selecting **Yes** for this option will also synchronize administrative accounts in e107 with Zen Cart. If you want the administrators to be the same for both e107 and Zen Cart, select **Yes** in this field.

- **Gender:** This field indicates what will be the default value for the **Salutation** field in Zen Cart while synchronizing the accounts between e107 and Zen Cart. If the account in e107 does not have a gender indication, this default value will be used.

- **Disable ZenCart Newsletter (no matter the user's choice):** Both e107 and Zen Cart have newsletters. While registering, you may decide to use only e107 newsletters. Selecting **Yes** in this field will disable Zen Cart newsletters for the user accounts. Select **Yes** only when you use e107 newsletter for advertising your products.

- **Default value for missing Extended User fields:** If your e107 users have extended fields, specify the defaults for those.

The main configuration for bridging e107 and Zen Cart is configuring the database options. However, it is also automated, and can be used easily. You can configure the Zen Cart database connection from **Plugins | ZenCart Bridge | ZenCart Connection**.

ZenCart Connection	
DB Options	
Zencart server root path for auto-detection: The relative path from e107 root to the ZenCart root.	[auto-detect] *Example 1:* http://mysite.com/e107/ [e107] | http://mysite.com/zen/ [zenCart] => **../zen/** *Example 2:* http://mysite.com [e107] | http://mysite.com/zen/ [zenCart] => **zen/** *Example 3:* http://mysite.com/ [e107] | http://mysite.com/ [zenCart] => **./** **ZenCart DB Connection status** OK
Host:	[ ]
User:	[ ]
Password:	[ ]
Database:	zencart
ZenCart Table Prefix:	[ ]
	Save

The following are the options for the database configuration:

- **ZenCart server root path for auto-detection**: You can use auto detection for Zen Cart database connection settings by mentioning the Zen Cart installation path. For example, if your Zen Cart installation is in the /shop directory of your webserver root, then you have to type http://yourserver.com/shop/ in this field. Then, click the **autodetect** button. It will locate the configuration.php file and read the database connection information from this file. Once it is detected, you are done.

- **Host**: If auto-detection does not work, type the database host name, for example, **localhost**, in this field.

- **User**: Type the database username in this field. This username will be used to connect to the database. So, make sure that this user has permission to do so.

- **Password**: Type the password used for the above user account.

- **Database**: Type the name of the database. If you are using cPanel and a shared Linux server, remember that the database names are prefixed with usernames. For example, if you have an account named bob, the database will be named **bob_zencart**.

- **ZenCart Table Prefix**: Your Zen Cart tables may use a prefix. If so, type the prefix in this field. Generally, for separate databases, table prefixes are not used. But when you are using the same database for separate CMSs, table prefixes, such as zen_ are used.

The Zen Cart Bridge works well with e107. However, it acts only as bridge. Using e107, users can also login and purchase products from the Zen Cart shop. This kind of bridge is good when you have kept the shop as a linked site with the e107 site.

 For better performance, it is suggested that you use the same database both for Zen Cart and e107. But, don't forget to use the zen_ prefix for the Zen Cart tables.

phpBB

phpBB is a bulletin board service for creating communities of common interest. This is widely used on the Internet, and I hope you have seen one or two by this time. You can integrate a phpBB bulletin board service with a Zen Cart shop. This can be done while you are installing Zen Cart.

If you want the forum or bulletin board service, download and install phpBB. You can download phpBB2 or phpBB3 from www.phpbb.com/downloads/. Install phpBB on the same server. Then, start installing Zen Cart. There will be a step asking you whether you want to integrate phpBB or not. Choose **Yes** in this screen, and then specify the phpBB directory path. This way, phpBB will be integrated to Zen Cart during installation.

If you do not integrate phpBB during the Zen Cart installation, you can do it at a later stage. Whenever you think that you need to add a forum to your shop, just install the phpBB forum and follow these instructions to integrate it with the Zen Cart shop.

1. Install phpBB and test whether it works properly. For ease of configuration, it is recommended that you install phpBB to the root of your server, perhaps like this:

   http://mysite.com/forums or http://mysite.com/phpbb.

2. Edit the `/includes/configure.php` file for Zen Cart and enter the path to your phpBB folder on this line:

   ```
   define('DIR_WS_PHPBB', '/phpBB2/');
   ```

   It needs to be the full exact path to your forum folder, including the `/var/www/client/public_html/` (or whatever it is on your server). Look at your **DIR_FS_CATALOG** for a hint, and then adjust by adding your phpBB or forum to that. Or it may be in a different folder. If it is in different folder, you can just mention `../phpBB2/`, or something similar. Remember to include the '/' at the end.

3. In Zen Cart's Admin area, go to **Configuration | My Store**, and set **Enable phpBB Linkage?** to **True**. Now, any new user created will be asked to select a forum username during signup.

Login Details

Email Address:	abu.hasan@suhreedsarkar.com	*
Forum Nick Name:	hasan	*
Password:	xxxxx	* (at least 5 characters)
Confirm Password:	xxxxx	*

Integration with phpBB means, when a user registers with Zen Cart, the same account is created on the phpBB. While creating an account on Zen Cart, the user is prompted to choose a nickname for the phpBB forum. Users can also see a link to the phpBB in the Information sidebox. Clicking on this link will take you to the phpBB forum where a user can login using his or her nickname and password.

Summary

In this chapter, we have learned about the integration of Zen Cart with other CMSs. We have discussed the necessity of integration, characteristics of successful integration, and ways to integrate CMS. Then, we have seen ways to integrate Zen Cart with other CMSs such as Drupal, WordPress, Gallery2, e107, and phpBB. Bridge or connectors are used for such integration. The development of such bridges or connectors for other CMSs such as Joomla! are under consideration. Keep an eye on those community forums for solutions.

In the next chapter, we are going to discuss maintenance and troubleshooting tasks in Zen Cart.

9
Maintenance and Troubleshooting

Maintenance and troubleshooting are important aspects for any web application. You need to perform some regular maintenance activities to keep your Zen Cart shop active, and trouble free. Sometimes, you also may face problems operating the shop. This chapter discusses maintenance and troubleshooting issues in Zen Cart. In this chapter, you will learn:

- How to backup and restore files and databases for Zen Cart
- How to harden security for Zen Cart
- How to solve common problems

Only common problems and troubleshooting techniques are discussed in this chapter. As a user of Zen Cart you may face different types of problems. For more information and solutions of such problems, the best place to raise the issues is Zen Cart Forum (`http://www.zen-cart.com/forum`). You may also consult the sites listed in the *Appendix*.

Website Maintenance Settings

Some maintenance activities to your Zen Cart online shop may interrupt its service. For example, when you are backing up or restoring databases and files, and installing and configuring some third-party contributions , the site may become unavailable to the customers, or it may be malfunctioning. Plan the maintenance activity in advance and schedule the activity for the time when the website traffic is expected to be minimal and the least number of customers will be affected.

Zen Cart has a built-in mechanism to notify visitors about scheduled maintenance. You can configure these settings in the administration panel from **Configuration | Website Maintenance**.

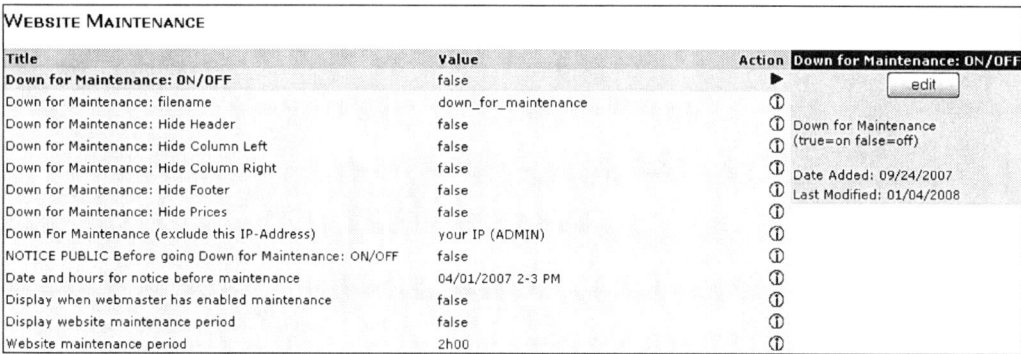

Taking the Shop Down for Maintenance

Whenever you want to do some maintenance, first take the shop offline. Click on **Down for Maintenance: ON/OFF** and set its value to **true**. Visitors to your site will then see a message on the front page about the maintenance.

Customizing for Maintenance Messages

By default, the name of the file displayed during maintenance is `down_for_ maintenance`. You can change the messages shown in this page by editing its language file, `/includes/languages/english/down_for_maintenance.php`. Its display can be customized by editing a corresponding template file `/includes/ templates/template_default/templates/tpl_down_for_maintenance.php`. You can also decide whether the header, footer, left column, right column, and the product price will be displayed or not by configuring these options from the **Configuration | Website Maintenance** page.

Excluding the Admin from being Blocked

Bringing the shop down for maintenance means you want to do some activities and also experiment with the shop. Therefore, it is necessary that at least you access the shop while it is blocked for the others. You can exclude yourself (admin) from being blocked during this down period by entering your IP address into the **Down For Maintenance (exclude this IP-Address)** field. You can type multiple IP addresses separated by a comma (,).

WEBSITE MAINTENANCE			
Title	Value	Action	**Down For Maintenance (exclude this IP-Address)**
Down for Maintenance: ON/OFF	true	①	Please make any necessary changes
Down for Maintenance: filename	down_for_maintenance	①	
Down for Maintenance: Hide Header	true	①	**Down For Maintenance (exclude this IP-Address)** This IP Address is able to access the website while it is
Down for Maintenance: Hide Column Left	true	①	Down For Maintenance (like webmaster)
Down for Maintenance: Hide Column Right	true	①	To enter multiple IP Addresses, separate with a comma. If you do not know your IP Address, check in the Footer
Down for Maintenance: Hide Footer	true	①	of your Shop.
Down for Maintenance: Hide Prices	true	①	your IP (ADMIN)
Down For Maintenance (exclude this IP-Address)	your IP (ADMIN)	▶	
NOTICE PUBLIC Before going Down for Maintenance: ON/OFF	false	①	update cancel
Date and hours for notice before maintenance	04/01/2007 2-3 PM	①	
Display when webmaster has enabled maintenance	false	①	
Display website maintenance period	false	①	
Website maintenance period	2h00	①	

Notice for Maintenance

It is good to inform the visitors about your scheduled maintenance in advance. Set the **NOTICE PUBLIC Before going Down for Maintenance: ON/OFF** field to **true**. By default, it is **false**, and whenever you set the **Down for Maintenance: ON/OFF** field to **true**, the value of this field becomes **false** automatically. Setting this value to **true** will display a notice for scheduled maintenance. Now is the time to set the schedule. Click on the **Date and hours for notice before maintenance** field, and set the date and time of maintenance. Then, a notice will be displayed in the header of your online shop before taking it down for maintenance.

Showing Downtime

You can show visitors when the shop was taken down for maintenance and what the estimated downtime is. Informing your visitors about this will encourage them to come back. Set the fields, **Display when webmaster has enabled maintenance** and **Display website maintenance period**, to **true**. You can also set the duration of the maintenance period in the **Website maintenance period** field.

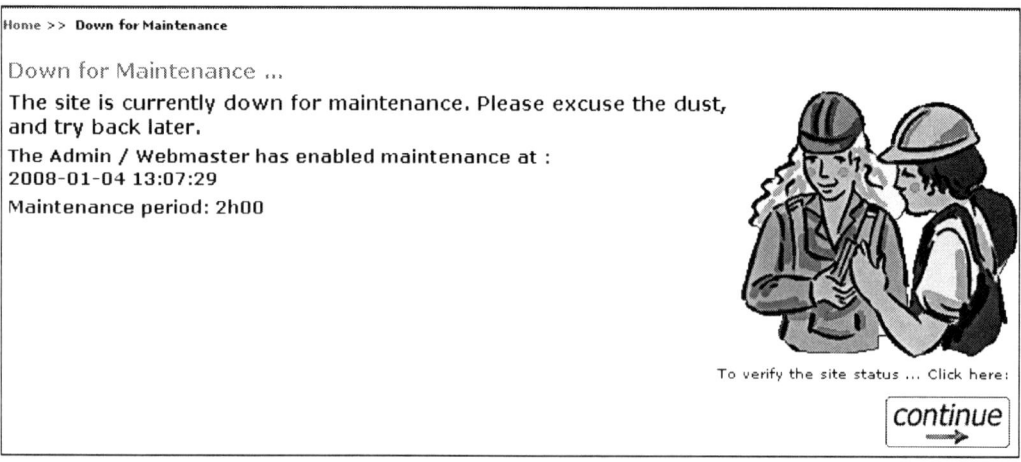

Backing Up Files and Databases

Backing up files and databases is the first step in maintenance activities. While setting up the Zen Cart shop and customizing it, you will change a lot of files which will not be the same as the original ones that came along with the Zen Cart installation package. By this time, you also know that all information you enter into your Zen Cart shop are stored in the database. Therefore, to be on the safe side, it is better to back up the files and databases regularly.

Why do you Need a Backup?

Backup has no value in normal time, but it seems invaluable when you have a problem. When your store is not working due to some recent changes in the files or databases, and you want to revert to the previous version of files and/or database (which was working fine), backup seems to be worth a million dollars.

For the following reasons you need to back up your files and databases regularly:

- Your web server may be compromised, or it may be out of order any time. In that case, you can start your online shop on another web server if you want to have a back up of all the files (modified .php files, product images, and so on) and databases.

- Sometimes, you may have a problem after modifying files. For example, you are customizing the look and feel of your Zen Cart shop, and suddenly you find that after editing some files and uploading them to the web server, your Zen Cart shop is not displaying the front page but is throwing errors. The backup of the files will help you revert to the previous version of files, and resolve the problem.

- Problems may also occur after installing third-party contributions. Some third-party contributions may overwrite some core files of Zen Cart. In which case, the backed up files will help you revert to the working version.

Backing Up Database

There is no built-in mechanism in Zen Cart to backup its database. You have to use phpMyAdmin, other MySQL tool, or third-party contributions to back up whole databases for Zen Cart. If you have access to phpMyAdmin, please follow these steps to backup your Zen Cart database:

1. Login to phpMyAdmin.
2. From the list of databases, select the Zen Cart database. Usually, it is **zencart**.
3. Click on the **Export** tab.

4. In the **Export** section, click on **Select All,** or select your desired tables by clicking on the table names. For selecting multiple tables, press *Ctrl* and click on the table names in the list.

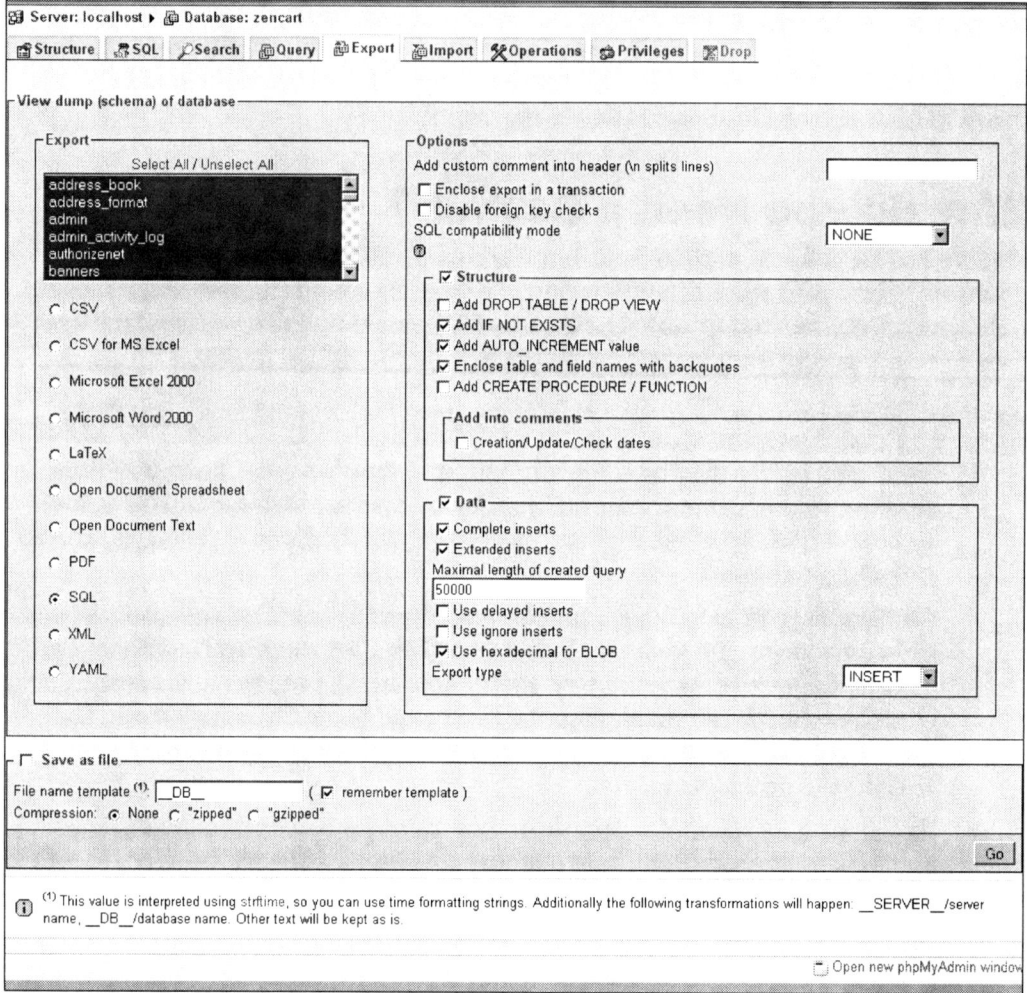

5. Uncheck the **Structure** checkbox for not including table structures. If you want to include a table structure, select **Add IF NOT EXISTS** in the **Structure** section. This will add a statement which will ensure that a table is created only when it does not exist. Selecting this option is especially advantageous for backups.

6. In the **Data** section, keep the default settings, that is, **Complete Inserts**, **Extended Inserts, Use Hexadecimal for Blobs** checked.

7. Click on **Save as File**, as you are going to save the export on your computer. You can also use a template for the filename. The default is **__DB__**, which names the file after the database. You can save the file as **zipped** or **gzipped** by selecting these options in the **Compression** field.

8. Click on the **Go** button. If you have selected **Save as File**, a **Save To** dialog box will be displayed. Browse a location on your computer to save the file.

There is a third-party contribution for Zen Cart to facilitate backing up of the Zen Cart database from within Zen Cart. Download **Backup Admin MySQL Plugin v.1.3** from Zen Cart website's download section. Installation is as simple as extracting and copying the `admin` folder to the Zen Cart root folder.

Backup Admin MySQL Plugin v.1.3 uses two MySQL programs: `mysql` and `mysqldump`. These two programs usually reside in the `/usr/bin` directory. This path is indicated in the `/admin/includes/languages/english/backup_mysql.php` file. If you are using a windows server, you may need to edit this. If MySQL backup Admin Tool is not working, open the `/admin/includes/languages/english/backup_mysql.php` file and change the following lines:

```
define('LOCAL_EXE_MYSQL',     '/usr/bin/mysql');
define('LOCAL_EXE_MYSQLDUMP', '/usr/bin/mysqldump');
```

Usually, on a Windows server, these paths will look like `c:/mysql/bin/mysql.exe` and `c:/mysql/bin/mysqldump.exe`. Be sure about the actual path on your Windows server and replace the previous lines accordingly.

 For creating backups, the `admin/backups` directory should have read/ write permission. If you are using a Linux server, apply **CHMOD 777** on the `admin/backups` directory.

You can run this backup tool from the administration area. Select **Tools | Database Backup – MySQL**. The **Database Backup Manager – MySQL** screen will be displayed.

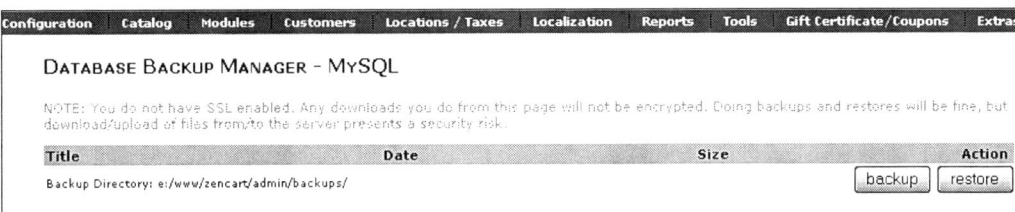

If you are not using SSL, a warning message will be displayed saying that any downloads from this page will be unencrypted. Click on the **backup** button to create a new backup of the Zen Cart database. The **New Backup** dialog box will be displayed. If you want to skip the locking of the database during a backup, check the **Skip Lock option** radio button. Generally, the backup generated is stored in the `admin/backups` folder, and you can download that by clicking the down arrow icon before the name of the backup. If you want to download the backup file directly to your computer without storing it on the web server, check **Download without storing on server**.

Backing up Files

Backing up files is as simple as backing up any web application. You may need to keep a backup of the initial snapshot, then do some backup for only the changed files. Once you have set up a Zen Cart shop, take the base snapshot. Then after customizing the shop, that is customizing the look and feel and installing third-party modules, you need to take backups.

Zen Cart themes are using overrides, and this override system does not modify or replace original files. Therefore, while adding a new template, you can just care about those new files in the template. Similarly, after adding Zen Cart third-party contributions, you can take a backup of the new files.

Although, in principle, no third-party contribution is supposed to touch the files in the original installation, some contributions still do some modifications to the original files. Be sure about such overwrites or modifications before installing the contributions. Also, keep a backup of the original files before installing such contributions.

Product data are very much important for any online shop. You must ensure that product data are always backed up and readily available for restoration whenever necessary. While product information such as description, price, and so on are stored in the database, product images are not stored in the database. Generally, product images are stored in the `images` directory under the Zen Cart installation directory of your web server. Therefore, you also need to backup this folder whenever you see that a large number of products have been added to the catalogue.

If you are using Linux hosting and cPanel, you can back up files (and also Zen Cart database) easily from cPanel. Follow these steps to backup files and database from cPanel:

1. Login to **cPanel**.

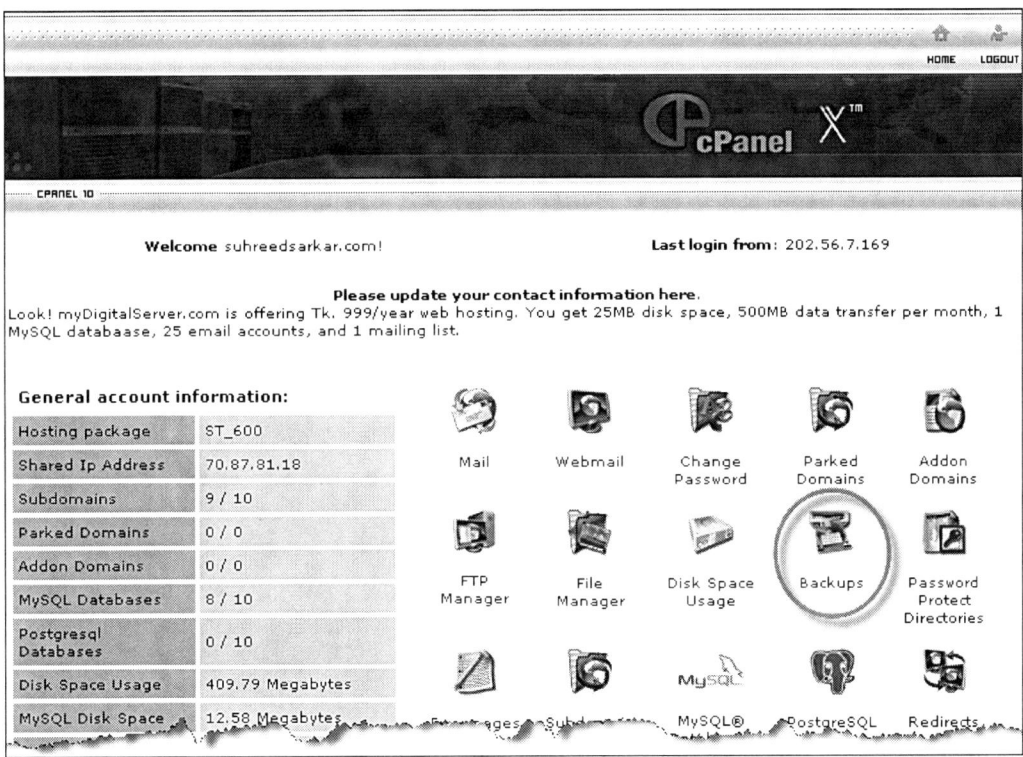

2. Click on the **Backups** icon in **cPanel**'s main page. The **Backups** page will be displayed. You can download the directory and database backups from this page.

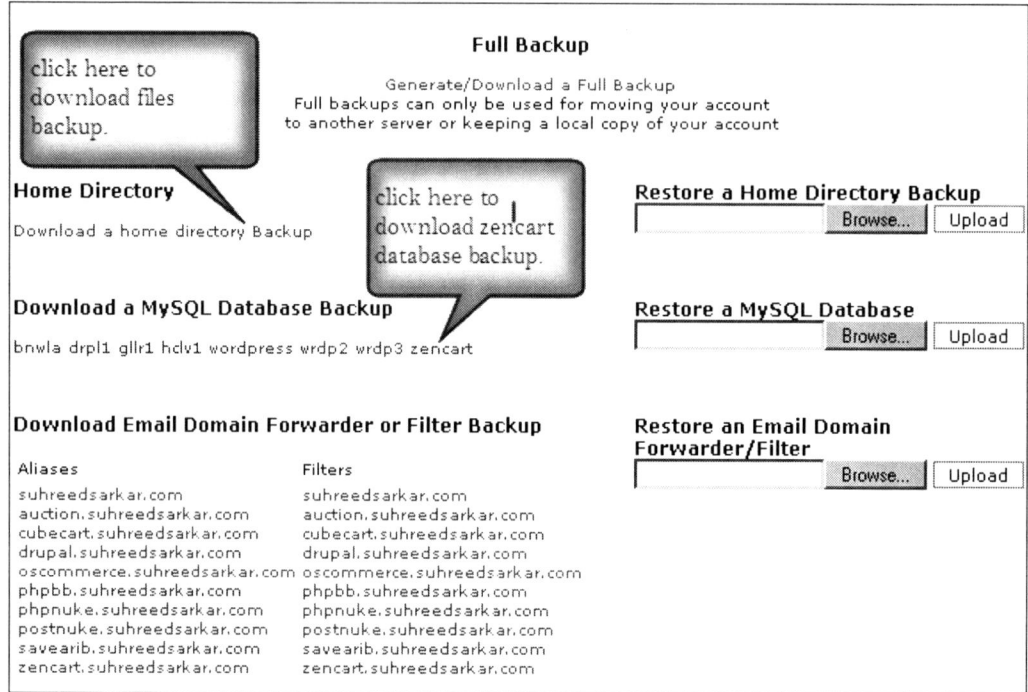

3. In the **Home Directory** section, click on the **Download a home directory Backup** link. This will start download of the backup. Save the file on your computer.

4. To back up the database, click on the Zen Cart database name under the **Download a MySQL Database Backup** section. This will save the SQL dump of the database in a compressed format. Save the file on your computer.

Restoring Database and Files

If you have backed up the database using **phpMyadmin** or **Database Backup Tool Plugin**, you can restore those backups from phpMyAdmin, or the Database Backup Tool Plugin.

Restoring database from phpMyAdmin is actually executing a query or importing the dump. Follow these steps to restore from a backup:

1. Login to **phpMyAdmin**.
2. Select the **zencart** database.
3. Click on the **Import** tab.

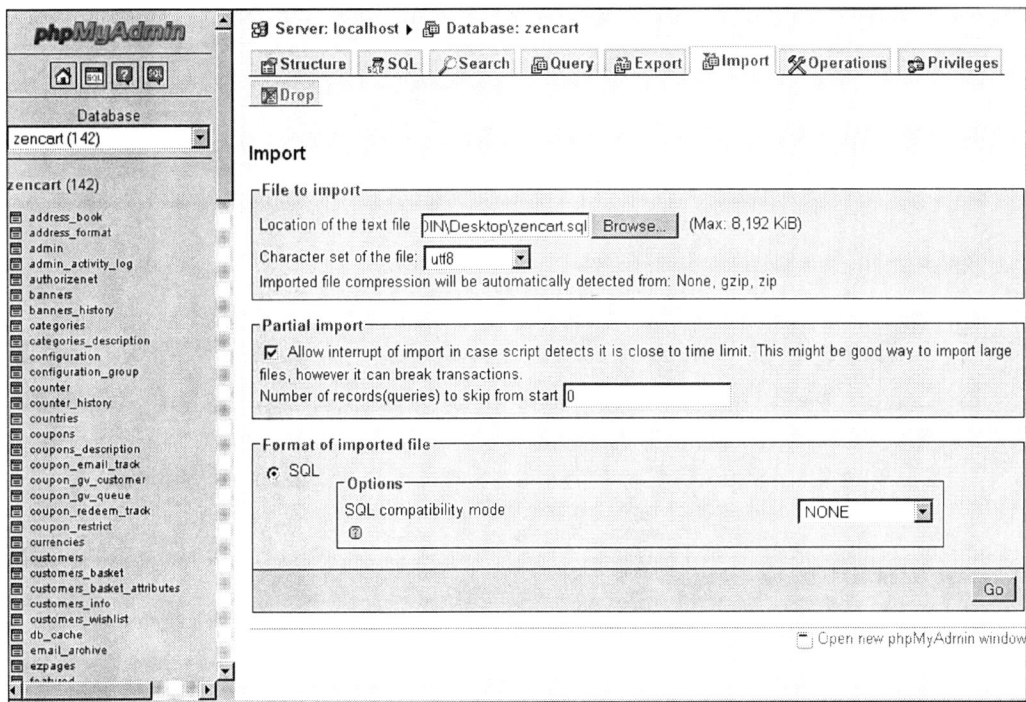

4. In the **File to Import** section, click on the **Browse** button and select the backup file which you want to restore.
5. Click on the **Go** button.

The database will be restored. If there is any record existing in the database, an error message will indicate the problem with that record. Remember that importing a large database may take some time.

Restoring database backups made by Database Backup Tool Plugin is much easier. Once the backup is generated, that will be listed on the **Database Backup Manager – MySQL** screen.

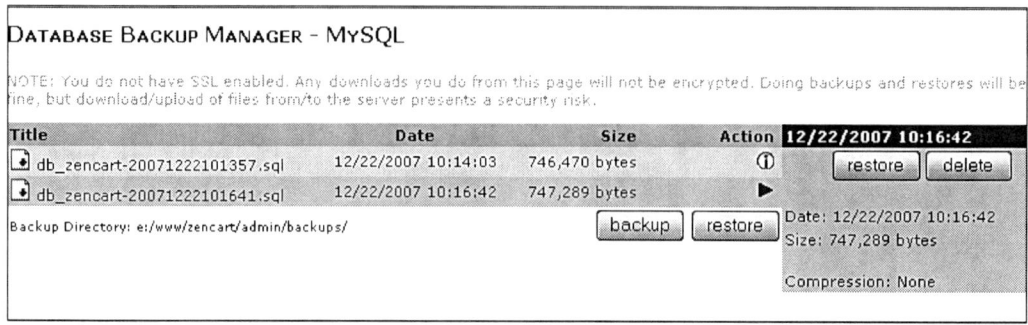

For restoring a database backup follow these steps:

1. Click on the database backup which you want to restore. On the right side, two options will be shown: **restore** and **delete**.

2. Click on the **delete** button to delete the database backup. You may delete it if you are sure that you will never need the backup in future.

3. Click on the **restore** button to restore that database backup. Details of information about that backup set will be shown.

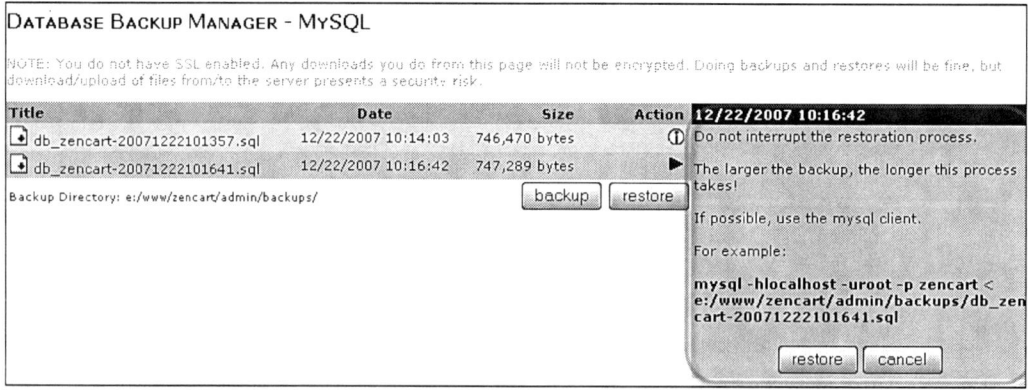

4. Again, click on the **restore** button on this dialog box to restore the backup.

Finally, the database will be restored. It may take some time depending on the size of the database you are restoring.

Note that, you have to click on the **restore** button shown to the right side box. If you click on the **restore** button shown in the following screenshot, the list of backups will show you options to restore from a file on your computer. Click on the **Browse...** button, select the .sql file from where you want to restore, and click on the **restore** button.

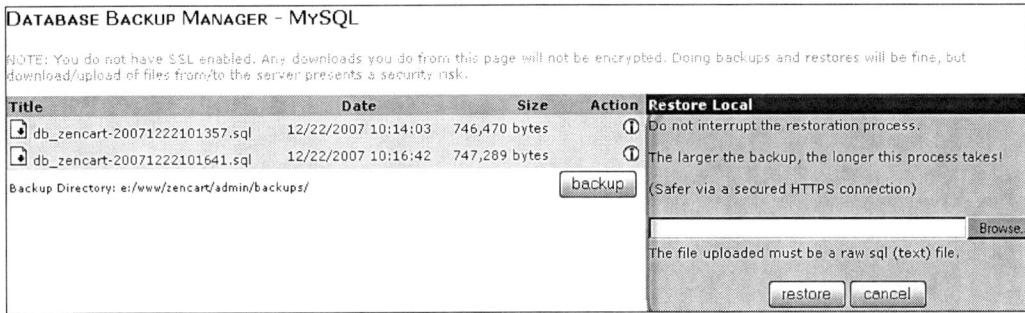

Restoring file backups is as simple as uploading the files from the backup set to Zen Cart's directory on the web server. You can do this using web-based uploading tools or FTP programs.

As you have seen you can use cPanel for database and files backup and restoration. We have discussed how to backup home directory and Zen Cart database from cPanel. Follow the steps below to restore those backups:

1. Login to **cPanel**.

2. Click on the **Backups** icons in the **cPanel** main page. The **Backups** page will be displayed.

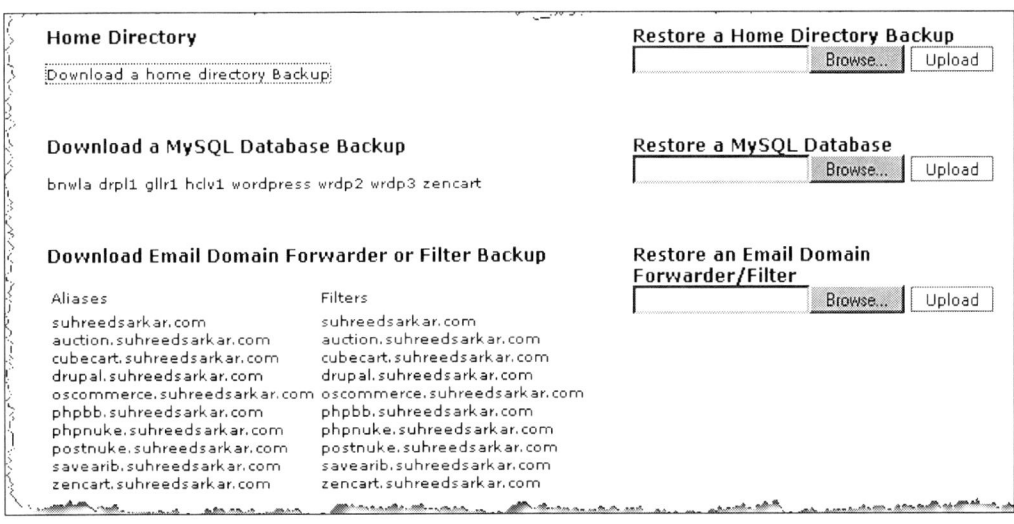

3. To restore files, click on the **browse** button in the **Restore a Home Directory Backup** section, select the backup file saved on your computer, and then click the **Upload** button. The file will be uploaded, extracted and restored as per the directory structure.

4. To restore a database, click on the **browse** button in the **Restore a MySQL Database** section, select the database backup file saved on your computer, and then click the **Upload** button. The database will be restored to its original.

 From cPanel backup, you cannot backup or restore selectively. As an alternative to this, you can use the FTP programs to download the backups and upload to the web server for restoring old files.

Auditing and Hardening Security

Auditing is the process of examining logs to ensure that there is no security breach or attempts to compromise security. While using Zen Cart for online stores you must ensure that it is secure and safe for both the customers and the owner. The following sections discuss ways to ensure security of your Zen Cart shop.

Common Security Settings

After installation and configuration of Zen Cart, you need to take appropriate security measures to protect your online shop. The following sections highlights some common steps for securing your online shop.

Use SSL whenever Possible

Secure Socket Layer (**SSL**) enables your site to communicate securely over the internet. Plain HTTP is not secure as it sends information over the internet unencrypted. Anybody on the internet can capture the data stream and know what you are sending or receiving. This is especially insecure for changing the passwords for the Zen Cart admin account. As you know, the Zen Cart admin account password is the key to controlling your online shop. If anybody can capture this password, he or she gets the controls of your shop.

For safeguarding communication over your online shop, use SSL. SSL sends and receives data, which you exchange with your online shop. It ensures that the configuration options you are using and the changes you are making to your site remain confidential by encrypting all transmissions from and to your computer.

For using SSL on your Zen Cart shop, you need a SSL certificate. Some hosting providers give you the shared SSL certificate at economy rate. But using such certificates is not secure, as compared to using a dedicated SSL certificate. Although there are some added expenses, it is recommended that you use a dedicated SSL certificate for your online shop. While you are searching for hosting for Zen Cart shop, also check whether that host supports SSL, and can install the SSL certificate. Whenever possible, also try to have a Secure FTP service such as FTP over SSL/TLS (FTPS) instead of the non-secure FTP.

Delete/Rename Sensitive Folders

Some folders in Zen Cart are more sensitive than the others. The first folder you should take care of is `zc_install`. The installation scripts remain in this folder, and anybody can start the installation of Zen Cart by pointing the browser to this folder. This folder should be removed from your web server on finishing the Zen Cart installation. Delete this folder completely instead of renaming it.

The second folder that you should take care of is the `admin` folder. This is the administration area for your Zen Cart shop. As hackers know that Zen Cart uses this folder as an administration area, they may attempt to access this often. You can make their attempts unsuccessful by renaming this folder. Give a name that is hard to guess; do not rename it as `myadmin`, or `newadmin`. Instead, use some randomly generated names, say `ctkobn`. You also need to reflect the name in the `/admin/includes/configure.php` file. Open this file in text editor, and find all instances of `admin` and replace them with the new name, that is, `ctkobn`. You need to change the following sections:

```
define('DIR_WS_ADMIN', '/admin/');
define('DIR_WS_CATALOG', '/');
define('DIR_WS_HTTPS_ADMIN', '/admin/');
define('DIR_WS_HTTPS_CATALOG', '/');

define('DIR_FS_ADMIN', '/home/suhreed/public_html/admin/');
define('DIR_FS_CATALOG','/home/suhreed/public_html/');
```

After the admin folder is renamed, the previous lines will look as follows:

```
define('DIR_WS_ADMIN', '/ctkobn/');
define('DIR_WS_CATALOG', '/');
define('DIR_WS_HTTPS_ADMIN', '/ctkobn/');
define('DIR_WS_HTTPS_CATALOG', '/');

define('DIR_FS_ADMIN', '/home/suhreed/public_html/ctkobn/');
define('DIR_FS_CATALOG', '/home/suhreed/public_html/');
```

Always remember to keep the ending '/' intact while you are typing the new folder in the above lines. Deleting the ending '/' will create problems.

You have to use new URLs to access the administration area after renaming the admin folder. Point your browser to the new URL such as, http://www.yourdomain.com/ctkobn and check whether you can access the administration area.

Set Appropriate Permissions to Files and Directories

Permissions set to sensitive folders are files that can enhance security of your online shop. Some files needs to be read-only while some folders may have write permission. The first file you should secure is configure.php. If you are using Linux hosting, then apply CHMOD 644 on both /admin/includes/configure.php and /includes/configure.php. If you need to change these file in future, first change these permissions, and then edit and save. Once the changes are made, apply CHMOD 644 on them again. On the Windows server, set permissions to these files as read-only. Also ensure that the IUSR_machine_name account has limited access permissions to these files.

For all other directories and files, set them as read-only, except for the /images and /cache directories. The /images directories and sub-directories under it should be writable by the server process as product images are uploaded to these directories. If you make these directories read-only, you will not be able to upload product images while adding a new product from the administration area. The /cache directory is used to cache queries; therefore, it needs to be writable by the server process.

From the **Tools | Define Pages Editor** in the administration area, you can edit pages for Zen Cart. Once you have finished editing define pages, you should make the /includes/languages/english/html_includes/ directory read-only. When you make them read-only, others cannot change them. However, if you want to modify some files from **Tools | Define Pages Editor** again, you have to make those directories and files writable first.

Another way to protect your folders from being browsed directly is by using the .htaccess file. In several directories, you will find that there is a .htaccess file and a blank index.html file. These are there to ensure security for those folders. The .htaccess file in a particular folder generally prevents direct access to that folder or some .php files. The blank index.html file is there for added security. In case .htaccess is not uploaded to that directory, index.html protects the directory from being browsed directly.

Always Use Secure Passwords

As mentioned earlier, security of your whole online shop depends entirely upon the strength and privacy of your admin password. If the password is well publicized and/or can be guessed easily, then the security of your entire online shop is thwarted. For strengthening the security of your shop, follow these guidelines for passwords:

1. Always use a complex password—a complex password should contain alphanumeric characters and some special characters.

2. Never use your name, or the names of your spouse, son, or daughter as the password. Do not use a birth date, telephone number, social security number, and so on for the password. These are known to others and can be guessed easily.

3. Do not write down your password in front of your computer, or in public places. Always keep the password memorized. If you really need to keep it in writing, keep it under lock and key.

4. Do not share your password with others. If necessary, create separate admin account for others and ensure that they are also aware of the security and importance of their password.

5. Generate random passwords. There are lots of free password generators that can be used for this purpose. You may also use some tools to test the strength of your password.

6. Change your password time to time. Changing it frequently lowers the risk of being discovered by others.

7. Do not send your password to someone by email, or over the telephone.

Remember that your online shop is secure as long as you protect your administration area by maintaining a strong and secret password for your admin account.

Securing Access to the Administration Panel

Unlike osCommerce, the administration area of Zen Cart is well protected by default. Whenever anyone wants to access the administration area, he or she needs to provide the username and password for an administrative account. Normal users or shoppers cannot login to this area. You do not need to edit `.htaccess` or any other file for securing this area.

The main administrative account is created during installation. The master administrator has full access to all areas of the administration area. Using this account name and password, you can login to the administration area.

It is not wise to use the same username and passwords for all people administering the online shop. Instead, create a separate administrative account. Once you are logged in to the administrative username and password, you can create other administrative accounts. Follow these steps for creating administrative accounts:

1. Login to the administrative area.

2. Select **Tools | Admin Settings**.

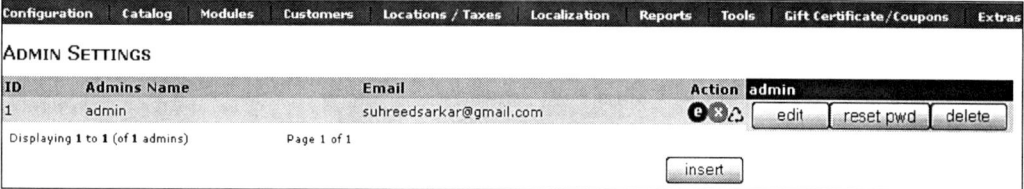

3. Click on the **insert** button.

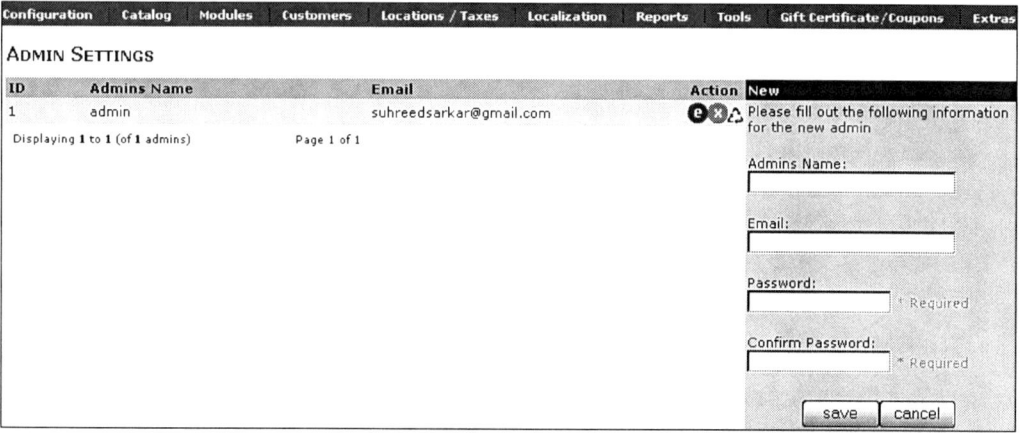

4. In the **New** box, type the name of the account, the email address, the password, and confirm the password. The email address used for this account is very important for the retrieval of the forgotten password.

5. Finally click on the **save** button when done.

You can also reset the password for administrative accounts. For resetting the password for any administrative account, select that account and click on the **reset pwd** button. Then, the **Reset Password** box will be displayed. Type the new password and confirm that by retyping it. Then, click the **save** button.

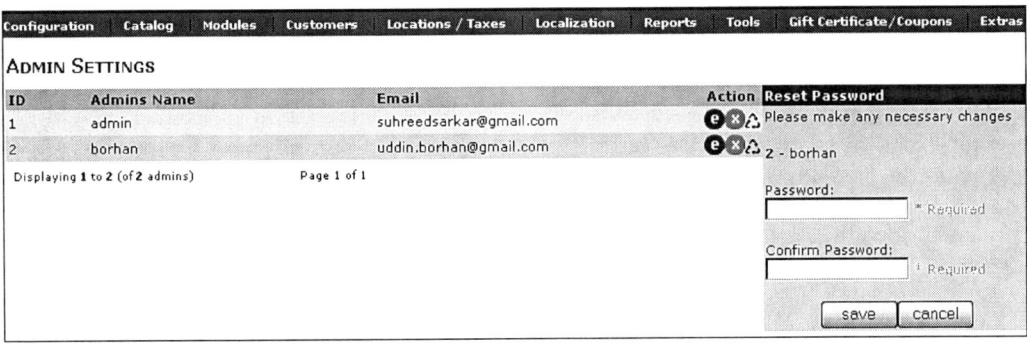

 Do not use the same admin account for multiple people sharing the password. Instead, create separate admin accounts for each user and ask that person to keep his or her password a secret. Make each person responsible for maintaining their login secret.

User Authentication and Security

Zen Cart has built-in user authentication and security mechanisms for controlling access to catalogues. You can configure your store to allow product browsing by all—both registered and unregistered users. At the same time, you can configure your store to require registration for placing orders. Unregistered users can browse the products, and even add products to their carts, but they must register and log in to Zen Cart to check out. This is a standard setting for online shops.

Register Globals Setting

Unlike osCommerce, Zen Cart runs with Register Globals **on** or **off**. It is not required to be on, as it is in osCommerce. Although, Zen Cart can run with register globals on, for better security, it is recommended that you keep it off. However, you may find some hosts which enable this setting to support other applications.

During Zen Cart installation, you will be notified whether Register Globals is on or not. If it is on, you may make it off through editing .htaccess. In the .htaccess file in the webroot, you have to add the following lines:

```
# to turn off register_globals
php_value register_globals 0
```

Session Handling

Session handling is an important aspect for any web application such as a shopping cart. Zen Cart has its built-in mechanism to handle session. In fact, Zen Cart uses session handling infrastructure of PHP. It handles login security and keeps the information on each visitor to the Zen Cart shopping cart separately.

Session Save Path

Zen Cart stores session information in a directory. This directory needs to be writable by the web server process. The session save path is configured during installation. If you forget the path and want to know the session save path, open **phpMyAdmin**, click on **SQL** tab and run the following query:

```
SELECT configuration_value FROM configuration WHERE configuration_key
                                      = 'SESSION_WRITE_DIRECTORY';
```

As a result of this query, a directory path will be displayed. This is the session save path. If you see that the directory does not exist, or you want to change the path, just replace /path/to/session/save in the following query and run it:

```
UPDATE configuration SET configuration_value =
                  '/path/to/session/save' WHERE configuration_key =
                                      'SESSION_WRITE_DIRECTORY';
```

When you have the correct session save path set, you need to make sure that you have the correct permissions set for it. Set permissions to 777 for this directory. Remember that if you are using a prefix for your database tables, you will need to apply that to the above queries.

Session Referer Setting

Make sure that session.referer_check is disabled. You can check this with phpinfo(), or from **Tools | Server Info**. If it is enabled, turn it off. You can disable session.referer_check by any of the following methods:

- php.ini file: Edit your php.ini file and set session.referer_check = off.

- .htaccess file: In your .htaccess file, add php_value session.referer_check none.

- ini_set() command: You can also use the ini_set() command to disable it. Open the includes/application_top.php and admin/includes/application_top.php files, and add ini_set('session.referer_check', ''); after the license information in these files.

The session.use_trans_sid Setting

By default, Zen Cart will be able to handle the session correctly unless the `session.use_trans_sid` setting is enabled on your server. If this setting is enabled, Zen Cart will not be able to hook into it properly to access its services in a way that lets it identify data related to Zen Cart.

As it is absolutely required for proper session handling of Zen Cart, you must keep this turned `off` on your server. Sometimes, your webhost provider may permit you to configure it through `.htaccess`. In that case, you may resolve this issue as follows:

1. In the webroot, that is the directory where `index.php` and `install.txt` are located, create a new file named `.htaccess`. If you have an existing file named `.htaccess`, then you just need to modify it as stated in the next step.

2. In the `.htaccess` file, add the following lines:

    ```
    # to turn off session-trans-sid
    php_value session.use_trans_sid 0
    ```

Adding the above lines and saving it will allow your server to allow Zen Cart to use PHP session handling mechanism.

Common Problems and Troubleshooting

While running your Zen Cart shop, you may face some common problems which can be broadly categorized as PHP and configuration related problems and Zen Cart related problems. The following sections highlight such problems.

PHP Related Problems

If there is any problem in configuring your Zen Cart shop, you may encounter various error and warning messages. Some of the common warning messages, their causes and remedies are discussed below.

Warning:
Cannot modify header information—headers already sent by (output started at `<path/to/output_file>:<line number>`) in `<path/to/current_file>` on line `<number>`.

You may encounter this message after modifying some .php files. This warning shows up if you leave a space or extra line at the beginning, or the end of a .php file. The file causing a problem is indicated by its name and line number. Look at after *output started at* and within brackets in the error message above. Fixing this error is as easy as removing that extra space or extra line. Open that file and go to the line number as reported in the error message. Then ensure that no space or extra line is present before `<?php` or after the `?>` tag.

Usually this kind of error happens when you are working with some custom editors such as Dreamweaver. For example, you have edited files using Dreamweaver and uploaded the files via Dreamweaver without using check-in features. You can avoid this error by using check-in features in Dreamweaver.

Sometimes 'header already sent' error appears after other error messages. In that case, always resolve other errors first, as the other error messages may cause the 'header already sent' error.

Warning:

Variable passed to `each()` is not an array or object in ... `/includes/classes/db/mysql/query_factory.php` on line 100

This error may be displayed if `magic_quotes_runtime` is enabled. To be sure, check your `phpinfo` and see if `magic_quotes_runtime` is enabled. If it is enabled, you need to turn it off. You can do this by editing the following files:

```
includes/application_top.php
admin/includes/application_top.php
```

Open the files in the editor, and just after the licensing terms, add the following lines:

```
if (get_magic_quotes_runtime()) {
        set_magic_quotes_runtime(0);
    }
```

Warning:

`main(<...>)`: failed to open stream: No such file or directory in `<...>`

This error occurs when some files included in the .php files are not found in the set path. For correcting this, first ensure that you have uploaded all files and set correct permissions, especially for the file in question. If that does not fix the problem, check your PHP `include_path`. You can see these paths along with the error messages you have received. You can also check this setting with `phpinfo()`.

On a Windows server, the `include_path` needs to start with `.;` and on a Unix/Linux server, it must start with `.:`. If the `include_path` does not contain this, you must configure it in `php.ini`, or in a `.htaccess` file.

In the `php.ini` file, add the following lines:

```
include_path = ".;Drive:\path\to\php\includes" //for windows server
include_path = ".:/path/to/php/includes" //for linux/unix server
```

Similarly, you configure it by editing the `.htaccess` file.

For Windows host, add the following line in the `.htaccess` file:

```
php_value include_path ".; Drive:\path\to\php\includes"
```

For Unix/Linux host, add the following line in the `.htaccess` file:

```
php_value include_path ".:/path/to/php/includes"
```

Warning:

`<restricted function>:open_basedir` restriction in effect. File (`<path to file>`) is not within the allowed path(s): (`<allowed paths>`) *in* `<file producing the error>` on line `<line>`

This error occurs when you try to access a directory on which you do not have access permission. To get rid of this error message, ensure that the directories listed in the error messages are configured to be accessible by Zen Cart. On a Windows server, the directories are shown separated by a semi-colon (`;`) and on Unix/Linux servers, these are separated by a colon (`:`).

You entered the wrong username or password.

This may happen when you are typing a wrong username or password. Remember that passwords are case-sensitive. So, ensure that the *Caps Lock* is not ON while you are typing your passwords. If you have really forgotten your password there is still hope to recover it, even if it is your admin account password.

The first attempt to recover a forgotten password will be to click on the **Resend Password** button and enter the admin email address. You will find this button on the admin login screen. Usually, you will get the password in your email box. If, for some reason, you do not receive the password, you can create a temporary password to login only if you have access to a Zen Cart database.

Login to your webhosting control panel, open **phpMyAdmin**, select the Zen Cart database and click on the **SQL** tab. In the query box, type the following query and click on **run**:

```
DELETE FROM zc_admin WHERE admin_name = 'Admin';
INSERT INTO zc_admin (admin_name, admin_email, admin_pass,
                      admin_level) VALUES ('Admin', 'admin@localhost',
                      '351683ea4e19efe34874b501fdbf9792:9b', 1);
```

Here `zc_` is the prefix for the Zen Cart tables. Your database may use different prefixes or none. In that case, replace `zc_` with the prefix you are using. Running this query will create a temporary admin account with a username admin and a password admin. You can now login to the administration area using these usernames and passwords.

It is important that, after you log in, delete this temporary admin account and create a new one from **Tools | Admin Settings**. Click on the **insert** button to create a new admin account. You have to provide the username, email address, and password for creating a a new admin account.

Warning:
`session.auto_start` is enabled — please disable this PHP feature in `php.ini` and restart the web server.

Enabling the `session.auto_start` setting starts a session automatically which creates a problem with proper session management. If you receive this warning, you have to disable this setting. You can do this by editing `php.ini` or the `.htaccess` file.

If you have access to the `php.ini` file, set the directive `session.auto_start` to 0, as follows:

```
session.auto_start = 0
```

In most of the cases you can edit the `.htaccess` file. If you do not see the `.htaccess` file in your Zen Cart directory, create one. Then add the following line to that `.htaccess` file and save it:

```
php_value session.auto_start 0
```

Your last resort will be to contact your host provider and ask them to disable this setting on the server.

Parse Error:

syntax error, unexpected `T_CONSTANT_ENCAPSED_STRING` in `/home/Suhreed/public_html/zencart/includes/languages/english/packt/product_info.php` on line 17

This error occurs when you forget to put a backslash (\) before a single quote (') in one of your `define()` statements in the language file. For example, the following line will result in similar error:

```
define('TEXT_SOMETHING','This is something simple that's used as an
        example');
```

Here a ' is not escaped, so this will fire an error message. To correct this error, escape the character as follows:

```
define('TEXT_SOMETHING','This is something simple that\'s used as an
        example');
```

This page contains both secure and non-secure items. Do you want to display the non-secure items?

Sometimes, you may have a symptom whereby clicking on a login link will result in a message saying that the page contains both secure and non-secure items. Usually this happens on all secure pages, especially in **My Account** and **Checkout** areas.

This problem occurs when:

- You have hard-coded actual URL links such as `http://xxxxxx` in your templates, instead of using relative paths to objects.
- You have added banners with the `http://` links and not marked them to skip display on the SSL pages
- You have added click-tracking tools to your site via JavaScript, which link to `http://` pages somewhere.

To solve the problem on your browser, view the source of the pages creating the problem and search for `src=http://`. When you find the links, edit the corresponding template files, and remove the hard-coded links. If they are caused by click-tracking scripts somewhere, try converting them to `https://` links, or contact the vendor for assistance with alternate scripts.

To be on the safe side, never hard-code a `http://` URL into any page on your site, always use the relative URL in such links. You can hard-code such URLs only when you are sure that doing so will not produce this sort of error, or when you are using only a non-secure mode, that is, without SSL. Be especially careful about the `<img src=...>` and `<script src=...>` tags.

Login Related Problems

You may face problems during login as a customer, or in the administration area. These problems are mainly due to some settings which control session handling and the authentication of users. The following sections highlight some common problems related to login.

Session Handling in Admin Area

It has been said earlier that Zen Cart's sessions are managed using the PHP session handling features. In general, it works as follows:

1. A session is generated upon login of a user. For customers, the session's name is `zenid`, and for admin users, it is `zenAdminId`.

2. On starting the session, PHP attempts to set a cookie in your browser. The cookie stores that session ID so that it does not need to be shown in the browser URL all the time. If the session ID is not in the cookie, it is shown as part of the URL; something like `&zenAdminID=243524524524525` is appended to the URL. If a cookie is set, the session ID is in the cookie, and the session name and number don't need to be appended to the URLs. Zen Cart needs this session ID to keep you logged in.

3. When you log out, or the session ID is lost, the session data is reset and your authentication data is removed. As the session ID is lost, you need to login again. This generates a new session ID.

Starting from Zen Cart v 1.3.8, a security token is generated, and embedded in the login form to identify that same person while logging again.

Understanding this session management helps you identify the cause. As discussed earlier, you may identify a problem while generating session ID, storing it in cookies, retrieving it from a cookie, or while re-using it. Session management problems may occur when Zen Cart cannot recognize the user's session ID:

- When cookies are blocked by a firewall, or a browser configuration. If you are using a firewall, first check whether it blocks cookies. If not, suspect the browser. By default, browsers receive cookies. However, in case of a problem, you should check the browser's configuration options.

- When PHP is configured wrongly, or has certain session settings set to methods incompatible with Zen Cart, such as `session-auto-start` and `transitive-sid`. You will get warning messages during installation if these PHP settings are found at that time. However, these may change after installation, and create problems to your Zen Cart's session management.

- When you have configured your site to store session data in files but your file system does not have permissions to write on the files. Appropriate permissions to the session file may be the problem.

- When you have configured your site to store session data in the database but the database table (that is **zc_sessions**) is corrupt, or the database storage is full and new records cannot be added.

Sometimes this may occur that you cannot remain logged in to the admin area. This shows the problems of handling PHP sessions in Zen Cart's administration area. First, try closing the browser windows, clearing the browser cache, cookies, and restart your computer. In most of the cases, this will solve your problem if that is due to caching of cookies in the browser. If the problem is not related to caching, it may also be due to incorrect SSL configuration. To solve such problems, edit your `/admin/includes/configure.php` file and change `ENABLE_SSL_ADMIN` to `false`. Then, clear browser cache, cookies, and try again.

Security Error during Login as Customer

If you have upgraded to Zen Cart v 1.3.8, you may receive an error message while trying to login, "There was a security error when trying to login".

This happens due to the fact that Zen Cart v1.3.8 has an added security feature to prevent spoofed external logins. All login forms have been designed to include a security token field. When a user tries to login, the security token is also submitted with the username and password. This security token needs to be current in order to login successfully. If the security token field is not the current one, or is outdated, then an error will be thrown.

If you have a customized template's login files, there is a possibility that the old files don't have that security token field with the login form. You need to merge new security features into the login file template.

In general, the following files are affected by this new security feature:

- `/includes/templates/CUSTOM_TEMPLATE/templates/tpl_login_default.php`
- `/includes/templates/CUSTOM_TEMPLATE/templates/tpl_timeout_default.php`

And for admin area the file will be: `/admin/login.php`.

In `tpl_login_default.php`, you find the following code block:

```
<label class="inputLabel" for="login-password">
  <?php echo ENTRY_PASSWORD; ?></label>
<?php echo zen_draw_password_field('password', '',
  zen_set_field_length(TABLE_CUSTOMERS, 'customers_password') . '
                       id="login-password"'); ?>
<br class="clearBoth" />
</fieldset>
```

You have to insert the following line of code before the code block shown above:

```
<?php echo zen_draw_hidden_field('securityToken',
                      $_SESSION['securityToken']); ?>
```

Similarly, you have to add the above line in the `tpl_timeout_default.php` file.

Additionally, if you have customized your `/includes/functions/sessions.php` file for some reason, you'll also need to merge the new changes for this core file into your customized version. In your old customized `/includes/functions/sessions.php` file, you will find the following code block:

```
function zen_session_start() {
    @ini_set('session.gc_probability', 1);
    @ini_set('session.gc_divisor', 2);
    if (defined('DIR_WS_ADMIN')) {
      @ini_set('session.gc_maxlifetime', (SESSION_TIMEOUT_ADMIN < 900
          ? (SESSION_TIMEOUT_ADMIN + 900) : SESSION_TIMEOUT_ADMIN));
    }
    return session_start();
}
```

For Zen Cart v 1.3.8, you need to change the line `return session_start();`. Now the code looks like this:

```
function zen_session_start() {
    @ini_set('session.gc_probability', 1);
    @ini_set('session.gc_divisor', 2);
    if (defined('DIR_WS_ADMIN')) {
      @ini_set('session.gc_maxlifetime', (SESSION_TIMEOUT_ADMIN < 900
          ? (SESSION_TIMEOUT_ADMIN + 900) : SESSION_TIMEOUT_ADMIN));
    }
    $temp = session_start();
    if (!isset($_SESSION['securityToken'])) {
      $_SESSION['securityToken'] = md5(uniqid(rand(), true));
    }
  if (ereg_replace('[a-zA-Z0-9]', '', session_id()) != '') session_
regenerate_id();
    return $temp;
  }
```

 The best way to reflect these changes in your custom template file is by using a file comparison, or a merging tool such as WinMerge. You can see the differences and merge them using this tool.

Forgotten Admin Password

The password for the administrator account is assigned during the installation of Zen Cart. Once the installation of Zen Cart is finished, you can log in to the administration area by using the admin account and its password. If you forget the password for the admin account, there is an easy way to get a new password. In the admin login page, click on **Resend Password**, and then type the administrator's email address and click on the **resend** button. A new password will be sent to that email address. You then can log in using that password.

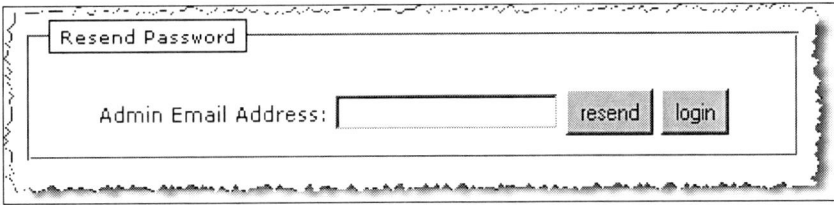

If for some reasons you cannot retrieve the admin password using the **Resend Password** feature, you have to create a temporary admin password for logging into the administration area. However, you need access to your MySQL database. Usually, you get cPanel and phpMyAdmin installed on your server.

For creating a temporary admin account and password to login to the administration area, follow these steps:

1. Login to **cPanel** and run **phpMyAdmin**.

2. Click on the **SQL** tab and run the following query:

   ```
   DELETE FROM admin WHERE admin_name = 'Admin';
   INSERT INTO admin (admin_name, admin_email, admin_pass,
       admin_level) VALUES ('Admin', 'admin@localhost',
       '351683ea4e19efe34874b501fdbf9792:9b', 1);
   ```

   If you are using a prefix to the Zen Cart database tables, add that prefix with the table name, for example, INSERT INTO zc_admin.

3. Running the above query will create an admin account with the password as *admin*. Now, you can log in to the admin area using the username admin and password admin.

4. Change the password and email address once you have logged in to the administration area.

Template Related Problems

Zen Cart templates are located in the /includes/templates/ folder. Under this, you will find a folder named classic, the files that exist there can be overridden by placing a copy of the file you wish to alter inside another folder named after your custom template. The name of custom template is defined in the template_info. php file.

The folder with the template_info.php file, a css folder and the .css files needs to be located at includes/templates/your_template. The other folders that are in the template_default can be created in your_template folder, such as includes/ templates/your_template/css and so on.

Once this is done, you should be able to see the template name from your administration area in **Tools | Template Selection**. If you do not see it there and cannot select it, you have done something incorrectly.

Remember that you need to put only the edited files in an override folder. As you edit more files in other locations, you will have several folders that are named after your template name. Note that, wherever there is a classic folder, you can create a template folder to keep your copied and edited files to have an override effect.

Image Related Problem

Sometimes, the images shown on your online shop may have problems due to inappropriate configurations related to image display or changes in the images directory. The following sections highlights two categories of problems related to images in the Zen Cart online shop.

Catalog Images Directory

When you are adding products to the catalogue and uploading the product image which is uploaded to the /images directory, or a sub-directory under the /images directory, the /images directory needs to be writable by Zen Cart. In other words, it means that you need to apply CHMOD 777 on this folder (including sub-directories) for write access. This should include all subdirectories for /images as well as their subdirectories such as:

- /images/large
- /images/medium
- /images/attributes
- /images/dvd
- /images/large/dvd
- /images/medium/dvd

If you do not set appropriate permissions (that is write access), you will not be able to upload product images.

The sub-directories in the /images directory needs to be created manually to be shown in the drop-down list while selecting image upload location, when adding products. Whenever you add a sub-directory, make sure that the sub-directory is writable to Zen Cart.

Image Distortion

Sometimes product images on your online shop may appear distorted. This happens when the size of your product image is large, but in your configuration display sizes have fixed height and width specifications. Distortion happens when your product images are not sized in the ratio of the specified height and width.

To get rid of image distortion, first set the image height and width proportions that you want to use throughout the online shop catalogue. Then, specify the height and width in the administration area from the **Configuration | Images** screen. Problems occur when any of the value for the following option pairs is set to 0:

- Small Image Width & Small Image Height
- Subcategory Image Width & Subcategory Image Height
- Category Icon Image Width – Product Info Pages & Category Icon Image Height – Product Info Pages
- Product Info – Image Width & Product Info – Image Height
- Image – Product Listing Width & Image – Product Listing Height
- Image – Product New Listing Width & Image – Product New Listing Height
- Image – New Products Width & Image – New Products Height
- Image – Featured Products Width & Image – Featured Products Height
- Image – Product All Listing Width & Image – Product All Listing Height

Also ensure that **Calculate Image Size** is set to **true,** and **Use Proportional Images on Products and Categories** is set to **1**. Choosing these options will allow your images to be resized according to their own proportions.

Trouble with E-mails

Emails are very important for an online shop. Customers are notified about the status of their orders through emails, administrators are also notified by e-mail about new orders. Email communication in Zen Cart works fine, once it is configured correctly. However, sometimes you may experience troubles in communicating through emails. The following sections highlight the email related problems in Zen Cart.

Emails are not Arriving

Sometimes you may face problem in sending emails from your Zen Cart shop. This may happen for various reasons. Mostly, it is related to mail server configuration. Sometimes, your mail server configuration requires a particular format in which messages are to be sent. In such cases, you may try the following options:

1. First check whether email transport methods are configured correctly. You can see email configuration options from **Configuration | E-mail Options**.

2. Enable the **Emails Must Be Sent From Known Domain?** option and also set the appropriate email address in the **Email Address (sent FROM)** field. Zen Cart will only send emails from domains specified in your from address.

3. Try a different E-mail Transport method. First try **php**. If that does not solve your problem, try SMTP and other methods. If you are using **sendmail**, try using **sendmail -f**. If SMTP does not work, try SMTPAUTH and provide correct login credentials for the SMTP server account.

4. Try to send the email to more than one email account. It may so happen that the problem resides in the receiving server. Try to send emails to a non-free email address; do not test only with Yahoo, Hotmail, or Gmail accounts. These email servers have built-in spam protection, and it is likely that the mail sent from your Zen Cart shop is redirected to a spam folder, or blocked entirely. Checking with some other email accounts will possibly help you find the exact cause.

5. If your email system has junk mail filters or spam protection, try searching for your mail in junk mails or spam folders. Try disabling the protection or filter temporarily, and send mails from Zen Cart again.

6. Another way to check whether a mail has been sent from your Zen Cart shop is to look at email archives. First, enable email archiving by setting the **E-mail Archiving Active?** option value to **true**. Enabling this will archive all emails you are sending from Zen Cart. However, there is no built-in mechanism to see archived emails from within the Zen Cart administration area. A contribution named **Email Archive Viewer** can be used for viewing archived emails. Download this contribution from the Zen Cart website, install it, and use it to see whether Zen Cart has really processed the email for sending. If it has been sent, and the email is not delivered to the recipient, the problem may be in some other place.

Remember that sending a mail involves PHP script for processing the email, email transport and network connectivity. You have to investigate and find the cause for non-delivery of the mail, and then take appropriate action to resolve the problem.

Email Transport Methods

Your emails may not be transmitted if you have not configured appropriate email transport. You can select email transport in the administration panel from **Configuration | Email Options**. In the **E-mail Transport Method** field, you can select the following methods:

1. **php**: If you choose this method, Zen Cart will send emails using the email transport method your web server is configured to use for PHP mail commands. In most cases, this will work fine. If this does not work, it is possible that the mail host for PHP is not configured.

2. **smtp** or **smtpauth**: Selecting this transport method will use simple mail transfer protocol (SMTP). Use **smtpauth** if your SMTP mail server requires authentication. If you are running your web server on a windows operating system, then **smtp** or **smtpauth** is your only choice. Remember that when you are using the **smtp** or **smtpauth** methods, you have to configure mail server address in **SMTP E-Mail Mail Host** and **SMTP E-Mail Mail Server Port**. For **smtpauth**, you need to configure **SMTP E-mail Account Mailbox** and **SMTP E-mail Account Password**. Double check these settings if you have problems with sending email using **smtp** or **smtpauth** transport methods.

3. **sendmail**: If you are not running the Windows web server, and the **php** transport method is not working, then you can try sendmail. Selecting this method will use sendmail as the email transport method. Before trying this method, be sure that your web server has sendmail installed. If you are using **cPanel** for linux hosting, you can see the sendmail path and be sure that it is installed and configured for email transportation.

4. **sendmail –f**: You should not try this at first. Use it when sendmail transport has some difficulties. This is usually used in some cases where your web server configuration has some tighter security requirements. For example, busy shared-hosting environments may need this option.

Bounce Handling

You may face problems with bounced emails from newsletter subscribers. By default, Zen Cart has no mechanism to handle bounced emails. If you see that newsletters/ emails have bounced back, the first thing you should do is turn off that particular subscriber. You can unsubscribe someone by going to the **Customers | Customers** screen. Enter email address in the search box in the upper right corner, and then press *Enter*. When you find the customer with that email address, click on that and edit the settings for that customer. Turn off subscription to newsletters.

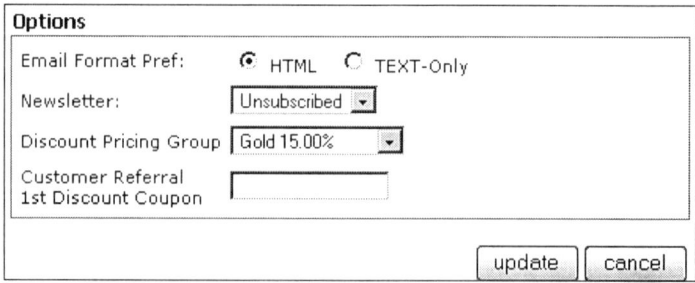

When you find that a customer's email address is not active, or newsletters bounce from a particular address, you can email that customer directly to test whether their account is really active or not. For your store's security, you should not allow any user without a valid email address.

Database Related Errors

Database connection errors are very rare if you continue to use the same server after installing Zen Cart. However, connection errors may occur when you are migrating to another server, or when you have upgraded your MySQL database server.

In case of database connection errors, you will get exact error messages indicating connectivity problems. This error may be connected to the server, or a specific database. You will find database connectivity related configurations in the `/includes/configure.php` file. Check the following settings in this file:

```
// define our database connection
  define('DB_TYPE', 'mysql');
  define('DB_PREFIX', '');
  define('DB_SERVER', 'localhost');
  define('DB_SERVER_USERNAME', 'root');
  define('DB_SERVER_PASSWORD', '');
  define('DB_DATABASE', 'zencart');
  define('USE_PCONNECT', 'false'); // use persistent connections?
```

The above defines mean:

- DB_TYPE : Database type – this is mysql in most of the cases.
- DB_PREFIX: If you are using the same database for some other application, using a prefix for Zen Cart tables will be useful. If you are using a separate database for Zen Cart, you may keep this blank.
- DB_SERVER: This is MySQL database server name. If the MySQL database server and the web server are the same, the value of this field will be localhost. If the servers are separate, mention the hostname of that server.

- DB_SERVER_USERNAME: This is the username which will be used to connect to the database. Ensure that this user has appropriate permissions to connect to, select from, insert into, delete from, and update from the Zen Cart database. If you are using cPanel in Linux hosting, a prefix is used before each database username. For example, if your hosting account name is suhreed, and you create a database user named user1, then the full name of the database user becomes suhreed_user1. Also remember that while installing Zen Cart from Fantastico, a database user and corresponding password are automatically generated which are used for connecting to Zen Cart database. This user account is automatically deleted when you uninstall it using Fantastico.

- DB_SERVER_PASSWORD: This is the password for the username mentioned in DB_SERVER_USERNAME. Always remember that passwords are case sensitive, so you need to type them carefully. The key thing in any connectivity problem should be to ensure the password's validity.

- DB_DATABASE: This is the type name of the database used for Zen Cart. Generally, it is named as zencart or zc. Be sure that database name is correctly mentioned in this field.

- USE_PCONNECT: Database connection can be persistent or non-persistent. Persistent connection remains open for some time. For a small number of users, this saves time in establishing connections again and again, and thus improves performance. But for a large number of requests to a database, a lot of memory may be used for maintaining persistent connection to database. If you see that a lot of memory is used up for a database, you may check this setting and set it to false.

If you are facing a problem with database connectivity, check whether the database itself is running. Try connecting to the database from another application. If you can connect to the database from other applications, then it is likely that you have a problem with the database configuration for Zen Cart. Check the above variables and test the results.

Summary

In this chapter, you have learned about common maintenance and troubleshooting activities in a Zen Cart online shop. Once you have set up, configured, and customized your online shop and taken it to live production, you need to carry out some routine maintenance tasks to keep it running. During maintenance, your shop may be down, which can be notified to your customers, from Zen Cart configuration. Regular maintenance activities help your shop to run smoothly. However, trouble may crop up any time. We discussed some common problems that you may face, in this chapter. This chapter has also introduced you to some security features of Zen Cart and ways to improve security.

A
Resources for Zen Cart

In the main text of this book, we have discussed how to install, configure and customize a Zen Cart shop. As you are customizing the Zen Cart shop, it is recommended that you do all development work in a development environment. In the whole process of customizing the Zen Cart shop, we have referred to several third-party contributions and web resources. This Appendix shows you how to setup a development environment in Windows PC and where to get the third-party contributions and other resources on the web.

Setting WAMP server

You need Apache-MySQL-PHP for running Zen Cart. You can use a hosting server for hosting Zen Cart shop. However, it is recommended that you do the customization of Zen Cart in a development environment. If you are using Windows PC, you can use one of the Apache-MySQL-PHP packages. Here we are going to discuss how you can set up and configure WAMP on your Windows computer.

Step 1. Get WAMP Server. WAMP server gives you Apache-MySQL-PHP. Point your browser to www.wampserver.com and download the latest version of WAMP Server.

Step 2. Install WAMP Server. Once WAMP Server is downloaded to your computer, double click on the installation file. It will be installed, by default, on c:\wamp. Under that, there will be a www directory, which is known as the web directory. This means all web applications you want to run, should be put inside this folder (c:\wamp\www).

Step 3. Run WAMP Server. You can configure your WAMP Sever to run when Windows starts. Alternatively, you can run it as and when needed. You can start WAMP Server from **Start | All Programs | Wamp Server | Start Wamp Server**. When WAMPServer started, you see WampServer icon in the system tray. Click on that icon, and you get the Wamp Server menu:

For starting all services (Apache, MySQL and PHP), click on **Start All Services**. For configuring PHP, go to **PHP**. You can create databases through **phpMyAdmin**. To see the default page in the web root, click on Localhost, or type `http://localhost/` in your browser's address bar. It will display a page like this:

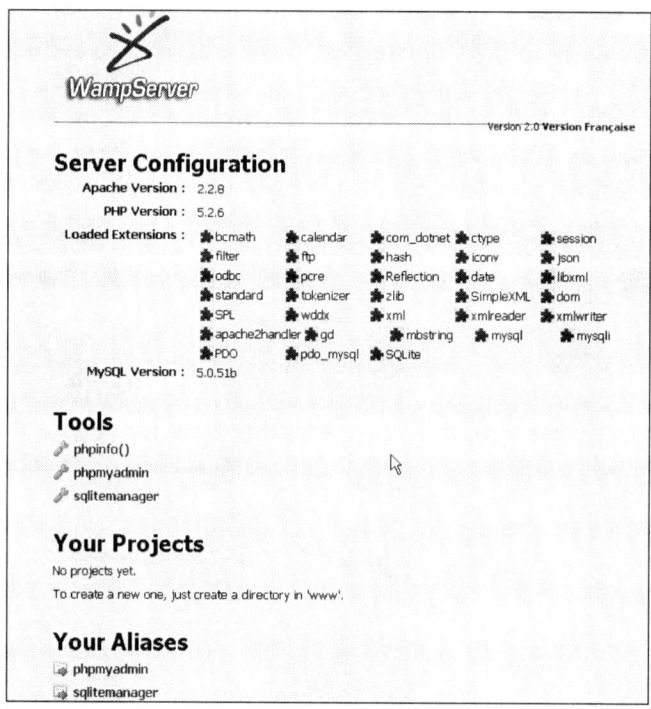

If it works fine, you are done! Your Wamp Server is working – so get ready for the next step.

Step 4. Get Zen Cart installation package. Now it is time to get Zen Cart installation package, by which you will install Zen Cart on your local computer. Open your browser, and type `www.zen-cart.com` in the address bar. You will see the Zen Cart home page. On the right side there is a download link for latest release (at present v.1.3.8a). Click on this link to download the latest release of Zen Cart.

If you want to download another version of Zen Cart, for example Zen Cart v.1.3.7, then go to `http://sourceforge.net/project/showfiles.php?group_id=83781`. Here you will get download links for all previous versions of Zen Cart. Click one of your choices and wait for completion of download.

Step 5. Unzip Zen Cart package files. Once download is complete, extract the Zip file on to your local disk. Generally, you will get a file named zen-cart-v1.3.8-full-fileset-11302007.zip. I hope that WinZip, WinRAR or some other compression utility is installed on your computer. If so, right click on the file and choose **Extract** here. It's better to copy the file in a folder named zencart. Unzipping the files will take some time. When finished, go to that `zencart` folder. You will see the admin, includes, and so on folders and some `.php` files. These all are needed for installing Zen Cart.

Step 6. Copy Zen Cart installation files to WAMP web root. Once you have unzipped the installation package, the whole folder should be copied to WAMP Server's webroot, i.e. `C:\wamp\www`. Wait until all the files are copied.

Step 7. Create database for Zen Cart. Before proceeding to Zen Cart installation, first create a database for Zen Cart. To create a database, click on WAMP Server icon and choose **phpMyAdmin** or type `http://localhost/phpmyadmin/` in your browser's address bar. This will open up **phpMyAdmin**.

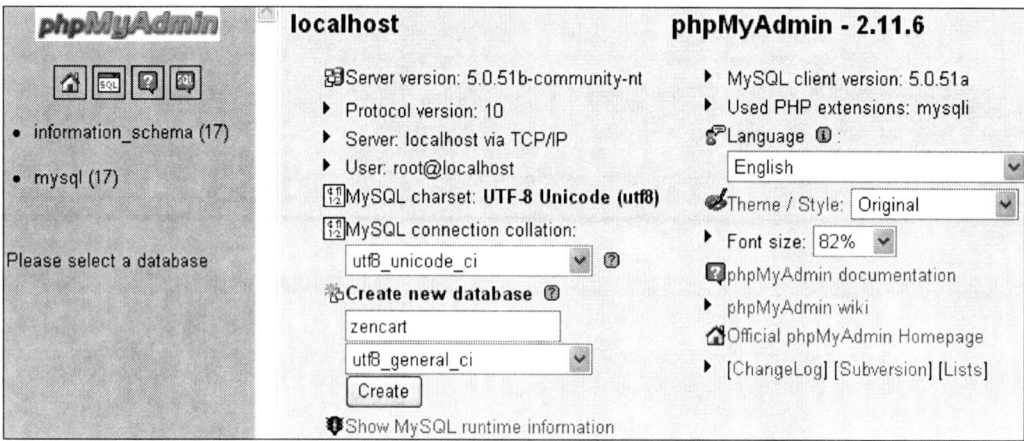

In the **Create new database** text box type the name of database you want to create. In this instance, type **zencart**. Now select collation from the next dropdown field. For the `zencart` database, select **utf8_general_ci**. Then click **Create**. You will see the **zencart** database listed in the left pane. You are done with creating the database, although no table has yet been defined. Zen Cart installation routine will create the necessary tables in this database.

Step 8. Start installation of Zen Cart. Now it is time to start installation of Zen Cart. Open your browser and type `http://localhost/zencart/zc_install/` in the address bar. This will start Zen Cart installation. Most of the options you can configure easily. In the database setup step, type the database name as **zencart**, and username **root**. Password will remain blank. The whole process of installing Zen Cart is detailed in Chapter 2, *Installation and Basic Configuration*.

Zen Cart Directory Structure

It is good to know about the default directory structure of Zen Cart. Following, is a list of directories and sub-directories, and a brief description of the directory contents. Remember that you may need to relocate or rename these directories for strengthening the security of your Zen Cart shop.

- `admin`: This directory contains files and sub-directories which are essential for the administration panel. This directory is, in fact, of same structure as the catalog part of the shop. It includes modules, languages, and all other sub-directories and files which are only used for the administration area of Zen Cart.

- `cache`: This folder is for caching SQL queries and only used when you have configured Zen Cart to store session information in files.

- `docs`: This folder contains some documents for providing help on Zen Cart installation and configuration.

- `downloads`: This folder is for storing downloadable contents of your online shop. You have to specify this folder by `DIR_WS_DOWNLOADS` and `DIR_FS_DOWNLOADS` directives in `/includes/configure.php file`.

- `editors`: This folder contains WYSIWYG editors for HTML text areas. Each editor will be in a separate subdirectory and configurable from the Zen Cart administration area.

- `email`: This directory contains e-mail templates only. All HTML files for templates and associated images will be in this directory.

- `extras`: This directory contains some extra files like PayPal IPN.

- `images`: This directory contains images for the Zen Cart online shop. Images for products, categories, and manufacturers can be stored in sub-directories under this. You can specify this folder by `DIR_WS_IMAGES` and `DIR_FS_IMAGES` directories in `/includes/configure.php` file.

- `includes`: This directory contains many important files for the Zen Cart online shop. It has a couple of sub-directories. You can specify this directory by `DIR_WS_INCLUDES` and `DIR_FS_INCLUDES` directives in `/includes/configure.php` file.

- `includes/auto_loaders`: This folder includes a file named `config.core.php` which lists files that requires automatic loading while Zen Cart shop starts.

- `includes/classes`: This directory contains class files for Zen Cart. Details of classes are discussed in the next section.

- `includes/classes/db`: This directory includes database related classes. The Zen Cart database abstraction layer will be found in two files `define_queries.php` and `query_factory.php` under `mysql` subdirectory.

- `includes/classes/support`: This directory contains support language files, such as `phpmailer.lang-cz.php`, `phpmailer.lang-pl.php`, and so forth for PHP mailing.

- `includes/extra_cart_actions`: This directory is for containing files manipulating extra actions for Cart. This directory is for overrides.

- `includes/extra_configures`: This directory contains extra configuration files. This is used for overrides.

- `includes/extra_datafiles`: This directory contains extra data files needed for contributions, and is used for overrides.
- `includes/functions`: This directory contains `.php` files which have functions defined for using in a Zen Cart shop. It has several functions in several files. `extra_functions` sub-directory in this directory gives you the opportunity to store extra functions for overriding.
- `includes/index_filters`: This directory contains functions used for filtering by product types.
- `includes/init_includes`: This directory contains the files needed for init subsystem. Whenever Zen Cart process starts, files in this directory are needed for initialization.
- `includes/languages`: This directory contains language files and directories for each language including template specific sub-directories. By default, `english.php` file, `english` and `classic` sub-directories are found. This directory has a lot of opportunities for applying overrides. At each level, you can apply template-specific overrides by putting modified language files.
- `includes/modules`: This directory contains files for modules. Some files are in the root of this directory whereas others are in sub-directories.
- `includes/templates`: This directory contains template directories and files.
- `js`: This directory contains JavaScript for Zen Cart.
- `media`: This directory contains digital products like music, songs, and so on.
- `pub`: This directory contains products which are publicly downloadable.
- `zc_install`: This directory contains files and sub-directories which are essential for installing and upgrading Zen Cart.
- `zc_install/demo`: This folder contains `.sql` scripts for demo products for Zen Cart installation.
- `zc_install/includes`: This directory contains necessary function and class files for the installation of Zen Cart.
- `zc_install/sql`: This directory contains `.sql` scripts for creating databases for Zen Cart shop and upgrading it from previous versions to a current version.

Zen Cart Community

You can get most of the information from Zen Cart's main site at `http://www.zen-cart.com`. This site has the following top links:

- **downloads**: This section contains categorized lists of contributions, modules, language packs, buttons, graphics, and templates to be used in Zen Cart.

- **showcase**: This section lists shops using Zen Cart. It's a good place to look into the design of Zen Cart shops used worldwide. You may visit some of these listed shops, to see the design flexibility of Zen Cart. You can also list your online shop by maintaining the Powered by Zen Cart link at the footer of your shop.

- **partners**: This section lists partner sites whose services can be used with Zen Cart. You will get domain registration, payment processing, affiliate programs, logo designs, google services, fun geek stuff—all in this section.

- **hosting**: This section gives you a list of hosting providers specializing in Zen Cart hosting. If you are new to Zen Cart and want to start a shop quickly, choose one of these hosting providers to get Zen Cart installed and configured quickly.

- **donate**: This section gives you options to donate to Zen Cart programmers through PayPal, mail check, or money order.

- **help(?)**: This is the FAQ section for Zen Cart. Before searching for help in the forum, first search in this section. This section will answer your questions in a more organized way and in article format, rather than the forum's conversational style.

Zen Cart Support

Most of the support for Zen Cart is available through the Zen Cart Forum and other related forum. Whenever you need support for Zen Cart first search for solutions in the following forums:

- `http://forum.zen-cart.com`—Main forum for getting support on Zen Cart. Your first place to search for help on Zen Cart.

- `http://www.zencartforum.com`—At Zen Cart Forum, you will find specific forums and threads for you to post your questions so that you get the most specific and focused responses.

- `http://wiki.zen-cart.com`—Zen Cart WiKi will provide you with clean documentation of Zen Cart installation, configuration, and customization. It is under development and many sections are yet to be written. A good place to search for information on Zen Cart.

Zen Cart Downloads

You can download Zen Cart packages from the homepage of Zen Cart's website. On the upper right side you will find a link to download the latest version of Zen Cart. You can download Zen Cart from the following links:

- `http://sourceforge.net/project/showfiles.php?group_id=83781&package_id=171544` This is the link for downloading Zen Cart v.1.3.8.

- `http://sourceforge.net/project/showfiles.php?group_id=83781.` From here you can download any version of Zen Cart. This page lists all versions of Zen Cart and enables you to choose your desired version. Follow this link, if you want to download any version of Zen Cart other than the most recent one.

- `http://www.zen-cart.com/index.php?main_page=index&cPath=40` This is Zen Cart's download section. Community-contributed additions for Zen Cart can be found here. However, remember that these contributions have no warranty expressed or implied. You have the freedom to download and use any contribution. You don't need to sign-up to downloading any contribution. All downloads are free to the public and you do not have to sign-in to download. You can also submit your contribution by creating an account and then logging in.

In the download section, contributions are stored in categories. Clicking on a category will show a list of contributions in that category. At present you will find the following categories:

- **Admin Tools**
- **Buttons and Graphics**
- **Language Packs**
- **Marketing Tools**
- **Other Modules**
- **Payment Modules**
- **Pricing Tools**
- **Privacy and Condition Statements**
- **Product Types**
- **Shipping Modules**
- **Sideboxes**
- **Template Alterations**

- **Template Packages**
- **Troubleshooting Tools**
- **Zones**

Some Essential Downloads

There are plenty of contributions to extend Zen Cart's functionality. Some of the important contributions are discussed in the main text of this book. Following are the list of such contributions:

- **Backup MySQL Plug-in** <http://www.zen-cart.com/index.php?main_page=download_contrib&contrib_id=81&update_id=2 >: This will allow you to backup and restore Zen Cart database from within Zen Cart's administration panel.

- **Easy Populate Free** < http://www.zen-cart.com/index.php?main_page=download_contrib&contrib_id=395&update_id=1 >: This contribution allows you to add or update products from a tab delimited text file, which can be edited in Microsoft Excel or in OpenOffice.org Calc.

- **Email Archive Manager** < http://www.zen-cart.com/index.php?main_page=download_contrib&contrib_id=198&update_id=5 >: Zen Cart archives e-mails sent to customers. However, there is no built-in feature to see these archived e-mails. This add-on will enable you to look up e-mails sent to customers. A great tool for Zen Cart shop administrators.

- **Better Together** < http://www.zen-cart.com/index.php?main_page=download_contrib&contrib_id=309&update_id=9 >: This contribution allows cross-selling at a discount. A product can be linked with another product, another product from a specific category, or any other product, with an associated discount (in dollars or % off) if both are purchased together. The associations must be hard coded, but once they are generic, logic can be added to the product_info page to display any available better together discount.

- **Cross Sell** < http://www.zen-cart.com/index.php?main_page=download_contrib&contrib_id=76&update_id=4 >: This module will allow you to add up to 6 optional products on your current products pages.

- **Cross Sell – Just Another Cross Sell Mod** <http://www.zen-cart.com/index.php?main_page=download_contrib&contrib_id=694&update_id=7>: This is an advanced cross-sell module which supports bi-directional cross-selling. Needs the original cross-sell module installed. Recent versions include both original and advanced cross-sell modules.

- **Cart Upsell/Cross-sell** <http://www.zen-cart.com/index.php?main_page=download_contrib&contrib_id=283&update_id=5>: This module is for upsell and cross-sell during checkout.

- **EZ Thumbnails** <http://www.zen-cart.com/index.php?main_page=product_contrib_info&cPath=40_47&products_id=704>: This module creates products and category thumbnails on the fly. Also creates sub-directories for storing thumbnails (if the source images are found in a sub-directory).

- **Image Handler 2 for v1.3.x** <http://www.zen-cart.com/index.php?main_page=product_contrib_info&cPath=40_47&products_id=117>: With the help of GD libraries or ImageMagick installed on your server, this contribution generates and resizes small, medium, and large images instantly on page request. This enables you to simply upload a single image or different images of medium and large sizes. This also enables you to watermark your images and create hover effects.

- **osCommerce Data importer** <http://www.zen-cart.com/index.php?main_page=product_contrib_info&cPath=40_41&products_id=918>: This script by Albert Savage is for importing osCommerce data into Zen Cart. You can import customers, products, product description, categories, category descriptions, category structure, specials, and reviews using this script. This script will run even when you have not completed installation of your Zen Cart shop.

- **osCommerce to Zen Cart migration script** <http://www.zen-cart.com/index.php?main_page=product_contrib_info&cPath=40_41&products_id=946>: This script by Michael Morris imports data from osCommerce to Zen Cart. However, it also erases all existing data on Zen Cart. Therefore, this script is suitable for importing data to a new Zen Cart shop.

- **Adsense Control Center** <http://www.zen-cart.com/index.php?main_page=product_contrib_info&cPath=40_60&products_id=780>: This module allows you to display Adsense ad on your shop. Through this control center, you can configure different ad units and configure them to be displayed on your pages.

- **Zen lightbox** <http://www.zen-cart.com/index.php?main_page=product_contrib_info&cPath=40_47&products_id=273>: This contribution adds lightbox support to Zen Cart. All large product images will be displayed within a lightbox. This eliminates the need for pop-up windows and makes your website much more user-friendly. Additional product images are displayed within a simple gallery interface.

Zen Cart Integration

Following sections give you some links to integration modules — for integrating Zen Cart and other CMS.

Joomla!

So far, there is no integration module for integrating Zen Cart with Joomla! However, an equivalent Joomla! component, VirtueMart <www.virtuemart.com>, can be used for an online shop attached with Joomla! website. You can import osCommerce or Zen Cart catalog to VirtueMart by using **osCommerce - Zen Cart Catalog Import Utility** in VirtueMart. For download and detail information, please visit: http://extensions.joomla.org/component/option,com_mtree/task,viewlink/link_id,3387/Itemid,35/

You can find discussions on Zen Cart - Joomla! integration at the Zen Cart forum thread: http://www.zen-cart.com/forum/showthread.php?t=47269

You can also follow development of JFusion plugin for integrating Zen Cart-Joomla! at http://www.jfusion.org/phpbb3/viewtopic.php?f=8&t=584.

Drupal

You can use a Drupal module, still in its development status, which integrates Drupal and Zen Cart. This module works with Drupal 5.x and Zen Cart v. 1.3.7. To downloading this, please visit the module's project page at http://drupal.org/project/zencart.

WordPress

WordPress-Zen Cart installation has been discussed in Chapter 8. Required resources for this are as follows:

- **WordPress on Zen Cart** module – You can download the WordPress on Zen Cart integration module from `http://www.zen-cart.com/index.php?main_page=download_contrib&contrib_id=681&update_id=1`.

- `http://www.sharpbrains.com/` - example of a WordPress and Zen Cart integrated site where WordPress is master and users can place orders through Zen Cart.

- `http://www.sharpbrains.com/get-started/brain-fitness-guide/` - Product pages are displayed in Zen Cart, although the users are redirected from WordPress.

Gallery2 Integration

Gallery2-Zen Cart installation has been discussed in Chapter 8. Required resources for this are as follows:

- Gallery2 Zen Cart Integration module is available at `http://www.zen-cart.com/index.php?main_page=product_contrib_info&cPath=40_47&products_id=581`.

- You can get details about gallery2 Integration module at `http://codex.gallery2.org/Gallery2:Modules:zencart`.

- Download link for Gallery2/Zen Cart integration module is `http://dakanji.com/g2stuff/zcg2-3_2_1a-full.zip`.

Zen Cart XOOPS Integration Module

XOOPS can be integrtated to Zen Cart by using the XOOPS Zen Cart integration module. This module is available at `http://www.xoops.org/modules/repository/visit.php?cid=22&lid=1626`.

e107 Plugins for Zen Cart Integration

e107 is a content management system written in PHP and using the popular open-source MySQL database system for content storage. It's completely free, totally customizable, and in constant development. You can integrate Zen Cart with e107 by installing Zen Cart Bridge and Zen Cart User-Sync Plug-ins for e107. Download these from the following links:

- Zen Cart Bridge `http://plugins.e107.org/e107_plugins/psilo/psilo.php?artifact.178`
- Zen Cart User-Sync `http://plugins.e107.org/e107_plugins/psilo/psilo.php?artifact.172`

Templates

There are lots of templates for Zen Cart, which may be suitable for your shop. The following are the sources where you can get such templates:

- **Zen Cart Templates Preview** < `www.zencarttemplates.info` > - You can test drive all the free templates available for the current version of Zen Cart at this site. This is a good place to view the template before downloading and customizing it for your shop.

- **Powered by Zen Cart** < `http://www.poweredbyzencart.com/` > - PoweredbyZencart.com provides premium Zen Cart templates to set up your own Zen Cart store. You can buy professionally designed templates suitable for your store from this template store.

- **Template Monster** < `www.templatemonster.com` > Zen Cart Templates available in Template Monster provide you with simple solutions in setting up your own Zen Cart store. From its large collection, you can easily find a Zen Cart template that best suits your business.

- **Zen Cart Hall of fame** <`http://www.zencarttemplates.info/hoff.php`> Look at this site to see some of the innovative designs for Zen cart. This page lists famous and much praised design innovations for Zen Cart templates.

Consulting

While customizing and extending your Zen Cart shop, you need consulting services for Zen Cart. The following links will help you find consultants for Zen Cart:

- **How to hire a Zen Cart consultant**: Tips for hiring a Zen Cart consultant and looking at skills in such hiring. Read at `http://thecartblog.com/2008/01/13/how-to-hire-a-zen-cart-consultant/`.

- `http://www.zencartconsulting.com`: Zen Cart Consulting provides Zen Cart customization and development services. It has developed a bunch of modules for Zen Cart to enhance it's features.

- `http://www.zen-cart.com/forum/forumdisplay.php?f=146`: Check this forum for searching Zen Cart hosting services. Normally you will find a linux host supporting Zen Cart. Zen Cart has some certified hosting service providers, which can be used for hosting Zen Cart-based shops.

Besides these, you can get competent consultants at `www.elance.com`, `www.getafreelancer.com` and `www.getacoder.com`. Visit these sites and search for Zen Cart experts.

Index

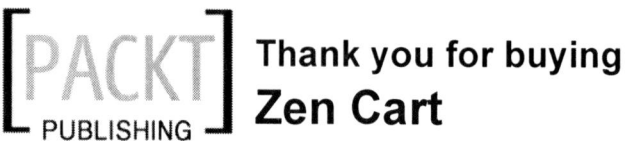

Thank you for buying
Zen Cart

Packt Open Source Project Royalties

When we sell a book written on an Open Source project, we pay a royalty directly to that project. Therefore by purchasing Zen Cart, Packt will have given some of the money received to the Zen Cart Project.

In the long term, we see ourselves and you—customers and readers of our books—as part of the Open Source ecosystem, providing sustainable revenue for the projects we publish on. Our aim at Packt is to establish publishing royalties as an essential part of the service and support a business model that sustains Open Source.

If you're working with an Open Source project that you would like us to publish on, and subsequently pay royalties to, please get in touch with us.

Writing for Packt

We welcome all inquiries from people who are interested in authoring. Book proposals should be sent to authors@packtpub.com. If your book idea is still at an early stage and you would like to discuss it first before writing a formal book proposal, contact us; one of our commissioning editors will get in touch with you.

We're not just looking for published authors; if you have strong technical skills but no writing experience, our experienced editors can help you develop a writing career, or simply get some additional reward for your expertise.

About Packt Publishing

Packt, pronounced 'packed', published its first book "Mastering phpMyAdmin for Effective MySQL Management" in April 2004 and subsequently continued to specialize in publishing highly focused books on specific technologies and solutions.

Our books and publications share the experiences of your fellow IT professionals in adapting and customizing today's systems, applications, and frameworks. Our solution-based books give you the knowledge and power to customize the software and technologies you're using to get the job done. Packt books are more specific and less general than the IT books you have seen in the past. Our unique business model allows us to bring you more focused information, giving you more of what you need to know, and less of what you don't.

Packt is a modern, yet unique publishing company, which focuses on producing quality, cutting-edge books for communities of developers, administrators, and newbies alike. For more information, please visit our website: www.PacktPub.com.

Deep Inside osCommerce

ISBN: 1-847190-90-1   Paperback: 400 pages

Ready-to-use recipes to customize and extend your
e-commerce website

1. osCommerce expert "Monika in Germany" lets
   you in on her secrets on how to hack your way
   to that perfect osCommerce site

2. Create new modules and custom-code your
   default osCommerce installation

3. Add extensions and features like
   category driven designs and individual
   shipping modules

Selling Online with Drupal
e-Commerce

ISBN: 978-1-847194-06-0   Paperback: 264 pages

Walk through the creation of an online store with
Drupal's e-Commerce module

1. Set up a basic Drupal system and plan
   your shop

2. Set up your shop, and take payments

3. Optimize your site for selling and
   better reporting

4. Manage and market your site

Please check **www.PacktPub.com** for information on our titles

Printed in the United Kingdom by
Lightning Source UK Ltd., Milton Keynes
139711UK00001B/78/P